# Cooking Light

# Comfort Food

# Cooking Light

# Comfort Food

### Home-Cooked, Delicious Classics Made Light

Oxmoor House

©2011 by Time Home Entertainment Inc.
135 West 50th Street, New York, NY 10020

ISBN-13: 978-0-8487-3464-0
ISBN-10: 0-8487-3464-5
Library of Congress Control Number: 2010933261
Printed in the United States of America
First printing 2011

Be sure to check with your health-care provider
before making any changes in your diet.

## Oxmoor House

VP, Publishing Director: Jim Childs
Editorial Director: Susan Payne Dobbs
Brand Manager: Michelle Turner Aycock
Senior Editor: Heather Averett
Managing Editor: Laurie S. Herr

## Cooking Light® Comfort Food

Project Editor: Georgia Dodge
Senior Designer: Emily Albright Parrish
Test Kitchens Director: Elizabeth Tyler Austin
Assistant Directors, Test Kitchens: Julie Christopher, Julie Gunter
Test Kitchens Professionals: Wendy Ball, Allison E. Cox,
Victoria E. Cox, Margaret Monroe Dickey,
Allyson Moreland Haynes, Callie Nash, Kathleen Royal Phillips,
Catherine Crowell Steele, Lean Van Deren
Photography Director: Jim Bathie
Senior Photo Stylist: Kay E. Clarke
Associate Photo Stylist: Katherine Eckert Coyne
Assistant Photo Stylist: Mary Louise Menendez
Senior Production Manager: Greg A. Amason
Production Manager: Tamara N. Wilder

### Contributors

Copy Editor: Jacqueline Giovanelli
Proofreader: Lauren Brooks
Indexer: Mary Ann Laurens
Interns: Sarah Bélanger, Christine T. Boatwright,
Blair Gillespie, Allison Sperando, Caitlin Watzke

## Cooking Light®

Editor: Scott Mowbray
Creative Director: Carla Frank
Deputy Editor: Phillip Rhodes
Food Editor: Ann Taylor Pittman
Special Publications Editor: Mary Simpson Creel, MS, RD
Associate Food Editors: Timothy Q. Cebula, Julianna Grimes
Associate Editors: Cindy Hatcher, Brandy Rushing
Test Kitchens Director: Vanessa T. Pruett
Assistant Test Kitchens Director: Tiffany Vickers Davis
Chief Food Stylist: Charlotte Autry
Senior Food Stylist: Kellie Gerber Kelley
Recipe Testers and Developers: Robin Bashinsky,
Adam Hickman, Deb Wise
Art Director: Fernande Bondarenko
Junior Deputy Art Director: Alexander Spacher
Associate Art Director: Rachel Lasserre
Designer: Chase Turberville
Photo Director: Kristen Schaefer
Senior Photographer: Randy Mayor
Senior Photo Stylist: Cindy Barr
Photo Stylist: Leigh Ann Ross
Copy Chief: Maria Parker Hopkins
Assistant Copy Chief: Susan Roberts
Research Editor: Michelle Gibson Daniels
Editorial Production Director: Liz Rhoades
Production Editor: Hazel R. Eddins
Art/Production Assistant: Josh Rutledge
Administrative Coordinator: Carol D. Johnson
CookingLight.com Editor: Allison Long Lowery
Nutrition Editor: Holley Johnson Grainger, MS, RD
Production Assistant: Mallory Daugherty

To order additional publications,
call 1-800-765-6400 or 1-800-491-0551.

For more books to enrich your life,
visit oxmoorhouse.com

To search, savor, and share thousands
of recipes, visit myrecipes.com

**Cover:** Company Pot Roast (page 205)
**Back cover:** Coconut Banana Bread with Lime Glaze (page 70)

# about this book

**Welcome to a fresh and healthy approach to comfort food** from *Cooking Light,* America's leading food magazine. At *Cooking Light* we're passionate about making healthy taste great, and for years we've been helping our readers transform their favorite recipes into healthier versions that still retain all the memorable and enticing flavors that they've grown to love.

*Cooking Light Comfort Food* is an amazing assortment of over 200 classic recipes that fit into a well-balanced diet—yet no one will guess these dishes are light! Organized by Breakfast, Lunch, Dinner, and Sides & Desserts, this book makes it easy to choose a variety of flavorful recipes—from buttermilk biscuits to French onion soup, fried chicken, mashed potatoes, and strawberry shortcake!

There is something for everyone—no matter your craving—in this inviting book of light, warming comfort-food dishes that are equally as good for your body as they are for your soul. In addition to the classic comfort-food recipes, these additional features are woven within:

- **A beautiful color photograph** of every recipe showcases delicious food at its finest.
- **"5 Ways With…"** features recipes that provide you with five uniquely different variations of timeless classics like mashed potatoes, meat loaf, and mac and cheese.
- **"Recipe Makeovers"** highlights reader recipes and tells you how the *Cooking Light* staff made them healthier—while keeping the dish supremely satisfying at the same time.
- **"30 Minutes or Less"** icons flag all the super-quick and easy recipes.
- **"What Makes it Light?"** info shows you exactly what makes that particular recipe lighter than a traditional recipe, giving you ideas on how to lighten up your own recipes.
- **A nutritional analysis** for every recipe gives you confidence that it's healthy.

# breakfast

## 8

77

210

# dinner

## 162

# lunch

92

304

# sides&desserts

# breakfast

**Traditionally served for breakfast in Mexico,** huevos rancheros piles crisp corn tortillas with protein-rich eggs, spicy salsa, and shredded cheese. Serve your eggs whichever way you like them best—with fresh tomato salsa, salsa verde, or both. You can also use white, yellow, or blue corn tortillas to change things up.

# Huevos Rancheros

4 (6-inch) corn tortillas
Cooking spray
1 cup chopped onion
½ cup chopped green bell pepper
3 garlic cloves, minced
¼ cup canned chopped green chiles
2 teaspoons New Mexico chile powder
1 teaspoon ground cumin
1 teaspoon dried oregano
½ teaspoon hot sauce
1 (14.5-ounce) can diced tomatoes, undrained
4 large eggs
¼ cup fresh salsa or ¼ cup salsa verde
¼ cup (1 ounce) shredded Monterey Jack cheese
Cilantro sprigs (optional)

**1.** Preheat oven to 350°.
**2.** Coat tortillas with cooking spray; place on a baking sheet. Bake at 350° for 12 minutes or until crisp.
**3.** Heat a large nonstick skillet over medium-high heat. Coat pan with cooking spray. Add onion, bell pepper, and garlic; sauté 3 minutes. Add green chiles and next 5 ingredients. Bring to a boil; cook 3 minutes or until thick.
**4.** Heat a large nonstick skillet over medium-low heat. Coat pan with cooking spray. Add eggs to pan; cook 3 minutes or until done.
**5.** Place 1 tortilla on each of 4 plates. Top each tortilla with ½ cup tomato mixture and 1 egg. Spoon 1 tablespoon fresh salsa or salsa verde over each serving; sprinkle each serving with 1 tablespoon cheese. Garnish with cilantro sprigs, if desired. **YIELD:** 4 servings.

CALORIES 222; FAT 8.6g (sat 3.1g, mono 2.8g, poly 1.3g); PROTEIN 11.7g; CARB 26.7g; FIBER 5.5g; CHOL 219mg; IRON 2.5mg; SODIUM 376mg; CALC 174mg

## what makes it light

- uses baked, not fried, corn tortillas
- uses less cheese than traditional recipes
- uses cooking spray instead of butter or oil to fry eggs
- doesn't use refried beans, which can be high in fat, like many traditional recipes

**The creamy cheese and sour cream** add salty notes to these tacos. Round out your breakfast with fresh mango slices.

# Egg and Cheese Breakfast Tacos with Homemade Salsa

1 cup chopped tomato
¼ cup chopped red onion
2 tablespoons chopped fresh cilantro
1 teaspoon minced jalapeño pepper
¼ teaspoon kosher salt
4 teaspoons fresh lime juice, divided
1 teaspoon minced garlic, divided
1 cup organic refried beans
¼ teaspoon ground cumin
1 tablespoon 1% low-fat milk
6 large eggs, lightly beaten
Cooking spray
¼ cup chopped green onions
8 (6-inch) corn tortillas
½ cup (2 ounces) shredded Monterey Jack cheese with jalapeño peppers
8 teaspoons reduced-fat sour cream

**1.** Combine first 5 ingredients in a small bowl. Stir in 2 teaspoons juice and $^1/_2$ teaspoon garlic. Combine beans, remaining 2 teaspoons juice, remaining $^1/_2$ teaspoon garlic, and cumin in another bowl.

**2.** Combine milk and eggs in a medium bowl; stir with a whisk. Heat a large nonstick skillet over medium-high heat. Coat pan with cooking spray. Add green onions to pan; sauté 1 minute, stirring frequently. Stir in egg mixture; cook 3 minutes or until soft-scrambled, stirring constantly. Remove from heat.

**3.** Warm tortillas according to package directions. Spread 1 tablespoon bean mixture on each tortilla. Spoon about 2 tablespoons egg mixture down center of each tortilla. Top each serving with 1 tablespoon tomato mixture, 1 tablespoon cheese, and 1 teaspoon sour cream. **YIELD:** 4 servings (serving size: 2 tacos).

CALORIES 334; FAT 13.3g (sat 5.5g, mono 4.2g, poly 2.3g); PROTEIN 19g; CARB 34g; FIBER 6.5g; CHOL 289mg; IRON 2.9mg; SODIUM 407mg; CALC 201mg

## what makes it light

- uses low-fat milk
- uses reduced-fat sour cream
- uses homemade salsa instead of bottled

**Perfect for either breakfast or a light dinner,** this dish uses white cornmeal for a creamy polenta. If you can find it, use imported Italian white polenta since the grain is very fine, resulting in a soft texture. Make an extra batch of salsa as a topping for bruschetta.

# Poached Eggs with White Corn Polenta

Salsa:
- ⅓ cup chopped bottled roasted red bell peppers
- 1 tablespoon chopped fresh basil
- ½ teaspoon extra-virgin olive oil
- ⅛ teaspoon salt
- 1 large plum tomato, seeded and diced (about ⅓ cup)

Polenta:
- 4 cups water
- 1½ cups frozen white corn kernels, thawed
- 1 cup white cornmeal or dry polenta

- ½ teaspoon salt, divided
- 3 tablespoons grated fresh Parmesan cheese
- 1 teaspoon butter
- ¼ teaspoon freshly ground black pepper

Eggs:
- 4 large eggs
- Cooking spray

Remaining Ingredients:
- 2 bacon slices, cooked and crumbled
- Freshly ground black pepper (optional)

**1.** To prepare salsa, combine bell pepper, basil, oil, ⅛ teaspoon salt, and tomato; set aside.

**2.** To prepare polenta, bring 4 cups water to a boil in a medium saucepan. Add corn, cornmeal, and ¼ teaspoon salt. Cook 2 minutes or until cornmeal mixture returns to a boil, stirring constantly. Reduce heat to low; cook 20 minutes or until thick, stirring frequently. Stir in remaining ¼ teaspoon salt, Parmesan cheese, butter, and black pepper. Cover and keep warm.

**3.** To prepare eggs, while polenta cooks, add water to a large skillet, filling two-thirds full; bring to a boil. Reduce heat; simmer. Break eggs into each of 4 (6-ounce) custard cups coated with cooking spray. Place custard cups in simmering water in pan. Cover pan; cook 6 minutes. Remove custard cups from water; carefully remove eggs from custard cups.

**4.** Spoon about 1 cup polenta onto each of 4 plates; top each serving with about 3 tablespoons salsa and 1 poached egg. Sprinkle evenly with bacon. Garnish with black pepper, if desired. **YIELD:** 4 servings.

CALORIES 307; FAT 10.3g (sat 3.4g, mono 4g, poly 1.6g); PROTEIN 14.2g; CARB 40.5g; FIBER 4.6g; CHOL 221mg; IRON 1.9mg; SODIUM 664mg; CALC 78mg

## what makes it light

- uses only ½ slice bacon per serving
- eggs are poached so no fat is used to cook them
- uses only 1 teaspoon butter in the polenta compared to several tablespoons in traditional recipes

**Here's an omelet that cooks up beautifully** and is chock-full of healthy vegetables wrapped in warm melted cheese.

# Mushroom and Bell Pepper Omelet with Fontina

1 teaspoon olive oil, divided
Cooking spray
¼ cup chopped green onions
½ medium green bell pepper, thinly sliced
2 cups sliced shiitake mushrooms (about 6 ounces)
½ cup chopped seeded plum tomato
½ teaspoon salt, divided

⅛ teaspoon black pepper
2 teaspoons chopped fresh parsley
8 large eggs
2 large egg whites
½ teaspoon butter
½ cup (2 ounces) shredded fontina cheese
¼ cup reduced-fat sour cream
Chopped fresh parsley (optional)

**1.** Heat ¹/₂ teaspoon oil in a large nonstick skillet coated with cooking spray over medium-high heat. Add green onions; sauté 1 minute. Add bell pepper; sauté 1 minute. Add mushrooms; cook 3 minutes, stirring frequently. Stir in tomato, ¹/₄ teaspoon salt, and black pepper; cook 30 seconds. Remove vegetable mixture from pan; cover and keep warm.

**2.** Place ¹/₄ teaspoon salt, parsley, eggs, and egg whites in a bowl; stir well with a whisk to combine.

**3.** Place ¹/₂ teaspoon oil and butter in skillet over medium-high heat until butter melts. Add egg mixture to pan; cook until edges begin to set (about 2 minutes). Slide front edge of a spatula between edge of omelet and pan. Gently lift edge of omelet, tilting pan to allow some uncooked egg mixture to come in contact with pan. Repeat procedure on opposite edge of omelet. Continue cooking until the center is just set (about 7 minutes).

**4.** Spoon vegetable mixture evenly over ¹/₂ of omelet; top vegetable mixture with cheese. Loosen omelet with a spatula; fold in half. Carefully slide omelet onto a serving platter. Cut omelet into 4 wedges; top with sour cream. Garnish with additional parsley, if desired. Serve immediately.

**YIELD:** 4 servings (serving size: 1 wedge and 1 tablespoon sour cream).

CALORIES 272; FAT 17.7g (sat 7.3g, mono 6.5g, poly 1.8g); PROTEIN 19.4g; CARB 7.1g; FIBER 1.3g; CHOL 448mg; IRON 2.4mg; SODIUM 576mg; CALC 145mg

## what makes it light

- uses a minimal amount of oil
- uses healthy vegetables
- uses some egg whites instead of all whole eggs
- uses reduced-fat sour cream
- uses creamy fontina instead of high-fat cheese

"My family loves this dish. It is delicious, and after making it on a weekend for breakfast, we have **leftovers that are easy to heat up and enjoy during the week**. It is a great dish to serve when you have guests, too.

**from cookinglight.com**

# Garden Vegetable Crustless Quiche

1½ cups egg substitute
3 large eggs
1½ cups (6 ounces) shredded reduced-fat extrasharp cheddar cheese, divided
1½ cups (6 ounces) shredded reduced-fat Monterey Jack cheese, divided
½ cup 1% low-fat milk
2.25 ounces all-purpose flour (about ½ cup)
1 teaspoon baking powder
½ teaspoon salt

1 (16-ounce) carton fat-free cottage cheese
Cooking spray
4 cups sliced zucchini (about 3)
2 cups diced potato with onion (such as Simply Potatoes)
1 cup finely chopped green bell pepper (about 1)
1 (8-ounce) package presliced mushrooms
½ cup chopped fresh parsley
2 tomatoes, thinly sliced

**1.** Preheat oven to 400°.

**2.** Beat egg substitute and eggs in a large bowl until fluffy. Add $^3/_4$ cup cheddar cheese, $^3/_4$ cup Jack cheese, milk, flour, baking powder, salt, and cottage cheese.

**3.** Heat a large nonstick skillet over medium-high heat. Coat pan with cooking spray. Add zucchini and next 3 ingredients; sauté 5 minutes or until tender. Add zucchini mixture and parsley to egg mixture. Pour mixture into a 3-quart casserole dish coated with cooking spray or 2 (10-inch) quiche pans. Top with remaining $^3/_4$ cup cheddar cheese and $^3/_4$ cup Jack cheese. Arrange tomato slices over cheese. Bake at 400° for 15 minutes. Reduce oven temperature to 350° (do not remove dish from oven), and bake 35 minutes or until lightly browned and set. **YIELD:** 10 servings.

CALORIES 230; FAT 7.7g (sat 4.6g, mono 1.3g, poly 0.3g); PROTEIN 23g; CARB 18.1g; FIBER 1.9g; CHOL 84mg; IRON 2.1mg; SODIUM 716mg; CALC 382mg

## what makes it light

- uses egg substitute
- uses reduced-fat extrasharp cheddar cheese
- uses reduced-fat Monterey Jack
- uses low-fat milk
- uses fat-free cottage cheese
- uses cooking spray instead of oil to sauté vegetables

"Delicious! Rich, creamy, and satisfying. I used a store-bought crust to save time and added a shallot to the green onions since I had one on hand. I might add more shallots and spinach next time. The smoked Gouda was delicious!"

from cookinglight.com

# Spinach, Green Onion, and Smoked Gouda Quiche

**Crust:**

    6 tablespoons butter, softened
    2 tablespoons 1% low-fat milk
    ¼ teaspoon salt
    1 large egg yolk
    5.6 ounces all-purpose flour (about 1¼ cups)

**Filling:**

    1 tablespoon extra-virgin olive oil
    ½ cup thinly sliced green onions
    3 cups fresh baby spinach
    1 cup 1% low-fat milk
    ¾ cup (3 ounces) grated smoked Gouda cheese
    ¾ teaspoon salt
    Dash of grated nutmeg
    3 large eggs

**1.** To prepare crust, place butter in a large bowl; beat with a mixer at medium speed until light and fluffy. Combine milk, salt, and egg yolk in a small bowl; stir well with a whisk. Add milk mixture to butter, 1 tablespoon at a time, beating well after each addition. Add flour; beat just until combined. Press mixture into a 4-inch circle on plastic wrap; cover. Chill 1 hour.

**2.** Preheat oven to 350°.

**3.** Unwrap and place chilled dough on a lightly floured surface. Roll dough into a 10-inch circle. Fit dough into a 9-inch pie plate. Freeze 15 minutes. Bake at 350° for 25 minutes or until lightly browned. Cool.

**4.** To prepare filling, heat oil in a large skillet over medium-high heat. Add onions; sauté 5 minutes or until tender. Add spinach; sauté 2 minutes.

**5.** Combine 1 cup milk and remaining ingredients in a bowl; stir well with a whisk. Stir in spinach mixture. Pour filling into crust. Bake at 350° for 35 minutes. Cut into 10 wedges.

**YIELD:** 10 servings (serving size: 1 wedge).

CALORIES 205; FAT 12.9g (sat 6.8g, mono 4.3g, poly 0.8g); PROTEIN 7.3g; CARB 15.4g; FIBER 1.1g; CHOL 113mg; IRON 1.5mg; SODIUM 405mg; CALC 120mg

## what makes it light

- uses butter instead of shortening in the crust
- uses low-fat milk in the filling
- uses a small amount of smoked Gouda cheese, which gives rich flavor

**Breakfast casseroles are ideal for overnight guests.** Assemble this one the night before, and bake in the morning.

# Mushroom, Bacon, and Swiss Strata

12 ounces ciabatta bread, cut into 1-inch cubes (about 7 cups)
2 tablespoons butter
2 cups chopped onion
2 (8-ounce) packages presliced mushrooms
Cooking spray
1½ cups (6 ounces) shredded reduced-fat Swiss cheese
8 center-cut bacon slices, cooked and crumbled
3 cups 1% low-fat milk
1½ cups egg substitute
2 teaspoons chopped fresh thyme
½ teaspoon freshly ground black pepper
¼ teaspoon salt
Thyme sprigs (optional)

**1.** Preheat oven to 350°.

**2.** Arrange bread in a single layer on a jelly-roll pan. Bake at 350° for 20 minutes or until toasted. Place bread cubes in a large bowl.

**3.** Melt butter in a large nonstick skillet over medium-high heat. Add onion and mushrooms to pan; sauté 10 minutes or until liquid evaporates and vegetables are tender. Add onion mixture to bread; toss well to combine. Arrange half of bread mixture in a 13 x 9–inch baking dish coated with cooking spray. Sprinkle with half of cheese and half of bacon; top with remaining bread mixture, cheese, and bacon.

**4.** Combine milk and next 4 ingredients, stirring with a whisk. Pour milk mixture over bread mixture. Cover and refrigerate 8 hours.

**5.** Preheat oven to 350°.

**6.** Remove strata from refrigerator; let stand at room temperature 15 minutes. Bake strata, covered, at 350° for 30 minutes. Uncover and bake an additional 15 minutes or until set. Let stand 10 minutes before serving. Garnish with thyme sprigs, if desired. **YIELD:** 8 servings.

CALORIES 313; FAT 10.4g (sat 5g, mono 4.2g, poly 0.8g); PROTEIN 21.7g; CARB 35.5g; FIBER 2.7g; CHOL 25mg; IRON 1.9mg; SODIUM 737mg; CALC 318mg

## what makes it light

- uses reduced-fat Swiss cheese
- uses low-fat milk
- uses egg substitute
- uses center-cut bacon, which is a leaner, lower-fat choice than regular bacon

# Brie and Egg Strata

2 teaspoons olive oil
2 cups chopped onion
1½ cups diced unpeeled Yukon gold
   potato (1 large)
1 cup chopped red bell pepper
1 cup halved grape tomatoes
1 teaspoon salt, divided
¾ pound ciabatta bread, cut into 1-inch
   cubes, toasted

Cooking spray
4 ounces Brie cheese, rind removed
   and chopped
1 cup egg substitute
2 large eggs
1 teaspoon herbes de Provence
¼ teaspoon freshly ground black pepper
3 cups 1% low-fat milk
2 tablespoons chopped fresh parsley

**1.** Heat oil in a large nonstick skillet over medium-high heat. Add onion, potato, and bell pepper; sauté 4 minutes or until tender. Stir in tomatoes; sauté 2 minutes. Stir in $^{1}/_{2}$ teaspoon salt. Combine onion mixture and bread.

**2.** Arrange half of bread mixture into a 13 x 9–inch baking dish coated with cooking spray. Sprinkle with half of Brie. Top with remaining bread mixture and remaining Brie.

**3.** Combine egg substitute and eggs in a medium bowl. Add remaining $^{1}/_{2}$ teaspoon salt, herbes de Provence, and pepper. Add milk, stirring with a whisk until well blended. Pour egg mixture over bread mixture. Let stand 30 minutes.

**4.** Preheat oven to 350°.

**5.** Bake at 350° for 50 minutes or until set. Sprinkle with parsley. Serve immediately. **YIELD:** 12 servings (serving size: 1 piece).

CALORIES 205; FAT 6.9g (sat 2.7g, mono 3g, poly 0.8g); PROTEIN 10.8g; CARB 26.1g; FIBER 1.7g; CHOL 47mg; IRON 2mg; SODIUM 534mg; CALC 120mg

## what makes it light
- vegetables and potato add fiber and flavor
- uses a reduced amount of Brie
- uses low-fat milk

# recipe makeover
# breakfast casserole

**The Reader:** Lisanne Kaplan

**The Story:** Breakfast is a favorite meal in the Kaplan house, "enjoyed in pajamas with mugs of good coffee and lively conversation," Lisanne says. But with work, school, and activities with her children, Lisanne needs a make-ahead meal that will be a more healthful, energizing start to the day than the casserole she first found in one of her favorite cookbooks.

**The Dilemma:** This heavyweight casserole called for 1½ pounds pork sausage, 1½ cups full-fat cheese, and nine whole eggs. Each serving had 10 grams of saturated fat and a whopping 204 milligrams of cholesterol. And the sausage and cheese contributed about 900 milligrams of sodium (or 40 percent of the daily recommended intake) per serving.

**The Solution:** Since breakfast turkey sausage has about one-third the fat and half the calories of pork sausage, we use 12 ounces of the flavorful poultry sausage. This eliminates three grams of saturated fat, and using a bit less turkey sausage shaves 187 milligrams of sodium and 20 milligrams of cholesterol per serving. Instead of using nine large eggs, we combine three eggs with two cups egg substitute to offer a fluffy egg texture and taste without missing another two and a half grams of fat (one gram saturated) and 115 milligrams of cholesterol in each portion. The swap from whole milk to 1% low-fat milk trims another gram of fat. The last big change involves using a bit less cheese, and finely shredding reduced-fat extra-sharp cheddar to better distribute the smaller amount and perk up the flavor. Since we halved the original amount of salt, a bit of ground red pepper adds a little spiciness and zest to the casserole while shaving some sodium.

**The Feedback:** Without exception, the Kaplan family agrees—their traditional casserole is improved, with a fluffier texture and more pronounced egg and sausage flavor. No one missed the casserole's greasy edge. "Using finely shredded sharp cheese was a great tip; the flavorful cheese was more evenly distributed throughout the dish," Lisanne says.

|  | BEFORE | AFTER |
|---|---|---|
| Calories per serving | 346 | 184 |
| Fat | 25.8g | 6.8g |
| Percent of total calories | 67% | 33% |

"Fabulous recipe! Made this for Christmas breakfast and it tasted exactly like my mom's full-fat version made with cream and pork sausage. Everyone loved this casserole and was amazed that this was a lighter version of our traditional favorite. My husband has hinted that he would like this throughout the year. My new favorite breakfast casserole recipe!

from cookinglight.com

# Sausage and Cheese Breakfast Casserole

Cooking spray
12 ounces turkey breakfast sausage
2 cups 1% low-fat milk
2 cups egg substitute
1 teaspoon dry mustard
¾ teaspoon salt
½ teaspoon freshly ground black pepper

¼ teaspoon ground red pepper
3 large eggs
16 (1-ounce) slices white bread
1 cup (4 ounces) finely shredded reduced-fat extrasharp cheddar cheese
¼ teaspoon paprika

**1.** Heat a large nonstick skillet over medium-high heat. Coat pan with cooking spray. Add sausage to pan; cook 5 minutes or until browned, stirring and breaking sausage to crumble. Remove from heat; cool.

**2.** Combine milk and next 6 ingredients in a large bowl, stirring with a whisk.

**3.** Trim crusts from bread. Cut bread into 1-inch cubes. Add bread cubes, sausage, and cheddar cheese to milk mixture, stirring to combine. Pour bread mixture into a 13 x 9–inch baking or 3-quart casserole dish coated with cooking spray, spreading egg mixture evenly in baking dish. Cover and refrigerate 8 hours or overnight.

**4.** Preheat oven to 350°.

**5.** Remove casserole from refrigerator; let stand 30 minutes. Sprinkle casserole evenly with paprika. Bake at 350° for 45 minutes or until set and lightly browned. Let stand 10 minutes.

**YIELD:** 12 servings (serving size: about 1 cup).

CALORIES 184; FAT 6.8g (sat 3.2g, mono 1.5g, poly 0.8g); PROTEIN 15.9g; CARB 14g; FIBER 0.6g; CHOL 76mg; IRON 2.2mg; SODIUM 636mg; CALC 181mg

"Wow! I was hesitant because the idea of tomatoes in this was not appealing to me, but this was great. **Only had hot Rotel, but my in-laws are from Texas and love hot.** It was great. They couldn't believe it was light. Can't wait to make again."

**from cookinglight.com**

# Southwestern Breakfast Casserole

1 (8½-ounce) package corn muffin mix
3 cups (½-inch) cubed white bread
8 ounces hot turkey Italian sausage
1 cup chopped onion
2½ cups fat-free milk
1 teaspoon ground cumin
⅛ teaspoon black pepper

1 (10-ounce) can diced tomatoes and green chiles, undrained
1 (8-ounce) carton egg substitute
Cooking spray
1 cup (4 ounces) shredded reduced-fat Monterey Jack or mild cheddar cheese, divided

**1.** Prepare corn muffin mix according to package directions; cool. Crumble muffins into a large bowl; stir in bread. Set aside.
**2.** Remove casings from sausage. Cook sausage and onion in a large nonstick skillet over medium heat until browned, stirring to crumble. Drain.
**3.** Combine milk, cumin, pepper, tomatoes, and egg substitute; stir with a whisk until well blended. Add sausage mixture; stir well. Stir into bread mixture. Spoon half of bread mixture into an 11 x 7–inch baking dish coated with cooking spray. Top with $1/2$ cup cheese. Spoon remaining bread mixture over cheese. Cover and refrigerate 8 hours or overnight.
**4.** Preheat oven to 350°.
**5.** Bake casserole at 350° for 20 minutes or until set. Top with $1/2$ cup cheese, and bake an additional 20 minutes or until set. Let stand 10 minutes before serving. **YIELD:** 8 servings.

CALORIES 271; FAT 7.6g (sat 2.7g, mono 2.6g, poly 1.7g); PROTEIN 14.7g; CARB 33.9g; FIBER 1.6g; CHOL 22mg; IRON 2.1mg; SODIUM 700mg; CALC 290mg

## what makes it light
- uses turkey Italian sausage
- uses fat-free milk
- uses egg substitute
- uses reduced-fat Monterey Jack cheese

# recipe makeover
## stuffed french toast

**The Reader:** Kristi Wold

**The Story:** As a practice manager for a thriving medical group, Kristi knows the value of efficiency, which is partly why she loves this recipe. You can throw it together the night before and pop it into the oven shortly before brunch—perfect for a hectic schedule. With layers of smooth cream cheese stuffing and cinnamon-raisin bread, the puddinglike dish wins raves from coworkers whenever Kristi takes it to the office. The dish has only one drawback—its nutritional profile.

**The Dilemma:** The original recipe contained one pound of cream cheese, a quart of half-and-half, and eight eggs. Sure, it was delicious, but consuming 27 grams of fat in one sitting is no way to start the day.

**The Solution:** We knew this recipe could stand some serious downsizing. By combining fat-free and ⅓-less-fat cream cheeses to replace the regular cream cheese, we trimmed the fat by more than 100 grams without losing any richness. Reducing the half-and-half and making up the difference with 1% milk cut another 60 grams of fat, while using egg substitute instead of eggs brought the number down another 23 grams. The lightened version remained so rich and flavorful that it rated even higher than the original in our Test Kitchens.

**The Feedback:** Kristi gives the lightened dish an excellent review. She likes it better than the original, not only because the new version has a smoother consistency but also because she can enjoy it more since it isn't so heavy and filling. As for the folks at work who'd adored the original dish—they liked the lightened version more. One doctor told Kristi, "Your dessert was really good." When she replied that it wasn't really a dessert, he said, "Well, it could be." That's what we call creative management.

| | BEFORE | AFTER |
|---|---|---|
| Calories per serving | 502 | 340 |
| Fat | 27.3g | 11.3g |
| Percent of total calories | 49% | 30% |

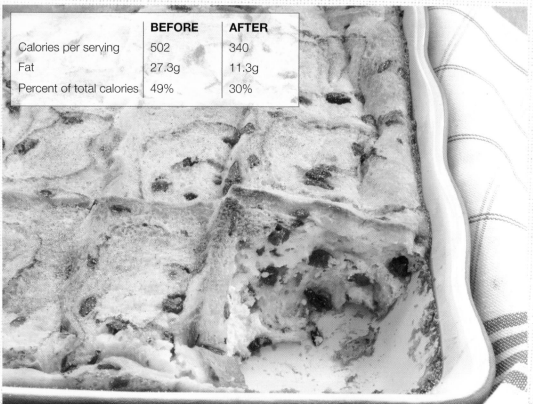

**This stuffed french toast is probably best described** as a combination of crème brulee, cheesecake, and bread pudding all wrapped up into one—only we recommend it for breakfast, not dessert!

# Stuffed French Toast

24 (1-ounce) slices cinnamon-raisin bread
Cooking spray
3 cups 1% low-fat milk
2 cups egg substitute, divided
1 cup half-and-half
1 cup sugar, divided

1 tablespoon vanilla extract
⅛ teaspoon ground nutmeg
1 (8-ounce) block fat-free cream cheese, softened
1 (8-ounce) block ⅓-less-fat cream cheese, softened
Bottled cinnamon-sugar (optional)

**1.** Trim crusts from bread. Arrange half of the bread in a 13 x 9–inch baking dish coated with cooking spray.
**2.** Combine milk, $1^1/2$ cups egg substitute, half-and-half, and $^1/2$ cup sugar in a large bowl, stirring with a whisk. Pour half of milk mixture over bread in dish.
**3.** Place $^1/2$ cup egg substitute, $^1/2$ cup sugar, vanilla, nutmeg, and cheeses in a food processor or blender; process until smooth. Pour cream cheese mixture over moist bread in dish. Top with remaining bread; pour remaining milk mixture over bread. Cover and refrigerate 8 hours or overnight.
**4.** Preheat oven to 350°.
**5.** Uncover and bake at 350° for 55 minutes. Let stand 10 minutes before serving. Sprinkle with cinnamon-sugar, if desired. **YIELD:** 12 servings (serving size: 1 piece).

CALORIES 340; FAT 11.3g (sat 5.1g, mono 3.3g, poly 0.9g); PROTEIN 16.7g; CARB 43.2g; FIBER 1.5g; CHOL 26mg; IRON 3.7mg; SODIUM 447mg; CALC 197mg

**BREAKFAST**

## Strawberry-Filled French Toast with Caramel and Pecans

**Sauce:**
- ½ cup granulated sugar
- 3 tablespoons water
- 1 tablespoon butter
- ½ cup evaporated fat-free milk
- ½ teaspoon vanilla extract
- ⅛ teaspoon salt

**French Toast:**
- Cooking spray
- 1 (12-ounce) loaf French bread, cut into 16 (¼-inch-thick) slices
- ½ cup strawberry preserves
- 2 cups fat-free milk
- ¾ cup egg substitute
- 1 tablespoon vanilla extract
- ⅛ teaspoon salt
- ¼ teaspoon ground cinnamon
- ⅛ teaspoon ground nutmeg
- 2 large eggs
- 3 tablespoons chopped pecans
- 2 tablespoons powdered sugar

**1.** To prepare sauce, combine granulated sugar and water in a medium, heavy saucepan. Cook over medium-low heat 5 minutes or until sugar dissolves. Cover and cook over medium heat 1 minute. Uncover and cook 3 minutes or until light golden (do not stir).

**2.** Remove from heat, and let stand 1 minute. Add butter; stir until melted. Add evaporated milk; stir constantly. Place pan over medium heat; cook 3 minutes or until caramel melts and mixture is smooth, stirring constantly. Remove from heat; stir in vanilla and salt.

**3.** To prepare French toast, pour sauce into a 13 x 9–inch baking dish coated with cooking spray. Arrange 8 bread slices in dish. Spread preserves evenly over bread; top with remaining bread.

**4.** Combine milk and next 6 ingredients. Pour milk mixture over bread; sprinkle with pecans.

**5.** Preheat oven to 350°.

**6.** Bake, uncovered, at 350° for 35 minutes or until top is golden. Let cool 5 minutes. Sprinkle with powdered sugar. **YIELD:** 8 servings (serving size: 1 piece).

CALORIES 332; FAT 6.7g (sat 1.7g, mono 2.9g, poly 1.5g); PROTEIN 11.9g; CARB 55.2g; FIBER 1.6g; CHOL 58mg; IRON 2mg; SODIUM 453mg; CALC 164mg

1

## Marmalade French Toast Casserole

Grapefruit or mixed fruit marmalade will work just as well as the orange marmalade called for in the recipe. Serve the casserole with honey or pancake syrup warmed with orange rind and a splash of orange juice (add one teaspoon rind and two tablespoons juice per ½ cup syrup). This easy casserole can be assembled in less than 15 minutes and stored in the refrigerator overnight.

    3 tablespoons butter, softened
    1 (16-ounce) sourdough French bread
      loaf, cut into 24 (½-inch) slices
Cooking spray
    1 (12-ounce) jar orange marmalade
  2¾ cups 1% low-fat milk
    ⅓ cup sugar
    1 teaspoon vanilla extract
    ¼ teaspoon ground nutmeg
    6 large eggs
    ⅓ cup finely chopped walnuts

**1.** Spread softened butter on one side of each bread slice. Arrange 12 bread slices, buttered sides down, slightly overlapping in a single layer in a 13 x 9–inch baking dish coated with cooking spray. Spread marmalade evenly over bread; top with remaining 12 bread slices, buttered sides up.
**2.** Combine milk and next 4 ingredients, stirring with a whisk. Pour egg mixture over bread. Cover and refrigerate 8 hours or overnight.
**3.** Preheat oven to 350°.
**4.** Sprinkle casserole with walnuts. Bake at 350° for 45 minutes or until golden. Let stand 5 minutes before serving. **YIELD:** 12 servings (serving size: 1 piece).

CALORIES 293; FAT 9g (sat 3.2g, mono 2.2g, poly 2.3g); PROTEIN 9.1g; CARB 46.4g; FIBER 1.6g; CHOL 116mg; IRON 2.2mg; SODIUM 315mg; CALC 132mg

## Baked Coconut French Toast with Tropical Fruit Compote ▼

**Compote:**

- 1½ cups chopped fresh pineapple
- 1 cup chopped peeled mango
- 1 cup chopped peeled papaya
- 1 cup chopped peeled kiwifruit
- 3 tablespoons sugar
- 3 tablespoons fresh lime juice

**French Toast:**

- 16 (1-inch-thick) slices diagonally cut French bread baguette (about 10 ounces)
- Cooking spray
- 1¼ cups light coconut milk
- 1¼ cups egg substitute
- ½ cup sugar
- 1 tablespoon vanilla extract
- ½ cup flaked sweetened coconut

**1.** To prepare compote, combine first 6 ingredients. Cover and chill 8 hours or overnight.
**2.** To prepare French toast, arrange bread in a single layer in a 13 x 9–inch baking dish coated with cooking spray. Combine light coconut milk, egg substitute, ½ cup sugar, and 1 tablespoon vanilla, stirring with a whisk, and pour evenly over bread. Turn bread over to coat. Cover and refrigerate 8 hours or overnight.
**3.** Preheat oven to 350°.
**4.** Remove bread mixture from refrigerator, and uncover. Turn bread slices over, and sprinkle evenly with flaked coconut. Let stand at room temperature 15 minutes. Bake, uncovered, at 350° for 30 minutes or until coconut is golden. Serve warm with fruit compote. **YIELD:** 8 servings (serving size: 2 french toast slices and ½ cup compote).

CALORIES 349; FAT 8.6g (sat 3.5g, mono 1.5g, poly 2.5g); PROTEIN 8.6g; CARB 60.3g; FIBER 4.1g; CHOL 0mg; IRON 1.8mg; SODIUM 309mg; CALC 44mg

## Easy French Toast Casserole ▼

- ⅔ cup packed dark brown sugar
- 2 tablespoons butter
- 2 tablespoons dark corn syrup
- Cooking spray
- 1½ cups 1% low-fat milk
- ½ cup egg substitute
- 1 teaspoon vanilla extract
- ¼ teaspoon salt
- ⅛ teaspoon grated orange rind
- 2 large eggs
- 6 (1½-inch-thick) slices French bread
- 6 tablespoons frozen fat-free whipped topping, thawed
- 1 to 2 teaspoons Grand Marnier (orange-flavored liqueur)
- 2 tablespoons finely chopped pecans, toasted

**1.** Combine first 3 ingredients in a small, heavy saucepan over medium heat. Cook 5 minutes

3

4

or until bubbly and sugar dissolves, stirring constantly. Pour sugar mixture into bottom of a 13 x 9–inch baking dish coated with cooking spray. Spread mixture evenly over bottom of pan. Set aside; cool completely.

**2.** Combine milk and next 5 ingredients in a large shallow bowl; stir with a whisk. Dip 1 bread slice in milk mixture; arrange bread slice over sugar mixture in dish. Repeat procedure with remaining 5 bread slices. Pour any remaining egg mixture over bread slices. Cover and refrigerate overnight.

**3.** Preheat oven to 350°.

**4.** Bake at 350° for 30 minutes or until lightly browned.

**5.** While casserole bakes, combine whipped topping and Grand Marnier. Place 1 bread slice, caramel side up, on each of 6 plates; top each serving with 1 tablespoon topping and 1 teaspoon pecans. **YIELD:** 6 servings.

CALORIES 352; FAT 8.8g (sat 3.5g, mono 2.8g, poly 0.9g); PROTEIN 11.1g; CARB 58.1g; FIBER 1.2g; CHOL 83mg; IRON 2.6mg; SODIUM 466mg; CALC 191mg

## Overnight Caramel French Toast ▶

This is one of *Cooking Light* Test Kitchens Director Vanessa Pruett's favorite holiday brunch dishes. She adapted this recipe from an old family favorite by reducing the amount of butter and eggs, and switching to low-fat milk while still keeping it decadent and rich.

      1  cup packed light brown sugar
      ½  cup light-colored corn syrup
      ¼  cup butter
          Cooking spray
    10  (1-ounce) slices French bread (soft bread such as Pepperidge Farm)
    2½  cups 1% low-fat milk
      1  tablespoon all-purpose flour
    1½  teaspoons vanilla extract
      ¼  teaspoon salt
      2  large eggs
      2  tablespoons granulated sugar
      1  teaspoon ground cinnamon

**1.** Combine first 3 ingredients in a small saucepan. Cook over medium heat 5 minutes or until mixture is bubbly, stirring constantly. Pour mixture evenly into a 13 x 9–inch baking dish coated with cooking spray.

**2.** Arrange bread slices in a single layer over syrup in dish.

**3.** Combine milk and next 4 ingredients in a large bowl, stirring with a whisk. Pour egg mixture over bread slices. Cover and refrigerate 8 hours or overnight.

**4.** Preheat oven to 350°.

**5.** Combine 2 tablespoons granulated sugar and cinnamon. Sprinkle evenly over bread.

**6.** Bake at 350° for 50 minutes or until golden. Let stand 5 minutes before serving.

**YIELD:** 10 servings (serving size: 1 piece).

CALORIES 314; FAT 7.2g (sat 3.2g, mono 2.8g, poly 0.6g); PROTEIN 6.2g; CARB 57.4g; FIBER 1.1g; CHOL 57mg; IRON 1.6mg; SODIUM 360mg; CALC 128mg

**To make ahead,** cook the grits, spoon them into the baking dish, and refrigerate overnight. Let the baking dish stand at room temperature while you prepare the mushroom topping; top the grits, and bake as directed.

# Grits Casserole with Mushrooms, Prosciutto, and Provolone

5 cups water
1¼ cups stone-ground yellow grits
¾ cup (3 ounces) shredded sharp provolone cheese, divided
1 teaspoon salt, divided
Cooking spray
1½ teaspoons butter
¾ cup chopped onion
2 garlic cloves, minced
4 cups thinly sliced portobello mushrooms (about 6 ounces)

3 cups thinly sliced shiitake mushroom caps (about 4½ ounces)
1 teaspoon dried herbes de Provence
¼ teaspoon freshly ground black pepper
1 cup chopped prosciutto (about 3 ounces)
⅓ cup dry white wine
3 large eggs, lightly beaten
2 large egg whites, lightly beaten
1 tablespoon chopped fresh parsley

**1.** Bring water to a boil in a large saucepan; gradually stir in grits. Reduce heat, and simmer 30 minutes or until thick, stirring frequently. Remove from heat. Stir in ¼ cup cheese and ½ teaspoon salt. Spoon grits mixture into an 11 x 7–inch baking dish coated with cooking spray.
**2.** Preheat oven to 350°.
**3.** Melt butter in a large nonstick skillet over medium-high heat. Add onion and garlic; sauté 3 minutes or until tender. Add remaining ½ teaspoon salt, mushrooms, herbes de Provence, and pepper; cook 6 minutes or until mushrooms are tender, stirring frequently. Stir in prosciutto and wine; cook 5 minutes or until liquid almost evaporates. Remove from heat; cool slightly. Stir in eggs and egg whites. Spread mushroom mixture over grits mixture; sprinkle with remaining ½ cup cheese. Bake at 350° for 30 minutes or until cheese melts and grits are thoroughly heated, and let stand 5 minutes before serving. Sprinkle with parsley. **YIELD:** 6 servings.

CALORIES 287; FAT 9.6g (sat 4.4g, mono 3.1g, poly 0.9g); PROTEIN 16.3g; CARB 35.7g; FIBER 2.3g; CHOL 131mg; IRON 2.9mg; SODIUM 832mg; CALC 136mg

## what makes it light
• uses a minimal amount of butter
• uses a combination of eggs and egg whites

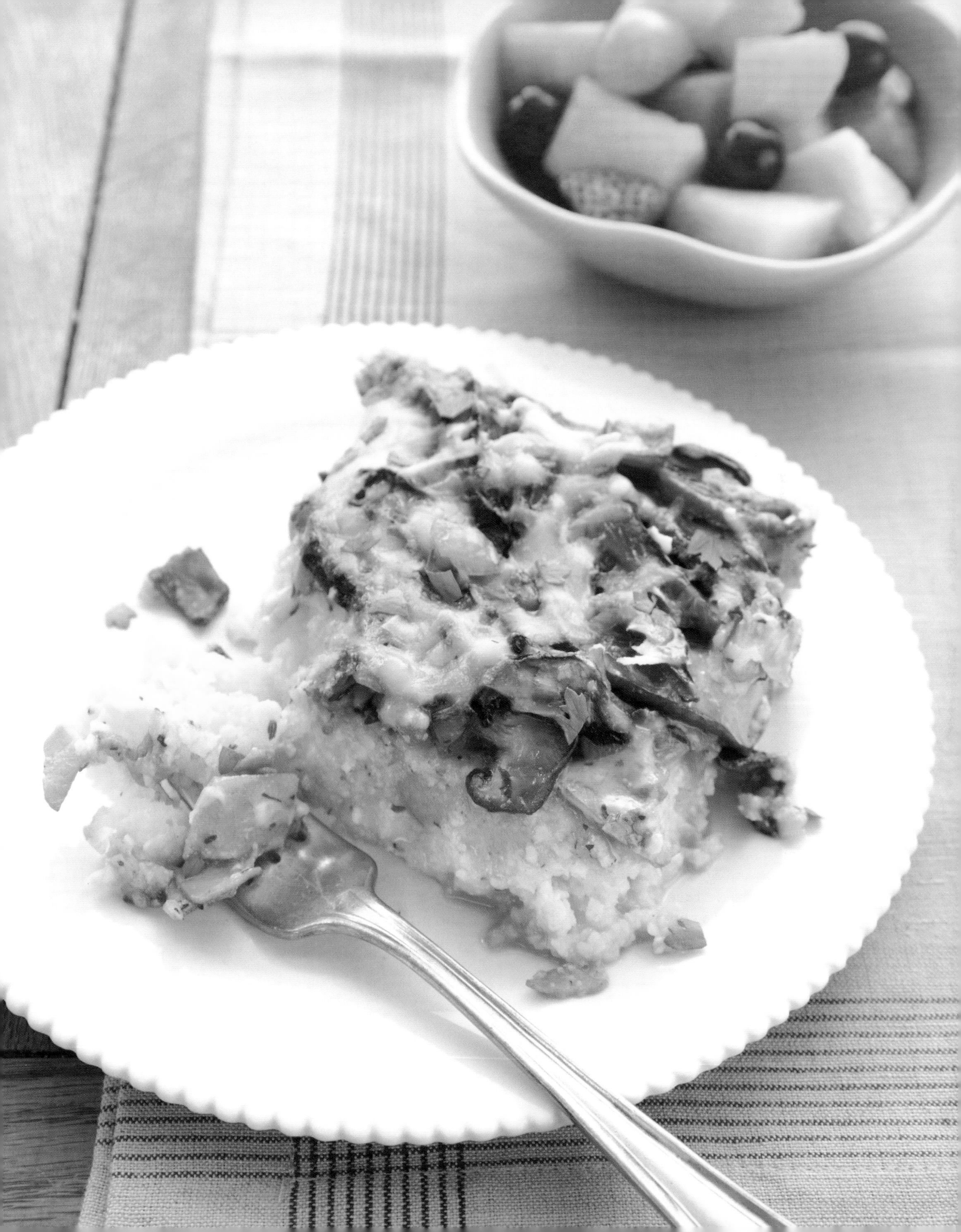

"I was looking for something different for breakfast and I stumbled upon this recipe. **I have fallen in love, and I drool on the mornings that I know I will be making this.** The combination of the goat cheese and fig preserves is divine, and the lemon zest gives the combo just a touch of freshness. I don't always have basil on hand, but it is still dynamite without it. Try it. You will not be disappointed.

**from cookinglight.com**

# Goat Cheese Sandwiches with Fig and Honey

2 teaspoons honey
¼ teaspoon grated lemon rind
1 (4-ounce) package goat cheese
8 (1-ounce) slices cinnamon-raisin bread

2 tablespoons fig preserves
2 teaspoons thinly sliced fresh basil
Cooking spray
1 teaspoon powdered sugar

**1.** Combine first 3 ingredients, stirring until well blended. Spread 1 tablespoon goat cheese mixture on each of 4 bread slices; top each slice with $1^1/_2$ teaspoons preserves and $^1/_2$ teaspoon basil. Top with remaining bread slices. Lightly coat outside of bread with cooking spray.

**2.** Heat a large nonstick skillet over medium heat. Add 2 sandwiches to pan. Place a cast-iron or heavy skillet on top of sandwiches; press gently to flatten. Cook 3 minutes on each side or until bread is lightly toasted (leave cast-iron skillet on sandwiches while they cook). Repeat with remaining sandwiches. Sprinkle with sugar. **YIELD:** 4 servings (serving size: 1 sandwich).

CALORIES 243; FAT 8.5g (sat 4.8g, mono 2.7g, poly 0.5g); PROTEIN 9.8g; CARB 33.1g; FIBER 2.5g; CHOL 13mg; IRON 2.2mg; SODIUM 326mg; CALC 78mg

## what makes it light

• uses cooking spray instead of oil to grill sandwiches

## Sweet Potato and Pecan Flapjacks

Cornmeal adds crunch, and mashed sweet potatoes lend creaminess to this weekend favorite. Yellow- or white-fleshed sweet potatoes have a dry and crumbly texture when baked and are not moist enough to make tender pancakes, so use the orange variety.

- 5.6 ounces all-purpose flour (about 1¼ cups)
- ¼ cup chopped pecans, toasted
- 3 tablespoons yellow cornmeal
- 2 teaspoons baking powder
- ½ teaspoon salt
- ½ teaspoon ground cinnamon
- 1 cup fat-free milk
- 1 cup mashed cooked sweet potato
- 3 tablespoons brown sugar
- 1 tablespoon canola oil
- ½ teaspoon vanilla extract
- 2 large egg yolks
- 2 large egg whites, lightly beaten
- Cooking spray

**1.** Weigh or lightly spoon all-purpose flour into dry measuring cups; level with a knife. Combine flour and next 5 ingredients in a large bowl, stirring with a whisk.
**2.** Combine milk, sweet potato, sugar, oil, vanilla, and egg yolks, stirring until smooth; add to flour mixture, stirring just until combined. Beat egg whites with a mixer at high speed until soft peaks form; then fold egg whites into batter. Let batter stand 10 minutes.
**3.** Heat a nonstick griddle or nonstick skillet over medium-high heat. Coat griddle or pan with cooking spray. Spoon about ¼ cup batter per pancake onto griddle or pan. Cook 2 minutes or until tops are covered with bubbles and edges look cooked. Carefully turn pancakes over, and cook 2 minutes or until bottoms are lightly browned. **YIELD:** 6 servings (serving size: 2 pancakes).

CALORIES 276; FAT 7.9g (sat 1.1g, mono 4.1g, poly 2.1g); PROTEIN 7.7g; CARB 43.7g; FIBER 2.8g; CHOL 71mg; IRON 2.7mg; SODIUM 419mg; CALC 166mg

1

## Blueberry Pancakes

For variety, substitute sliced bananas or chocolate chips for the blueberries for a special treat. Since these pancakes reheat well in the toaster oven, consider making a big batch to enjoy throughout the week.

2.25 ounces all-purpose flour (about ½ cup)
2.38 ounces whole-wheat flour (about ½ cup)
   1 tablespoon sugar
   1 teaspoon baking powder
   ½ teaspoon baking soda
   ⅛ teaspoon salt
   ⅛ teaspoon ground nutmeg
   ¾ cup vanilla fat-free yogurt
   2 tablespoons butter, melted
   2 teaspoons fresh lemon juice
   ½ teaspoon vanilla extract
   2 large eggs, lightly beaten
   1 cup fresh blueberries

**1.** Weigh or lightly spoon flours into dry measuring cups; level with a knife. Combine flours and next 5 ingredients in a large bowl, stirring well with a whisk. Combine yogurt and next 4 ingredients in a small bowl; add to flour mixture, stirring until smooth.
**2.** Pour about ¼ cup batter per pancake onto a hot nonstick griddle or nonstick skillet. Top each pancake with 2 tablespoons blueberries. Cook 2 minutes or until tops are covered with bubbles and edges look cooked. Carefully turn pancakes over; cook 2 minutes or until bottoms are lightly browned. **YIELD:** 4 servings (serving size: 2 blueberry pancakes).

CALORIES 272; FAT 8.8g (sat 4.5g, mono 2.5g, poly 0.8g); PROTEIN 9.5g; CARB 40.1g; FIBER 3.2g; CHOL 122mg; IRON 2mg; SODIUM 403mg; CALC 192mg

## Buttermilk Pancakes ▼

To freeze any leftovers, place wax paper between pancakes, and wrap them tightly in foil.

- 4.5 ounces all-purpose flour (about 1 cup)
- 2 tablespoons sugar
- 1 teaspoon baking powder
- ½ teaspoon baking soda
- ¼ teaspoon salt
- 1 cup low-fat buttermilk
- 1 teaspoon vegetable oil
- 1 large egg, lightly beaten
- Cooking spray

**1.** Weigh or lightly spoon flour into a dry measuring cup; level with a knife. Combine flour and next 4 ingredients in a large bowl, and make a well in center of mixture. Combine buttermilk, oil, and egg; add to flour mixture, stirring until smooth.

**2.** Spoon about ¼ cup batter onto a hot non-stick griddle or nonstick skillet coated with cooking spray. Turn pancakes when tops are covered with bubbles and edges look cooked.

**YIELD:** 9 (4-inch) pancakes (serving size: 1 pancake).

CALORIES 99; FAT 2.9g (sat 0.8g, mono 0.9g, poly 1g); PROTEIN 3.2g; CARB 14.9g; FIBER 0.4g; CHOL 25mg; IRON 0.8mg; SODIUM 211mg; CALC 69mg

## Carrot Cake Pancakes ▼

These cakey flapjacks feature warm spices and bright carrot flavor. This lightened version uses low-fat buttermilk and a small dab of honey butter to top the pancakes versus a typical pat of butter.

- 5.6 ounces all-purpose flour (about 1¼ cups)
- ¼ cup chopped walnuts, toasted
- 2 teaspoons baking powder
- 1 teaspoon ground cinnamon
- ¼ teaspoon salt
- ⅛ teaspoon freshly ground nutmeg
- Dash of ground cloves
- Dash of ground ginger
- ¼ cup brown sugar
- ¾ cup low-fat buttermilk
- 1 tablespoon canola oil
- 1½ teaspoons vanilla extract
- 2 large eggs, lightly beaten
- 2 cups finely grated carrot (about 1 pound)
- Cooking spray
- 3 tablespoons butter, softened
- 2 tablespoons honey

**1.** Weigh or lightly spoon flour into dry measuring cups, and level with a knife. Combine flour

and next 7 ingredients in a large bowl, stirring with a whisk. Combine $\frac{1}{4}$ cup brown sugar and next 4 ingredients; add sugar mixture to flour mixture, stirring just until moist. Fold in 2 cups carrot.

**2.** Heat a large nonstick skillet over medium heat. Coat pan with cooking spray. Spoon 4 ($\frac{1}{4}$-cup) batter mounds onto pan, spreading with a spatula. Cook 2 minutes or until tops are covered with bubbles and edges look cooked. Carefully turn pancakes over; cook 1 minute or until bottoms are lightly browned. Repeat procedure twice with remaining batter. Combine butter and honey in a small bowl; serve with pancakes. **YIELD:** 6 servings (serving size: 2 pancakes and about 2 teaspoons honey butter).

CALORIES 315; FAT 13.3g (sat 4.8g, mono 4.4g, poly 3.3g); PROTEIN 7.8g; CARB 41.6g; FIBER 2.2g; CHOL 78mg; IRON 2.3mg; SODIUM 381mg; CALC 177mg

5

## Hearty Pancakes ▶

Forget that these pancakes are supremely healthy—they are supremely satisfying! Any pancake aficionado will love to have these in the morning breakfast rotation. Ingredients such as whole-wheat flour, soy milk, golden raisins, and walnuts punch up the nutrition in these pancakes, making them heart-healthy.

 4.75 ounces whole-wheat flour (about 1 cup)
 1.1 ounces all-purpose flour (about $\frac{1}{4}$ cup)
 $\frac{1}{3}$ cup uncooked farina (such as Cream of Wheat)
 $\frac{1}{3}$ cup sugar
 1 teaspoon baking soda
 1 teaspoon baking powder
 $\frac{1}{2}$ teaspoon salt
 1$\frac{1}{2}$ cups vanilla soy milk
 $\frac{1}{4}$ cup applesauce
 1 large egg, lightly beaten
 Cooking spray
 $\frac{1}{2}$ cup golden raisins, divided
 $\frac{1}{2}$ cup coarsely chopped walnuts, divided
 $\frac{1}{4}$ cup maple syrup

**1.** Weigh or lightly spoon flours into dry measuring cups; level with a knife. Combine flours, farina, and next 4 ingredients in a large bowl, stirring with a whisk. Combine milk, applesauce, and egg in a medium bowl, stirring until well blended. Add milk mixture to flour mixture, stirring until well combined. Let batter stand 5 minutes.

**2.** Heat a nonstick griddle or skillet over medium heat; coat pan with cooking spray. Pour about $\frac{1}{4}$ cup batter per pancake onto pan; sprinkle each with 2 teaspoons raisins and 2 teaspoons walnuts. Cook 1 minute or until tops are covered with bubbles and edges look cooked. Carefully turn pancakes over, and cook 1 minute or until bottoms are lightly browned. Repeat procedure with remaining batter, raisins, and walnuts. Serve with syrup. **YIELD:** 6 servings (serving size: 2 pancakes and 2 teaspoons maple syrup).

CALORIES 347; FAT 9g (sat 1g, mono 1.3g, poly 5.1g); PROTEIN 8.8g; CARB 61.1g; FIBER 4.3g; CHOL 35mg; IRON 4.8mg; SODIUM 537mg; CALC 142mg

# waffles

1

## Bacon Maple Waffles

Crumbled bacon is cooked into maple-sweetened waffles, so every bite contains that classic pairing. If you're using a Belgian waffle maker, spread about ½ cup batter per waffle onto the waffle iron; you'll get about eight waffles.

9 ounces all-purpose flour (about
   2 cups)
1 tablespoon baking powder
½ teaspoon salt
1¼ cups 2% reduced-fat milk
3 tablespoons maple syrup
2 tablespoons butter, melted
4 bacon slices cooked, crumbled, and
   divided
3 large eggs, lightly beaten
Cooking spray
⅓ cup maple syrup

**1.** Weigh or lightly spoon flour into dry measuring cups; level with a knife. Place flour, baking powder, and salt in a bowl; stir with a whisk. Make a well in center of mixture. Combine milk, 3 tablespoons syrup, butter, 3 bacon slices, and eggs, stirring with a whisk. Add milk mixture to flour mixture; stir just until moist.

**2.** Coat a waffle iron with cooking spray; preheat. Spoon about ⅓ cup batter per waffle onto hot waffle iron, spreading batter to edges. Cook 4 to 5 minutes or until steaming stops; repeat procedure with remaining batter. Serve waffles with ⅓ cup syrup and remaining crumbled bacon. **YIELD:** 5 servings (serving size: 2 waffles and about 1 tablespoon syrup).

CALORIES 411; FAT 11.4g (sat 5.3g, mono 3.7g, poly 1.1g); PROTEIN 12.9g; CARB 64.5g; FIBER 1.4g; CHOL 149mg; IRON 3.7mg; SODIUM 754mg; CALC 284mg

## Banana-Cinnamon Waffles

Crown these lightly spiced waffles with cinnamon sugar, sliced bananas, and/or a drizzle of maple syrup. Buckwheat flour adds a somewhat tangy, robust nuttiness.

4.5 ounces all-purpose flour (about 1 cup)
2.38 ounces whole-wheat flour (about ½ cup)
1 ounce buckwheat flour (about ¼ cup)
¼ cup ground flaxseed
2 tablespoons sugar
1½ teaspoons baking powder
½ teaspoon ground cinnamon
¼ teaspoon salt
1½ cups fat-free milk
3 tablespoons butter, melted
2 large eggs, lightly beaten
1 large ripe banana, mashed
Cooking spray

**1.** Weigh or lightly spoon flours into dry measuring cups; level with a knife. Combine flours, flaxseed, and next 4 ingredients in a medium bowl, stirring with a whisk.
**2.** Combine milk, butter, and eggs, stirring with a whisk; add milk mixture to flour mixture, stirring until blended. Fold in mashed banana.
**3.** Coat a waffle iron with cooking spray; preheat. Spoon about ¼ cup batter per 4-inch waffle onto hot waffle iron, spreading batter to edges. Cook 3 to 4 minutes or until steaming stops; repeat procedure with remaining batter.
**YIELD:** 8 servings (serving size: 2 waffles).

CALORIES 215; FAT 7.4g (sat 3.3g, mono 1.9g, poly 1.4g); PROTEIN 7.3g; CARB 31.1g; FIBER 3.4g; CHOL 65mg; IRON 1.9mg; SODIUM 205mg; CALC 133mg

3

## Citrus Waffles with Marmalade Compote

**Compote:**
- ¼ cup reduced-sugar orange marmalade (such as Smucker's)
- 1 tablespoon fresh orange juice
- 1 teaspoon fresh lemon juice
- 1 teaspoon honey
- 2 cups fresh orange sections (about 2 oranges)

**Waffles:**
- 3.75 ounces all-purpose flour (about ¾ cup)
- 3.5 ounces whole-wheat flour (about ¾ cup)
- ½ cup packed brown sugar
- ¼ cup toasted wheat germ
- 1¼ teaspoons baking powder
- 1 teaspoon baking soda
- ¼ teaspoon salt
- ¼ teaspoon nutmeg
- 1⅓ cups buttermilk
- ⅓ cup water
- 2 tablespoons canola oil
- 1 teaspoon grated orange rind
- 1 large egg, lightly beaten
- Cooking spray
- Powdered sugar

**1.** To prepare compote, place marmalade, orange juice, lemon juice, and honey in a small saucepan over medium-low heat; cook 2 minutes or until marmalade melts. Reduce heat, and gently stir in orange sections; keep warm.

**2.** To prepare waffles, weigh or lightly spoon flours into dry measuring cups, and level with a knife. Combine flours and next 6 ingredients in a large bowl, stirring with a whisk. Combine buttermilk, ⅓ cup water, canola oil, orange rind, and egg in a small bowl. Add milk mixture to flour mixture, stirring just until moist. Coat a waffle iron with cooking spray; preheat. Spoon about ⅓ cup batter per 4-inch waffle onto hot waffle iron, spreading batter to edges. Cook 5 minutes or until steaming stops, and repeat procedure with remaining batter. Sift powdered sugar over tops of waffles. Serve with orange compote. **YIELD:** 6 servings (serving size: 2 waffles and ⅓ cup compote).

CALORIES 309; FAT 8.3g (sat 1.9g, mono 3.7g, poly 2.1g); PROTEIN 8.5g; CARB 52.5g; FIBER 4.5g; CHOL 43mg; IRON 2.3mg; SODIUM 492mg; CALC 169mg

## French Toast Waffles ▼

A waffle maker creates a crisp, brown French toast without a skillet. Just make sure you start with slightly hardened bread so that the toast won't be soggy. Serve this toast with fresh raspberries and maple syrup.

    Cooking spray
    1  cup fat-free milk
    1  tablespoon sugar
    1  tablespoon butter, melted
    1  teaspoon vanilla extract
    ½  teaspoon ground cinnamon
    2  large eggs
    16 (½-inch-thick) slices day-old French
       bread (about 7 ounces)

**1.** Coat waffle iron with cooking spray, and preheat.
**2.** Combine milk and next 5 ingredients, stirring well with a whisk. Place bread in a 13 x 9–inch baking dish; pour milk mixture over bread, turning to coat. Let stand 5 minutes.
**3.** Place 4 bread slices on hot waffle iron. Cook 3 to 5 minutes or until done; repeat procedure with remaining bread. **YIELD:** 4 servings (serving size: 4 waffles).

CALORIES 236; FAT 7g (sat 3g, mono 2.4g, poly 0.8g); PROTEIN 9.6g; CARB 32.5g; FIBER 1.6g; CHOL 115mg; IRON 1.7mg; SODIUM 395mg; CALC 129mg

## Honeyed Yogurt and Mixed Berries with Whole-Grain Waffles ▼

    2  cups vanilla low-fat yogurt
    2  tablespoons honey
    2  cups fresh raspberries
    1  cup quartered small strawberries
    1  cup fresh blackberries
    ⅓  cup sugar
    2  tablespoons fresh lemon juice
    4  frozen whole-grain waffles, toasted
    4  teaspoons toasted wheat germ

**1.** Drain yogurt in a fine sieve or colander lined with cheesecloth 10 minutes; spoon into a bowl. Add honey, stirring to combine.
**2.** Combine berries, sugar, and juice; let stand 5 minutes. Place 1 waffle on each of 4 plates; top each serving with 1 cup fruit mixture, about ⅓ cup yogurt mixture, and 1 teaspoon wheat germ. Serve immediately. **YIELD:** 4 servings (serving size: 1 waffle, 1 cup fruit mixture, about ⅓ cup yogurt mixture, and 1 teaspoon wheat germ).

CALORIES 377; FAT 6.8g (sat 2.3g, mono 2.3g, poly 1.6g); PROTEIN 11.5g; CARB 71.6g; FIBER 8.3g; CHOL 43mg; IRON 1.9mg; SODIUM 214 mg; CALC 345mg

4   5

This recipe falls into the 'dangerously good category.' For serving size it should say 'you will eat this until it is gone.' Highly recommended.

from cookinglight.com

# Sweet Potato and Canadian Bacon Hash

4 cups (¾-inch) diced peeled sweet potato (about 1 pound)
2 cups (¾-inch) diced red potato (about 8 ounces)
2 tablespoons vegetable oil
1 cup diced Canadian bacon (about 8 ounces)
1 cup chopped green bell pepper

⅔ cup chopped green onions
¾ teaspoon salt
½ teaspoon celery seed
½ teaspoon freshly ground black pepper
⅛ teaspoon grated whole nutmeg
¼ cup fat-free, lower-sodium chicken broth
1 tablespoon cider vinegar

**1.** Place potatoes in a saucepan, and cover with water. Bring to a boil. Reduce heat, and simmer 5 minutes. Drain.

**2.** Heat oil in a large nonstick skillet over medium heat. Add bacon; cook 4 minutes, stirring frequently. Add bell pepper and green onions; cook 2 minutes, stirring frequently. Add potatoes, salt, celery seed, pepper, and nutmeg; cook 4 minutes, gently stirring occasionally. Stir in broth and vinegar. Toss gently until liquid is absorbed. **YIELD:** 6 servings (serving size: about 1 cup).

CALORIES 207; FAT 6.8g (sat 1.4g, mono 2.1g, poly 3g); PROTEIN 8.8g; CARB 28g; FIBER 3g; CHOL 19mg; IRON 1.4mg; SODIUM 711mg; CALC 32mg

## what makes it light

• uses fat-free, lower-sodium chicken broth
• uses a minimal amount of salt
• uses Canadian bacon, which is a leaner choice than regular bacon

30 minutes or less

## what makes it light

- doesn't use butter like traditional recipes
- uses half the amount of cheese and sour cream as traditional recipes
- uses fat-free sour cream
- uses 30% reduced-sodium, 98% fat-free cream of mushroom soup

"Here in the Midwest a popular side for Sunday dinners and potlucks is a hash brown casserole much like this one. There are probably five not-light versions in every local cookbook. I was asked to bring that dish for a huge family get-together, so I substituted a double recipe of this casserole. It was the first thing to disappear. Everyone loved the bacon (not included in the traditional recipes that are popular in this area) and **everyone thought they were getting a bonus version, not a light version.**"

**from cookinglight.com**

# Hash Brown Casserole with Bacon, Onions, and Cheese

6 bacon slices
1 cup chopped onion
2 garlic cloves, minced
1 (32-ounce) package frozen Southern-style hash brown potatoes
1 cup (4 ounces) preshredded four cheese blend, divided (such as Kraft)
½ cup chopped green onions
½ cup fat-free sour cream
½ teaspoon salt
¼ teaspoon freshly ground black pepper
1 (10.75-ounce) can condensed 30% reduced-sodium, 98% fat-free cream of mushroom soup, undiluted
Cooking spray

**1.** Cook bacon in a large nonstick skillet over medium heat until crisp. Remove bacon from pan, and crumble. Discard drippings. Add 1 cup onion and garlic to pan; cook 5 minutes or until tender, stirring frequently. Stir in potatoes; cover and cook 15 minutes, stirring occasionally.
**2.** Combine crumbled bacon, $^{1}/_{4}$ cup cheese, green onions, sour cream, salt, pepper, and soup in a large bowl. Add potato mixture; toss gently to combine. Spoon mixture into an 11 x 7–inch baking dish coated with cooking spray. Sprinkle with remaining $^{3}/_{4}$ cup cheese. Cover with foil coated with cooking spray. Refrigerate 8 hours or overnight.
**3.** Preheat oven to 350°.
**4.** Remove casserole from refrigerator; let stand at room temperature 15 minutes. Bake casserole, covered, at 350° for 30 minutes. Uncover and bake an additional 30 minutes or until bubbly around edges and cheese begins to brown. **YIELD:** 6 servings (serving size: about 1 cup).

CALORIES 293; FAT 10g (sat 4.8g, mono 3.3g, poly 0.7g); PROTEIN 12.2g; CARB 41.4g; FIBER 4.7g; CHOL 31mg; IRON 0.2mg; SODIUM 720mg; CALC 214mg

> Super easy to make. **It is so much better than what you can buy in a box.** Much healthier, too! We've been eating a little of it each morning for breakfast with milk and sometimes as an after-workout snack with yogurt.
>
> **from cookinglight.com**

# Three-Grain Breakfast Cereal with Walnuts and Dried Fruit

½ cup maple syrup
⅓ cup honey
3 tablespoons canola oil
1½ tablespoons vanilla extract
4½ cups regular oats
1 cup uncooked quick-cooking barley
¾ cup chopped walnuts or pecans

½ cup wheat germ
1 teaspoon ground cinnamon
¼ teaspoon ground nutmeg
Cooking spray
1 (7-ounce) package dried mixed fruit, chopped (such as Sun-Maid brand)

**1.** Preheat oven to 325°.

**2.** Combine first 4 ingredients, stirring with a whisk.

**3.** Combine oats, barley, walnuts, wheat germ, cinnamon, and nutmeg in a large bowl. Add syrup mixture; stir well to coat. Spread oat mixture evenly onto a jelly-roll pan coated with cooking spray. Bake at 325° for 30 minutes or until browned, stirring every 10 minutes. Stir in dried fruit. Cool completely. **YIELD:** 24 servings (serving size: ⅓ cup).

CALORIES 185; FAT 5.8g (sat 0.6g, mono 1.7g, poly 2.8); PROTEIN 4.5g; CARB 31.3g; FIBER 4g; CHOL 0mg; IRON 1.6mg; SODIUM 4mg; CALC 24mg

## what makes it light

- uses canola oil, which is a healthy option
- doesn't use salt, which is in most store-bought cereals
- uses three types of whole grains to maximize health benefits

> This was a wonderful oatmeal and easy to make. The dried cherries gave it a sweet-tart flavor, and the brown sugar–hazelnut topping added just the right amount of sweetness. The hazelnut oil gave it a rich creamy texture and a nutty kick. Leftovers heated up nicely with a little extra water. Will make again and again.
>
> **from cookinglight.com**

# Cherry-Hazelnut Oatmeal

6 cups water
2 cups steel-cut (Irish) oats (such as McCann's)
⅔ cup dried Bing or other sweet cherries, coarsely chopped
¼ teaspoon salt

5 tablespoons brown sugar, divided
¼ cup chopped hazelnuts, toasted and divided
¼ teaspoon ground cinnamon
2 tablespoons toasted hazelnut oil

**1.** Combine first 4 ingredients in a medium saucepan; bring to a boil. Reduce heat, and simmer 20 minutes or until desired consistency, stirring occasionally. Remove from heat. Stir in 3 tablespoons sugar, 1 tablespoon nuts, and cinnamon. Place 1 cup oatmeal in each of 6 bowls; sprinkle each serving with 1 teaspoon sugar. Top each serving with $1^1/_2$ teaspoon nuts; drizzle with 1 teaspoon oil. **YIELD:** 6 servings.

CALORIES 350; FAT 11.1g (sat 1.1g, mono 6.8g, poly 2g); PROTEIN 8.9g; CARB 56.1g; FIBER 6.8g; CHOL 0mg; IRON 3mg; SODIUM 112mg; CALC 52mg

## what makes it light

- uses cherries, cinnamon, and a small amount of brown sugar to add natural sweetness
- uses fiber-rich oats

**what makes it light**

? • uses fat-free milk
• uses a minimal amount of salt

*"This makes an outstanding breakfast. I first had it at a trendy restaurant in Chicago and was able to locate the recipe to make at home. It can be made ahead and reheated for a later time. My family loves it!"*

**from cookinglight.com**

# Pan-Seared Oatmeal with Warm Fruit Compote and Cider Syrup

**Syrup:**

2 cups apple cider

**Compote:**

2 cups water

¼ cup packed brown sugar

½ teaspoon ground cinnamon

1 (7-ounce) package dried mixed fruit bits

**Oatmeal:**

3 cups water

1 cup fat-free milk

¼ cup packed brown sugar

½ teaspoon ground cinnamon

¼ teaspoon salt

1½ cups steel-cut (Irish) oats

Cooking spray

¼ cup butter, divided

**1.** To prepare syrup, bring cider to a boil in a small saucepan over medium-high heat. Cook until reduced to $^1/_3$ cup (about 20 minutes); set aside.

**2.** To prepare compote, combine 2 cups water, $^1/_4$ cup sugar, $^1/_2$ teaspoon cinnamon, and dried fruit in a medium saucepan; bring to a boil. Reduce heat, and simmer 20 minutes or until thick. Set aside, and keep warm.

**3.** To prepare oatmeal, combine 3 cups water, 1 cup milk, $^1/_4$ cup brown sugar, $^1/_2$ teaspoon cinnamon, and salt in a large saucepan. Bring to a boil over medium-high heat; stir in oats. Reduce heat, and simmer 20 minutes or until thick, stirring occasionally. Spoon oatmeal into an 11 x 7–inch baking dish coated with cooking spray; cool to room temperature. Cover and chill at least 1 hour or until set.

**4.** Using a sharp knife, cut oatmeal into 8 equal rectangles; cut each rectangle in half diagonally to form 16 triangles.

**5.** Melt 2 tablespoons butter in a large nonstick skillet over medium heat. Add 8 oatmeal triangles; cook 3 minutes on each side or until golden brown. Remove from pan; keep warm. Repeat procedure with remaining 2 tablespoons butter and oatmeal triangles. Place 2 oatmeal triangles on each of 8 plates, and top each serving with $3^1/_2$ tablespoons fruit compote and about 2 teaspoons syrup.

**YIELD:** 8 servings.

CALORIES 314; FAT 7.9g (sat 3.9g, mono 2.3g, poly 0.9g); PROTEIN 5.8g; CARB 58.7g; FIBER 2.8g; CHOL 16mg; IRON 2.4mg; SODIUM 167mg; CALC 76mg

**It's important to measure the flour correctly.** We recommend weighing it. Also, keep this tip in mind when cutting your biscuits: Cut the dough with a biscuit cutter dipped in flour, but be careful not to twist it. Twisting it could seal the edges of the dough and hinder the biscuits from rising. The buttermilk adds flavor and tenderness so you don't have to use as much butter in these flaky melt-in-your-mouth biscuits.

# Buttermilk Biscuits

9 ounces all-purpose flour (about 2 cups)
2 teaspoons baking powder
¼ teaspoon baking soda
¼ teaspoon salt

3 tablespoons plus 1 teaspoon chilled butter, cut into small pieces
¾ cup low-fat or nonfat buttermilk
Honey (optional)

**1.** Preheat oven to 450°.

**2.** Weigh or lightly spoon flour into dry measuring cups; level with a knife. Combine flour and next 3 ingredients in a bowl. Cut in butter with a pastry blender or 2 knives until mixture resembles coarse meal. Add buttermilk; stir just until dry ingredients are moist.

**3.** Turn dough out onto a lightly floured surface; knead 4 or 5 times. Roll dough to a $^{1}/_{2}$-inch-thickness; cut with a $2^{1}/_{2}$-inch biscuit cutter. Place on a baking sheet. Bake at 450° for 12 minutes or until biscuits are golden. Drizzle biscuits with honey, if desired. **YIELD:** 1 dozen (serving size: 1 biscuit).

CALORIES 102; FAT 2.6g (sat 1.2g, mono 1g, poly 0.2g); PROTEIN 2.7g; CARB 16.9g; FIBER 0.6g; CHOL 6mg; IRON 1.1mg; SODIUM 189mg; CALC 67mg

## what makes it light

- uses low-fat buttermilk
- uses less butter than traditional recipes

**This recipe puts a surprising but delicious twist on a classic Southern breakfast.** Vegetarian sausage has a firmer texture than pork sausage. Crumbling it helps distribute it evenly throughout the gravy. The gravy boasts 3 grams of soy protein per serving and is far healthier than a traditional meat-based sausage gravy.

# Biscuits and Vegetarian Sausage Gravy

1 (16.3-ounce) can reduced-fat refrigerated biscuit dough
1 tablespoon vegetable oil
½ (14-ounce) package meatless fat-free sausage (such as Lightlife Gimme Lean)

1.1 ounces all-purpose flour (about ¼ cup)
3 cups 1% low-fat milk
½ teaspoon salt
¼ teaspoon freshly ground black pepper

**1.** Prepare biscuits according to package directions.

**2.** Heat oil in a large nonstick skillet over medium-high heat. Add sausage; cook 3 minutes or until browned, stirring to crumble.

**3.** Weigh or lightly spoon flour into a dry measuring cup; level with a knife. Combine flour and 1% low-fat milk, stirring with a whisk until smooth. Add milk mixture, salt, and freshly ground black pepper to pan; bring to a boil over medium-high heat. Cover, reduce heat, and simmer 3 minutes or until thick. Split biscuits in half. Place 2 biscuit halves on each of 8 plates; top each serving with about ⅓ cup gravy. Serve immediately. **YIELD:** 8 servings.

CALORIES 268; FAT 8.7g (sat 2.4g, mono 4g, poly 1g); PROTEIN 11.4g; CARB 36.9g; FIBER 0.6g; CHOL 4mg; IRON 1mg; SODIUM 910mg; CALC 131mg

## ?what makes it light

• uses vegetarian sausage instead of pork sausage
• uses low-fat milk
• uses reduced-fat refrigerated biscuits

**Best light scones ever!** I even added a couple tablespoons of ground flaxseed, and they were great.

from cookinglight.com

# Sour Cream Scones

6.75 ounces all-purpose flour (about 1½ cups)
3 ounces whole-wheat flour (about ⅔ cup)
⅓ cup packed brown sugar
2 tablespoons granulated sugar
2 teaspoons baking powder
½ teaspoon baking soda
¼ teaspoon salt
⅔ cup reduced-fat sour cream
3 tablespoons butter, melted and cooled
1 large egg white
⅓ cup dried currants or raisins
Cooking spray
1 tablespoon granulated sugar
¼ teaspoon ground cinnamon
Lemon curd (optional)

**1.** Preheat oven to 400°.
**2.** Weigh or lightly spoon flours into dry measuring cups; level with a knife. Combine flours and next 5 ingredients in a large bowl; stir well with a whisk.
**3.** Combine sour cream, butter, and egg white in a small bowl. Add sour cream mixture to flour mixture, stirring just until moist. Stir in currants.
**4.** Turn dough out onto a lightly floured surface; knead lightly 6 to 12 times with floured hands. (Dough will be crumbly.) Divide dough in half. Pat each half into a 6-inch circle on a baking sheet coated with cooking spray. Cut each circle into 6 wedges; do not separate.
**5.** Combine 1 tablespoon granulated sugar and cinnamon. Lightly coat top of dough with cooking spray. Sprinkle with cinnamon mixture. Bake at 400° for 15 minutes or until lightly browned. Serve with lemon curd, if desired. **YIELD:** 1 dozen (serving size: 1 scone).

CALORIES 175; FAT 4.8g (sat 2.9g, mono 1.3g, poly 0.3g); PROTEIN 3.6g; CARB 30.2g; FIBER 1.4g; CHOL 14mg; IRON 1.3mg; SODIUM 219mg; CALC 81mg

## what makes it light
• uses reduced-fat sour cream
• uses almost half the amount of butter as traditional recipes
• uses egg white

This easy recipe turns out the most delicious, fluffy, rich-tasting scones. My local bakery's full-fat version can't beat them! I've also substituted about ¾ cup chopped dill for the ham and have gotten nothing but rave reviews.

**from cookinglight.com**

# Ham and Cheese Scones

- 9 ounces all-purpose flour (about 2 cups)
- 1 tablespoon baking powder
- 2 teaspoons sugar
- ¼ teaspoon salt
- ¼ teaspoon ground red pepper
- 3 tablespoons chilled butter, cut into small pieces
- ¾ cup (3 ounces) shredded reduced-fat extrasharp cheddar cheese
- ¾ cup finely chopped 33%-less-sodium ham (about 3 ounces)
- ¾ cup nonfat buttermilk
- 2 large egg whites
- Cooking spray

**1.** Preheat oven to 400°.

**2.** Weigh or lightly spoon flour into dry measuring cups; level with a knife. Combine flour, baking powder, sugar, salt, and pepper in a large bowl; cut in butter with a pastry blender or 2 knives until mixture resembles coarse meal. Stir in cheese and ham. Combine buttermilk and egg whites, stirring with a whisk. Add to flour mixture, stirring just until moist.

**3.** Turn dough out onto a lightly floured surface; knead lightly 4 to 5 times with floured hands. Pat dough into an 8-inch circle on a baking sheet coated with cooking spray. Cut dough into 8 wedges, cutting into but not through dough. Bake at 400° for 20 minutes or until lightly browned. **YIELD:** 8 servings (serving size: 1 scone).

CALORIES 217; FAT 7.2g (sat 4.1g, mono 1.6g, poly 0.4g); PROTEIN 10.4g; CARB 27.1g; FIBER 0.9g; CHOL 26mg; IRON 1.8mg; SODIUM 519mg; CALC 235mg

## what makes it light

- uses reduced-fat extrasharp cheddar cheese
- uses 33%-less-sodium ham
- uses nonfat buttermilk
- uses egg whites
- uses almost half the amount of butter as traditional recipes

# 5 ways with
# muffins

**1**

## Strawberry-Cinnamon Muffins

- 6.75 ounces all-purpose flour (about 1½ cups)
- ½ cup sugar
- 2½ teaspoons baking powder
- 1 teaspoon ground cinnamon
- ¼ teaspoon salt
- ⅔ cup vanilla fat-free yogurt
- ¼ cup butter, melted
- 3 tablespoons 1% low-fat milk
- 1 large egg, lightly beaten
- Cooking spray
- ¼ cup strawberry jam
- 1 tablespoon sugar
- ½ teaspoon ground cinnamon

**1.** Preheat oven to 375°.
**2.** Weigh or lightly spoon flour into dry measuring cups, and level with a knife. Combine flour and next 4 ingredients in a large bowl, stirring well with a whisk. Make a well in center of flour mixture. Combine yogurt, butter, milk, and egg in a bowl, stirring well with a whisk. Add yogurt mixture to flour mixture, stirring just until moist.
**3.** Place 12 foil cup liners in muffin cups; coat liners with cooking spray. Spoon 1 tablespoon batter into each liner. Top each with 1 teaspoon jam. Top evenly with remaining batter. Combine 1 tablespoon sugar and ½ teaspoon cinnamon; sprinkle over batter. Bake at 375° for 15 minutes or until a wooden pick inserted in center comes out clean. Cool in pan on a wire rack 15 minutes. Remove from pan; place on wire rack. **YIELD:** 1 dozen (serving size: 1 muffin).

CALORIES 165; FAT 4.4g (sat 2.6g, mono 1.3g, poly 0.3g); PROTEIN 3g; CARB 29g; FIBER 0.6g; CHOL 28mg; IRON 1mg; SODIUM 206mg; CALC 94mg

## Raspberry-Cream Cheese Muffins

One of our cookinglight.com readers said she had a serious problem with this recipe—it was super easy to make and she couldn't stop eating them. We think you'll discover the same "problem."

  ⅔ cup (5 ounces) ⅓-less-fat cream cheese, softened
  ⅓ cup butter, softened
  1½ cups sugar
  1½ teaspoons vanilla extract
  2 large egg whites
  1 large egg
  9 ounces all-purpose flour (about 2 cups)
  1 teaspoon baking powder
  ¼ teaspoon baking soda
  ½ teaspoon salt
  ½ cup low-fat buttermilk
  2 cups fresh or frozen raspberries
  ¼ cup finely chopped walnuts

**1.** Preheat oven to 350°.

**2.** Combine cream cheese and butter in a large bowl. Beat with a mixer at high speed until well blended. Add sugar; beat until fluffy. Add vanilla, egg whites, and egg; beat well.

**3.** Weigh or lightly spoon flour into dry measuring cups; level with a knife. Combine flour, baking powder, baking soda, and salt. With mixer on low speed, add flour mixture and buttermilk to cream cheese mixture, beginning and ending with flour mixture. Gently fold in raspberries and walnuts.

**4.** Place 24 foil cup liners in muffin cups. Spoon batter evenly into liners. Bake at 350° for 25 minutes or until a wooden pick inserted in center comes out clean. Remove from pans; cool on a wire rack. **YIELD:** 2 dozen (serving size: 1 muffin).

CALORIES 142; FAT 4.7g (sat 2.4g, mono 1.3g, poly 0.7g); PROTEIN 2.7g; CARB 22.6g; FIBER 1.1g; CHOL 19mg; IRON 0.7mg; SODIUM 138mg; CALC 31mg

2

## Sour Cream Muffins with Poppy Seed Streusel ▾

Keep these orange-scented muffins on hand for a quick breakfast or sweet snack.

Streusel:

- 3 tablespoons sugar
- 2 tablespoons all-purpose flour
- 1 tablespoon butter, melted
- 1 teaspoon poppy seeds

Muffins:

- 9 ounces all-purpose flour (about 2 cups)
- ¾ cup sugar
- 2 teaspoons baking powder
- 1 teaspoon baking soda
- ½ teaspoon salt
- ¾ cup nonfat buttermilk
- ¼ cup butter, melted
- 1 tablespoon grated orange rind
- 1 teaspoon vanilla extract
- 1 large egg, lightly beaten
- 1 (8-ounce) container reduced-fat sour cream
- Cooking spray

**1.** Preheat oven to 375°.
**2.** To prepare streusel, combine first 4 ingredients in a small bowl; set aside.
**3.** To prepare muffins, weigh or lightly spoon 9 ounces flour into dry measuring cups; level with a knife. Combine flour, ³⁄4 cup sugar, baking powder, baking soda, and salt in a medium bowl, stirring with a whisk. Make a well in center of mixture. Combine buttermilk and remaining ingredients except cooking spray in a small bowl; add to flour mixture, stirring just until moist. Spoon batter into 15 muffin cups coated with cooking spray. Sprinkle streusel evenly over batter. Bake at 375° for 18 minutes or until golden brown. Remove muffins from pans immediately; place on a wire rack. **YIELD:** 15 servings (serving size: 1 muffin).

CALORIES 180; FAT 6.3g (sat 3.2g, mono 2.3g, poly 0.4g); PROTEIN 3.3g; CARB 27.8g; FIBER 0.5g; CHOL 31mg; IRON 1mg; SODIUM 277mg; CALC 77mg

## Lemon-Blueberry Muffins ▾

- 9 ounces all-purpose flour (about 2 cups)
- ½ cup sugar
- 1 teaspoon baking powder
- ½ teaspoon baking soda
- ½ teaspoon salt
- ⅛ teaspoon ground nutmeg
- ¼ cup butter
- 1¼ cups low-fat buttermilk
- 1 large egg
- 1 tablespoon grated lemon rind
- 1 cup blueberries
- Cooking spray
- 1 tablespoon fresh lemon juice
- ½ cup powdered sugar

3

4

1. Preheat oven to 400°.
2. Weigh or lightly spoon flour into dry measuring cups; level with a knife. Combine flour and next 5 ingredients in a medium bowl; cut in butter with a pastry blender or 2 knives until mixture resembles coarse meal.
3. Combine buttermilk, egg, and rind; stir well with a whisk. Add to flour mixture; stir just until moist. Gently fold in blueberries.
4. Spoon batter into 12 muffin cups coated with cooking spray. Bake at 400° for 20 minutes or until muffins spring back when lightly touched. Remove muffins from pans immediately, and place on a wire rack to cool.
5. Combine lemon juice and powdered sugar in a small bowl. Drizzle glaze evenly over cooled muffins. **YIELD:** 1 dozen (serving size: 1 muffin).

CALORIES 187; FAT 4.8g (sat 2.7g, mono 1.4g, poly 0.3g); PROTEIN 3.7g; CARB 32.6g; FIBER 1g; CHOL 30mg; IRON 1.1mg; SODIUM 264mg; CALC 59mg

## Tropical Muffins with ▲ Coconut-Macadamia Topping

**Muffins:**
- 6 ounces all-purpose flour (about 1⅓ cups)
- 1 cup regular oats
- 1 teaspoon baking powder
- ½ teaspoon baking soda
- ½ teaspoon salt
- 1 cup mashed ripe banana (about 2 bananas)
- 1 cup low-fat buttermilk
- ½ cup packed brown sugar
- 2 tablespoons canola oil
- 1 teaspoon vanilla extract
- 1 large egg
- ½ cup canned crushed pineapple in juice, drained
- ⅓ cup flaked sweetened coconut
- 3 tablespoons finely chopped macadamia nuts, toasted
- Cooking spray

**Topping:**
- 2 tablespoons flaked sweetened coconut
- 1 tablespoon chopped macadamia nuts
- 1 tablespoon granulated sugar
- 1 tablespoon regular oats

1. Preheat oven to 400°.
2. To prepare muffins, weigh or lightly spoon flour into dry measuring cups; level with a knife. Combine flour and next 4 ingredients in a large bowl. Make a well in center of flour mixture. Combine banana and next 5 ingredients in a medium bowl; add to flour mixture, stirring just until moist. Stir in pineapple, ⅓ cup coconut, and 3 tablespoons nuts. Spoon batter into 12 muffin cups coated with cooking spray.
3. To prepare topping, combine coconut and remaining ingredients in a small bowl.
4. Sprinkle about 1 teaspoon topping over each muffin. Bake at 400° for 18 minutes or until muffins spring back when touched lightly in center. Remove muffins from pans immediately; place on a wire rack. **YIELD:** 1 dozen (serving size: 1 muffin).

CALORIES 205; FAT 6.7g (sat 1.7g, mono 3.4g, poly 1g); PROTEIN 4.3g; CARB 33.3g; FIBER 2g; CHOL 19mg; IRON 1.5mg; SODIUM 215mg; CALC 69mg

> **I have made this recipe hundreds of times** since it first came out in **Cooking Light** in 2003. I've received nothing but rave reviews from the people I've made it for, and it's my favorite recipe to make! It also doubles well. Moist and flavorful.
>
> **from cookinglight.com**

# Coconut Banana Bread with Lime Glaze

9 ounces all-purpose flour (about 2 cups)
¾ teaspoon baking soda
½ teaspoon salt
1 cup granulated sugar
¼ cup butter, softened
2 large eggs
1½ cups mashed ripe banana (about 3 bananas)

¼ cup plain low-fat yogurt
3 tablespoons dark rum
½ teaspoon vanilla extract
½ cup flaked sweetened coconut
Cooking spray
1 tablespoon flaked sweetened coconut
½ cup powdered sugar
1½ tablespoons fresh lime or lemon juice

**1.** Preheat oven to 350°.

**2.** Weigh or lightly spoon flour into dry measuring cups; level with a knife. Combine flour, baking soda, and salt, stirring with a whisk.

**3.** Place granulated sugar and butter in a large bowl; beat with a mixer at medium speed until well blended. Add eggs, 1 at a time, beating well after each addition. Add banana, yogurt, rum, and vanilla; beat until blended. Add flour mixture; beat at low speed just until moist. Stir in $1/2$ cup coconut. Spoon batter into a 9 x 5–inch loaf pan coated with cooking spray; sprinkle with 1 tablespoon coconut. Bake at 350° for 1 hour or until a wooden pick inserted in center comes out clean. Cool in pan 10 minutes on a wire rack; remove from pan. Combine powdered sugar and juice, stirring with a whisk; drizzle over warm bread. Cool completely on wire rack.

**YIELD:** 1 loaf, 16 servings (serving size: 1 slice).

CALORIES 193; FAT 4.6g (sat 2.8g, mono 1.1g, poly 0.3g); PROTEIN 2.9g; CARB 35g; FIBER 1.1g; CHOL 35mg; IRON 1mg; SODIUM 179mg; CALC 15mg

## what makes it light

• uses half the amount of butter as traditional recipes

**Blueberries and lemon are a natural match,** and they come together nicely in this fruit-filled snack cake. Almond paste, a sweet mixture of ground almonds and sugar, contributes a mildly nutty flavor and moist texture. You can find almond paste in the baking section of the grocery store. (Don't substitute marzipan, which is sweeter and has a smoother texture.) If it is hard, soften it by microwaving at HIGH 10 to 15 seconds.

# Blueberry-Lemon Coffee Cake

Cake:
- 6.75 ounces all-purpose flour (about 1½ cups)
- 2 teaspoons baking powder
- ¼ teaspoon baking soda
- ½ teaspoon salt
- ½ cup sugar
- ⅓ cup almond paste
- 2 tablespoons chilled butter, cut into small pieces
- 1 large egg
- 1 tablespoon lemon juice
- ¾ cup fat-free milk
- 1½ cups blueberries
- 2 teaspoons grated lemon rind
- Cooking spray

Topping:
- ¼ cup sugar
- 3 tablespoons sliced almonds, chopped
- 1½ tablespoons butter, melted
- ½ teaspoon ground cinnamon

**1.** Preheat oven to 350°.

**2.** To prepare cake, weigh or lightly spoon flour into dry measuring cups, and level with a knife. Combine flour, baking powder, baking soda, and salt in a small bowl, stirring with a whisk.

**3.** Place $1/2$ cup sugar, almond paste, and 2 tablespoons butter in a large bowl; beat with a mixer at medium speed until well blended. Add egg and lemon juice, beating well. Add flour mixture and fat-free milk alternately to sugar mixture, beginning and ending with flour mixture. Fold in blueberries and rind. Spoon batter into a 9-inch square baking pan coated with cooking spray.

**4.** To prepare topping, combine $1/4$ cup sugar and remaining ingredients in a small bowl, tossing with a fork until moist. Sprinkle topping evenly over batter. Bake at 350° for 35 minutes or until a wooden pick inserted in center comes out clean. Cool in pan on a wire rack. **YIELD:** 12 servings (serving size: 1 piece).

CALORIES 196; FAT 6.5g (sat 2.1g, mono 3.2g, poly 0.8g); PROTEIN 3.8g; CARB 31.6g; FIBER 1.4g; CHOL 27mg; IRON 1.2mg; SODIUM 243mg; CALC 82mg

**? what makes it light**
- uses fat-free milk
- uses a reduced amount of butter

> " Excellent low-fat coffee cake! **It has stayed fresh for over five days**—much longer than the full-fat sour cream coffee cake I used to make. This will be my new coffee cake recipe. "
>
> **from cookinglight.com**

# Sour Cream Coffee Cake

¾ cup old-fashioned rolled oats (about 2.5 ounces), divided
Cooking spray
4.5 ounces all-purpose flour (about 1 cup)
1 ounce whole-wheat flour (about ¼ cup)
1 teaspoon baking powder
½ teaspoon baking soda
¼ teaspoon salt
½ cup granulated sugar
½ cup packed brown sugar, divided

⅓ cup butter, softened
2 large eggs
1 teaspoon vanilla extract
1 (8-ounce) carton light sour cream (such as Daisy)
2 tablespoons finely chopped walnuts, toasted
½ teaspoon ground cinnamon
1 tablespoon chilled butter, cut into small pieces

**1.** Preheat oven to 350°.
**2.** Spread oats in a single layer on a baking sheet. Bake at 350° for 6 minutes or until oats are barely fragrant and light brown.
**3.** Coat a 9-inch springform pan with cooking spray; set aside.
**4.** Reserve ¼ cup oats; set aside. Place remaining oats in a food processor; process 4 seconds or until finely ground. Weigh or lightly spoon flours into dry measuring cups; level with a knife. Combine processed oats, flours, baking powder, baking soda, and salt; stir with a whisk.
**5.** Place granulated sugar, ¼ cup brown sugar, and ⅓ cup butter in a large bowl. Beat with a mixer at medium speed 3 minutes or until light and fluffy. Add eggs, 1 at a time, beating well after each addition. Beat in vanilla. Add flour mixture to sugar mixture alternately with sour cream, beginning and ending with flour mixture. (Batter will be slightly lumpy because of oats.) Spoon batter into prepared pan; spread evenly.
**6.** Combine remaining ¼ cup oats, remaining ¼ cup brown sugar, nuts, and cinnamon in a bowl. Cut in 1 tablespoon butter with a pastry blender or 2 knives until well blended. Sprinkle top of batter evenly with nut mixture. Bake at 350° for 38 minutes or until a wooden pick inserted in center comes out clean, top is golden, and cake begins to pull away from sides of pan. Cool cake in pan 10 minutes; remove from pan. **YIELD:** 10 servings (serving size: 1 piece).

CALORIES 276; FAT 11.5g (sat 6.5g, mono 2.5g, poly 1.2g); PROTEIN 5.5g; CARB 38.5g; FIBER 1.4g; CHOL 61mg; IRON 1.5mg; SODIUM 247mg; CALC 59mg

## what makes it light

- uses less sugar than traditional recipes

# recipe makeover
## pecan sticky rolls

**The Reader:** Angela Thompson

**The Story:** For more than 50 years, Angela Thompson's grandmother, Philomena Olivo, has delighted friends and family with her irresistible Pecan Sticky Rolls. These yeast-raised cinnamon buns are extravagant: The butter- and egg-enriched dough is formed into oversized bakery-style rolls smothered in a gooey brown sugar–butter sauce and topped with pecans. Angela recently had a private baking lesson with her grandmother during which Olivo divulged the secrets of this treasured family recipe. However, with the knowledge of just how much butter, sugar, and eggs go into the sweet pastry, Angela decided she needed an updated version to enjoy these special treats while adhering to her commitment to a healthful lifestyle.

**The Dilemma:** The dinner-plate-sized rolls contribute nearly half the 2,000 calories an average healthy adult needs in a day, according to the USDA Dietary Guidelines. Loaded with two cups sugar, one-half cup pecans, and nearly two sticks of butter, the rolls weighed in at more than 835 calories and about 36 grams of fat each, including 18 grams of saturated fat, about the maximum daily allotment, according to the USDA.

**The Solution:** Portion size was an issue here, so our first step was to increase the recipe's yield from six servings to 15 still generously sized rolls. Then we used fat-free milk instead of whole and one-half cup egg substitute in place of the egg to shave a few calories while maintaining the dough's richness. The filling and rich sauce are the high-fat and -calorie culprits, so we halved the butter in both components to trim 30 calories and five grams of fat (three grams saturated) per roll. To curb calories, we reduced the granulated sugar in the filling by one-third and the brown sugar in the sauce by one-fourth to drop another 20 calories per portion. Using dark brown sugar, which has a higher moisture content and stronger molasses flavor than light brown sugar offers richness and preserves the stickiness of the sauce. We also used fewer high-calorie pecans (and toasted them to intensify their flavor), cutting another 10 calories per serving.

|  | BEFORE | AFTER |
|---|---|---|
| Calories per serving | 835 | 275 |
| Fat | 35.6g | 7.6g |
| Percent of total calories | 38% | 25% |

**The Feedback:** "They were fabulous," Angela says. She reports many family members found the lightened rolls just as tasty as the originals. Even her grandmother admits, "I think these might be better than mine."

**This recipe earned our Test Kitchens' highest rating.** The dough for these rolls rises twice before being shaped.

# Pecan Sticky Rolls

**Dough:**
- ¾ cup warm fat-free milk (100° to 110°)
- ¼ cup granulated sugar
- ½ teaspoon salt
- 1 package dry yeast (about 2¼ teaspoons)
- ¼ cup warm water (100° to 110°)
- ½ cup egg substitute
- 3 tablespoons butter, melted and cooled
- 18 ounces all-purpose flour (about 4 cups), divided
- Cooking spray

**Sauce:**
- ¾ cup packed dark brown sugar
- 3 tablespoons butter, melted
- 2 tablespoons hot water
- ⅓ cup finely chopped pecans, toasted

**Filling:**
- ⅔ cup granulated sugar
- 1 tablespoon ground cinnamon
- 1½ tablespoons butter, melted

**1.** To prepare dough, combine first 3 ingredients in a large bowl.

**2.** Dissolve yeast in ¼ cup warm water in a small bowl; let stand 5 minutes. Stir yeast mixture into milk mixture. Add egg substitute and 3 tablespoons melted butter; stir until well combined.

**3.** Weigh or lightly spoon flour into dry measuring cups; level with a knife. Add 16.8 ounces (about 3¾ cups) flour to yeast mixture; stir until smooth. Turn dough out onto a lightly floured surface. Knead until smooth and elastic (about 8 minutes); add enough of remaining flour, 1 tablespoon at a time, to prevent dough from sticking to hands (dough will feel slightly soft and tacky).

**4.** Place dough in a large bowl coated with cooking spray; turn to coat top. Cover and let rise in a warm place (85°), free from drafts, 45 minutes. Punch dough down and turn over in bowl; lightly coat with cooking spray. Cover and let rise another 45 minutes. Punch dough down; cover and let rest 5 minutes.

**5.** To prepare sauce, combine brown sugar, 3 tablespoons butter, and 2 tablespoons hot water in a small bowl; stir with a whisk until smooth. Scrape sugar mixture into a 13 x 9–inch baking pan coated with cooking spray, spreading evenly over bottom of pan with a spatula. Sprinkle sugar mixture evenly with pecans, and set aside.

**6.** To prepare filling, combine ⅔ cup granulated sugar and cinnamon in a small bowl. Turn dough out onto a lightly floured surface; pat dough into a 16 x 12–inch rectangle. Brush surface of dough with 1½ tablespoons melted butter. Sprinkle sugar mixture evenly over dough, leaving a ½-inch border. Beginning with a long side, roll up dough jelly-roll fashion; pinch seam to seal (do not seal ends of roll). Cut roll into 15 slices (approximately 1 inch wide). Arrange slices, cut sides up, in prepared pan. Lightly coat rolls with cooking spray; cover and let rise in a warm place (85°), free from drafts, 30 minutes or until doubled in size.

**7.** Preheat oven to 350°.

**8.** Uncover rolls, and bake at 350° for 20 minutes or until lightly browned. Let stand 1 minute; carefully invert onto serving platter. **YIELD:** 15 servings (serving size: 1 roll).

CALORIES 275; FAT 7.6g (sat 3.8g, mono 2.6g, poly 0.8g); PROTEIN 4.9g; CARB 47g; FIBER 1.4g; CHOL 15mg; IRON 2.2mg; SODIUM 146mg; CALC 37mg

# 5 ways with
# cinnamon rolls

## Cinnamon Rolls

**Rolls:**

- 1 cup warm fat-free milk (100° to 110°)
- 6 tablespoons melted butter, divided
- ⅓ cup granulated sugar, divided
- 1 package quick-rise yeast
- 16.88 ounces all-purpose flour (about 3¾ cups)
- 1 large egg, lightly beaten
- ¼ teaspoon salt
- Cooking spray
- ⅔ cup packed brown sugar
- 1½ tablespoons ground cinnamon

**Icing:**

- 3 tablespoons butter, softened
- 2 tablespoons heavy cream
- ½ teaspoon vanilla extract
- 1 cup powdered sugar

1

**1.** To prepare rolls, combine milk, 3 tablespoons melted butter, 1 tablespoon granulated sugar, and yeast in a large bowl; let stand 5 minutes. Weigh or lightly spoon flour into dry measuring cups. Add egg and remaining granulated sugar to bowl. Stir in 4.5 ounces (1 cup) flour; let stand 10 minutes.

**2.** Add 11.25 ounces (about 2½ cups) flour and salt to milk mixture; stir until a soft dough forms (dough will be sticky). Turn out onto a lightly floured surface. Knead until smooth and elastic (about 6 minutes); add enough of remaining flour, 1 tablespoon at a time, to prevent dough from sticking to hands. Place dough in a large bowl coated with cooking spray; turn to coat top. Cover and let rise in a warm place (85°), free from drafts, 35 minutes or until doubled in size. (Gently press two fingers into dough. If indentation remains, dough has risen enough.) Punch dough down; cover and let rise 35 minutes or until doubled in size. Punch dough down; cover and let rest 5 minutes.

**3.** Combine brown sugar and cinnamon. Turn dough out onto a lightly floured surface; roll dough into an 18 x 11–inch rectangle. Brush remaining 3 tablespoons melted butter over dough; sprinkle evenly with brown sugar mixture. Beginning at one long side, roll up dough tightly, jelly-roll fashion; pinch seam to seal (do not seal ends of roll). Cut dough into 18 (1-inch) slices. Arrange 9 slices, cut sides up, in each of 2 (8-inch) square baking dishes coated with cooking spray. Cover and let rise 35 minutes or until doubled in size.

**4.** Preheat oven to 350°.

**5.** Uncover rolls. Bake at 350° for 22 minutes or until lightly browned. Cool 10 minutes in dishes on a wire rack. Turn rolls out onto wire rack; cool 5 minutes. Turn rolls over.

**6.** To prepare icing, combine 3 tablespoons softened butter and cream; stir with a whisk. Stir in vanilla. Gradually add powdered sugar; stir until blended. Spread icing over rolls; serve warm. **YIELD:** 18 servings (serving size: 1 roll).

CALORIES 234; FAT 6.8g (sat 4.1g, mono 1.8g, poly 0.4g); PROTEIN 3.8g; CARB 39.6g; FIBER 1.1g; CHOL 28mg; IRON 1.7mg; SODIUM 87mg; CALC 40mg

# Cinnamon-Date-Pecan Rolls with Maple Glaze

These frosted sweet rolls make a delectable breakfast or holiday brunch offering.

**Dough:**

- 1 teaspoon granulated sugar
- 1 package dry yeast (about 2¼ teaspoons)
- ¾ cup warm water (100° to 110°)
- ⅓ cup granulated sugar
- 3 tablespoons butter, melted
- ½ teaspoon salt
- 1 large egg
- 14.5 ounces all-purpose flour (about 3¼ cups)
- Cooking spray

**Filling:**

- ⅔ cup packed brown sugar
- 1 teaspoon ground cinnamon
- 1 teaspoon grated orange rind
- 2 tablespoons butter, melted
- ¾ cup chopped pitted dates
- ¼ cup chopped pecans, toasted

**Glaze:**

- 1 cup powdered sugar
- 2 tablespoons maple syrup
- 1 tablespoon fat-free milk

**1.** To prepare dough, dissolve 1 teaspoon granulated sugar and yeast in ¾ cup warm water; let stand 5 minutes. Combine ⅓ cup granulated sugar, 3 tablespoons butter, salt, and egg in a large bowl. Add yeast mixture; beat with a mixer at medium speed until blended.
**2.** Weigh or lightly spoon flour into dry measuring cups; level with a knife. Gradually add 3 cups flour to yeast mixture, beating mixture on low speed until a soft dough forms. Turn dough out onto a lightly floured surface. Knead until smooth and elastic (about 5 minutes); add enough of remaining flour, 1 tablespoon at a time, to prevent dough from sticking to hands. Place dough in a large bowl coated with cooking spray, turning to coat top. Cover and let rise in a warm place (85°), free from drafts, 1 hour or until doubled in size. Punch dough down; turn out onto a lightly floured surface.
**3.** To prepare filling, combine brown sugar, cinnamon, and rind in a small bowl. Roll dough into a 15 x 10–inch rectangle; brush with 2 tablespoons butter. Sprinkle brown sugar mixture over dough, leaving a ½-inch border. Sprinkle dates and pecans over sugar mixture. Beginning with a long side, roll up jelly-roll fashion; pinch seam to seal (do not seal ends of roll). Cut roll into 18 (½-inch) slices. Place slices, cut sides up, in a 13 x 9–inch baking pan coated with cooking spray. Cover and let rise in a warm place (85°), free from drafts, about 1 hour or until rolls have doubled in size.
**4.** Preheat oven to 375°.
**5.** Uncover dough. Bake at 375° for 20 minutes or until rolls are golden brown.
**6.** To prepare glaze, combine powdered sugar, syrup, and milk in a small bowl; stir with a whisk until smooth. Drizzle glaze over warm rolls. Serve immediately. **YIELD:** 18 rolls (serving size: 1 roll).

CALORIES 226; FAT 4.9g (sat 2.2g, mono 1.6g, poly 0.6g); PROTEIN 3.2g; CARB 43.4g; FIBER 1.5g; CHOL 20mg; IRON 1.5mg; SODIUM 96mg; CALC 21mg

# Cinnamon-Fruit Rolls

These rolls are good for busy mornings. Take them out of the freezer, let them stand 30 minutes, then bake 20 minutes.

Dough:
- 1 package dry yeast (about 2¼ teaspoons)
- ¼ cup warm water (100° to 110°)
- ½ cup fat-free milk
- ⅓ cup granulated sugar
- ¼ cup butter, melted
- 1 teaspoon vanilla extract
- ½ teaspoon salt
- 1 large egg, lightly beaten
- 16.88 ounces all-purpose flour (about 3¾ cups), divided
- Cooking spray

Filling:
- ⅔ cup packed brown sugar
- ½ cup golden raisins
- ½ cup chopped dried apricots
- ½ cup chopped pecans
- 1 tablespoon ground cinnamon
- 2 tablespoons butter, melted

Glaze:
- 1 cup powdered sugar
- 2 tablespoons fat-free milk

**1.** Dissolve yeast in warm water in a large bowl; let stand 5 minutes. Stir in ½ cup milk and next 5 ingredients. Weigh or lightly spoon flour into dry measuring cups; level with a knife. Add 3½ cups flour to yeast mixture; stir until blended. Turn dough out onto a floured surface. Knead until smooth and elastic (about 10 minutes); add enough of remaining flour, 1 tablespoon at a time, to prevent dough from sticking to hands (dough will feel sticky).

**2.** Place dough in a large bowl coated with cooking spray, turning to coat top. Cover and let rise in a warm place (85°), free from drafts, 1 hour or until doubled in size. (Gently press two fingers into dough. If indentation remains, dough has risen enough.) Punch dough down; cover and let rest 5 minutes.

**3.** To prepare filling, combine brown sugar, raisins, dried apricots, chopped pecans, and cinnamon.

**4.** Roll dough into an 18 x 10–inch rectangle on a floured surface. Brush 2 tablespoons melted butter over dough; sprinkle with 1½ cups filling, leaving a ½-inch border. Beginning with a long side, roll up jelly-roll fashion, and pinch seam to seal (do not seal ends of roll).

**5.** Place a long piece of dental floss under dough ¾ inch from end of roll. Cross ends of floss over top of roll; slowly pull ends to cut through dough. Repeat procedure to make 24 rolls. Coat 2 (9-inch) square foil baking pans with cooking spray. Sprinkle ½ cup filling into bottom of each pan. Place 12 rolls, cut sides up, in each pan. Cover and let rise 1½ hours or until doubled in size.

**6.** Preheat oven to 350°.

**7.** Uncover rolls. Bake at 350° for 20 minutes or until browned. Invert onto a serving platter.

**8.** To prepare glaze, combine powdered sugar and 2 tablespoons milk, stirring until smooth. Drizzle over warm rolls. **YIELD:** 24 servings (serving size: 1 roll).

CALORIES 193; FAT 5.1g (sat 2g, mono 1.9g, poly 0.8g); PROTEIN 3.1g; CARB 34.4g; FIBER 1.4g; CHOL 17mg; IRON 1.5mg; SODIUM 87mg; CALC 28mg

3

4

## Make-Ahead Ooey-Gooey Sticky Buns

    1 package dry yeast (about 2¼ teaspoons)
    1 teaspoon granulated sugar
    ¼ cup warm water (100° to 110°)
   18 ounces all-purpose flour (about
        4 cups), divided
    ¼ cup granulated sugar
    1 teaspoon ground nutmeg
    ¾ teaspoon salt
    1 cup evaporated fat-free milk, divided
    ¼ cup water
    1 large egg, lightly beaten
      Cooking spray
   1¼ cups packed dark brown sugar, divided
    ⅓ cup dark corn syrup
    2 tablespoons butter
    ¾ cup chopped pecans
    1 tablespoon ground cinnamon

**1.** Dissolve yeast and 1 teaspoon granulated sugar in ¼ cup warm water in a small bowl; let stand 5 minutes. Weigh or lightly spoon flour into dry measuring cups; level with a knife. Place 3¾ cups flour, ¼ cup granulated sugar, nutmeg, and salt in a food processor; pulse 2 times or until blended. Combine ⅔ cup milk, ¼ cup water, and egg. With processor on, slowly add milk mixture and yeast mixture through food chute; process until dough forms a ball. Process for an additional minute. Turn dough out onto a lightly floured surface; knead until smooth and elastic (about 8 minutes);

add enough of remaining flour, 1 tablespoon at a time, to prevent dough from sticking to hands.
**2.** Place dough in a large bowl coated with cooking spray, turning to coat top. Cover and let rise in a warm place (85°), free from drafts, 45 minutes or until doubled in size. Combine ⅓ cup milk, 1 cup brown sugar, corn syrup, and butter in a small saucepan; bring to a boil, stirring constantly. Remove from heat. Divide pecans evenly between 2 (9-inch) round cake pans coated with cooking spray. Top each with half of brown sugar mixture.
**3.** Punch dough down; let rest 5 minutes. Roll into a 24 x 10–inch rectangle on a lightly floured surface; coat entire surface of dough with cooking spray. Combine ¼ cup brown sugar and cinnamon in a small bowl; sprinkle evenly over dough. Beginning with a long side, roll up jelly-roll fashion; pinch seam to seal (do not seal ends of roll). Cut roll into 24 (1-inch) slices, using string or dental floss. Arrange 12 slices, cut sides up, in each prepared pan. Cover with plastic wrap coated with cooking spray, and let rise in refrigerator 8 to 24 hours or until doubled in size.
**4.** Preheat oven to 375°.
**5.** Bake rolls at 375° for 23 minutes. Run a knife around outside edges of pans. Place a plate upside down on top of pan; invert onto plate.
**YIELD:** 2 dozen (serving size: 1 bun).

CALORIES 188; FAT 4g (sat 0.5g, mono 2.1g, poly 1g); PROTEIN 3.7g; CARB 35.1g; FIBER 1g; CHOL 10mg; IRON 1.5mg; SODIUM 110mg; CALC 51mg

## Pumpkin-Cinnamon Streusel Buns

**Buns:**

- 1 package dry yeast (about 2¼ teaspoons)
- ¼ cup warm water (100° to 110°)
- 13.5 ounces all-purpose flour (about 3 cups), divided
- ½ cup canned pumpkin puree
- ½ cup 1% low-fat milk
- ¼ cup butter, melted
- 1 tablespoon granulated sugar
- 1¼ teaspoons salt
- ¼ teaspoon ground nutmeg
- Cooking spray
- 3 tablespoons granulated sugar
- 3 tablespoons brown sugar
- 2 tablespoons all-purpose flour
- 1½ teaspoons ground cinnamon
- 2 tablespoons chilled butter, cut into small pieces

**Glaze:**

- ¾ cup sifted powdered sugar
- 1 tablespoon hot water
- ¼ teaspoon vanilla extract

**1.** To prepare buns, dissolve yeast in warm water in a large bowl; let stand 5 minutes. Weigh or lightly spoon flour into dry measuring cups, and level with a knife. Add 2¾ cups flour, pumpkin, and next 5 ingredients to yeast mixture; beat with a mixer at medium speed until smooth. Turn dough out onto a floured surface. Knead until smooth and elastic (about 10 minutes); add enough of remaining ¼ cup flour, 1 tablespoon at a time, to prevent dough from sticking to hands (dough will feel tacky).

**2.** Place dough in a large bowl coated with cooking spray, turning to coat top. Cover and let rise in a warm place (85°), free from drafts, for 45 minutes or until doubled in size. (Gently press two fingers into the dough. If an indentation remains, dough has risen enough.)

**3.** Combine 3 tablespoons granulated sugar, brown sugar, 2 tablespoons flour, and cinnamon in a small bowl. Cut in butter with a pastry blender or 2 knives until mixture resembles coarse meal.

**4.** Punch dough down; cover and let rest 5 minutes. Roll dough into a 12 x 10–inch rectangle on a floured surface. Sprinkle with brown sugar mixture. Roll up rectangle tightly, starting with a long edge, pressing firmly to eliminate air pockets; pinch seam and ends to seal. Cut roll into 12 (1-inch) slices. Place slices in a 9-inch square baking pan coated with cooking spray. Cover and let rise 25 minutes or until doubled in size.

**5.** Preheat oven to 375°.

**6.** Bake rolls at 375° for 20 minutes or until golden brown. Cool 15 minutes in pan on a wire rack.

**7.** To prepare glaze, combine powdered sugar, 1 tablespoon water, and vanilla extract in a small bowl, stirring with a whisk until smooth. Drizzle glaze over buns. Serve warm. **YIELD:** 12 servings (serving size: 1 bun).

CALORIES 219; FAT 6.2g (sat 3.7g, mono 1.8g, poly 0.3g); PROTEIN 3.8g; CARB 36.9g; FIBER 1.2g; CHOL 16mg; IRON 1.6mg; SODIUM 311mg; CALC 24mg

# Maple-Glazed Sour Cream Doughnut Holes

6 tablespoons warm water (100° to 110°)
¼ cup granulated sugar
1⅛ teaspoons dry yeast
6.75 ounces all-purpose flour (about 1½ cups), divided
⅛ teaspoon salt
3 tablespoons sour cream

1 large egg, lightly beaten
Cooking spray
6 cups peanut oil
1½ cups powdered sugar
2 tablespoons maple syrup
2 tablespoons water

**1.** Combine first 3 ingredients in a large bowl. Let stand 5 minutes or until bubbly. Weigh or lightly spoon 5.63 ounces (about 1¼ cups) flour into dry measuring cups; level with a knife. Combine 5.63 ounces flour and salt. Add sour cream and egg to yeast mixture; stir until smooth. Add flour mixture; stir until a moist dough forms.

**2.** Turn dough out onto a lightly floured surface. Knead until smooth and elastic (about 3 minutes); add enough of remaining 1.13 ounces flour, 1 tablespoon at a time, to prevent dough from sticking to hands (dough will feel slightly sticky). Place dough in a clean bowl coated with cooking spray. Cover dough with plastic wrap. Let rise in a warm place (85°), free from drafts, 1 hour or until almost doubled in size.

**3.** Punch dough down. Divide dough into 36 equal portions; roll each portion into a ball. Cover dough with plastic wrap coated with cooking spray; let stand 30 minutes.

**4.** Clip a candy/fry thermometer onto side of a Dutch oven; add oil to pan. Heat oil to 375°. Combine powdered sugar, syrup, and 2 tablespoons water; stir until smooth. Place 9 dough balls in hot oil; fry 2 minutes or until golden and done, turning as necessary. Make sure oil temperature remains at 375°. Remove doughnut holes from pan; drain. Dip doughnut holes into syrup mixture; remove with a slotted spoon. Drain on a cooling rack over a baking sheet. Repeat procedure 4 times with remaining dough balls and syrup mixture. **YIELD:** 12 servings (serving size: 3 doughnut holes).

CALORIES 178; FAT 5.9g (sat 1.4g, mono 2.5g, poly 1.6g); PROTEIN 2.4g; CARB 29.3g; FIBER 0.5g; CHOL 19mg; IRON 0.9mg; SODIUM 33mg; CALC 11mg

# recipe makeover
# orange rolls

**The Reader:** Desiree Schneider

**The Story:** Ever since they began dating, Desiree had listened to her husband, Paul, reminisce about the gooey orange rolls of his childhood. So as a part of his 25th birthday celebration, she secretly obtained a copy of the recipe from her mother-in-law and surprised him by baking a batch of his favorite treat. Desiree describes them as "buttery yeast rolls drenched in a cooked sour cream glaze" and now understands why these delicious rolls were etched in Paul's memory.

**The Dilemma:** Desiree felt there was a good chance that Paul would overindulge in the rolls anytime she made them. We took her concerns to heart once we looked at the recipe and saw the ample amounts of sour cream and butter it called for.

**The Solution:** Our first alteration was simple, but it significantly lightened the rolls: Switching from regular to reduced-fat sour cream saved about 120 calories and 19 grams of fat in the recipe. Another 72 calories and almost 5 grams of fat were trimmed by using one egg instead of two. The biggest change occurred when we slashed the butter content, but we kept enough in the

dough to maintain the original's tender, almost pillowlike texture. We kept most of the butter originally in the glaze because it imparts rich flavor at first bite. Still, the rolls contain only half the butter of the original recipe, which knocks out a whopping 792 calories and 91 grams of fat. All the modifications make for a rich-tasting baked delight with only 178 calories per serving and about half the fat of the original.

**The Feedback:** The **Cooking Light** staff awarded the new and improved orange rolls with our Test Kitchens' highest rating. Desiree found the new dough easier to work with, plus **the light-ened rolls "have the same decadent flavor with none of that heavy feeling** after eating them. If I had not told Paul, I am certain he wouldn't have known any difference. Now when he's tempted to reach for a second roll, I won't feel nearly as bad knowing they've been lightened," she says.

|  | BEFORE | AFTER |
|---|---|---|
| Calories per serving | 218 | 178 |
| Fat | 10.2g | 5.6g |
| Percent of total calories | 41% | 28% |

**Keep any remaining rolls in the baking pan.** Cover pan with foil, and store it in the refrigerator. To reheat, place foil-covered pan in a 300° oven for 15 minutes or until rolls are warm.

# Orange Rolls

Dough:
- 1 package dry yeast (about 2¼ teaspoons)
- ½ cup warm water (100° to 110°)
- 1 cup sugar, divided
- ½ cup reduced-fat sour cream
- 2 tablespoons butter, softened
- 1 teaspoon salt
- 1 large egg, lightly beaten
- 15.75 ounces all-purpose flour (about 3½ cups), divided

Cooking spray
- 2 tablespoons butter, melted
- 2 tablespoons grated orange rind

Glaze:
- ¾ cup sugar
- ¼ cup butter
- 2 tablespoons fresh orange juice
- ½ cup reduced-fat sour cream

**1.** To prepare dough, dissolve yeast in warm water in a large bowl; let stand 5 minutes. Add ¼ cup sugar, ½ cup sour cream, 2 tablespoons softened butter, salt, and egg, and beat with a mixer at medium speed until smooth. Weigh or lightly spoon flour into dry measuring cups; level with a knife. Add 9 ounces flour (about 2 cups) to yeast mixture; beat until smooth. Add 4.5 ounces flour (about 1 cup) to yeast mixture, stirring until a soft dough forms. Turn dough out onto a floured surface. Knead until smooth and elastic (about 10 minutes); add enough of remaining flour, 1 tablespoon at a time, to prevent dough from sticking to hands (dough will feel sticky).

**2.** Place dough in a large bowl coated with cooking spray, turning to coat top. Cover and let rise in a warm place (85°), free from drafts, 1 hour and 15 minutes or until doubled in size. (Gently press two fingers into dough. If indentation remains, dough has risen enough.)

**3.** Punch dough down; cover and let rest 5 minutes. Divide dough in half. Working with 1 portion at a time (cover remaining dough to prevent drying), roll each portion of dough into a 12-inch circle on a floured surface. Brush surface of each circle with 1 tablespoon melted butter. Combine ¾ cup sugar and rind. Sprinkle half of sugar mixture over each circle. Cut each circle into 12 wedges. Roll up each wedge tightly, beginning at wide end. Place rolls, point sides down, in a 13 x 9–inch baking pan coated with cooking spray. Cover and let rise 25 minutes or until doubled in size.

**4.** Preheat oven to 350°.

**5.** Uncover dough. Bake at 350° for 25 minutes or until golden brown.

**6.** While rolls bake, prepare glaze. Combine ¾ cup sugar, ¼ cup butter, and orange juice in a small saucepan; bring to a boil over medium-high heat. Cook 3 minutes or until sugar dissolves, stirring occasionally. Remove from heat; cool slightly. Stir in ½ cup sour cream. Drizzle glaze over warm rolls; let stand 20 minutes before serving. **YIELD:** 2 dozen (serving size: 1 roll).

CALORIES 178; FAT 5.6g (sat 3.2g, mono 1.3g, poly 0.3g); PROTEIN 2.8g; CARB 30g; FIBER 0.6g; CHOL 24mg; IRON 1mg; SODIUM 146mg; CALC 23mg

## what makes it light

- uses ⅓-less-fat cream cheese
- uses fat-free milk
- uses light sour cream

"This is a wonderful recipe! **The bread is perfectly soft and sweet,** and the filling is a fantastic compliment—not to mention the beautiful presentation. I use seedless raspberry preserves at times and make this for all special occasions. A must try!"

**from cookinglight.com**

# Apricot-Cream Cheese Bread

**Dough:**
- ½ cup granulated sugar
- ⅓ cup butter
- ½ teaspoon salt
- 1 (8-ounce) carton light sour cream
- 2 packages dry yeast (about 4½ teaspoons)
- ½ cup warm water (100° to 110°)
- 2 large eggs, lightly beaten
- 18 ounces all-purpose flour (about 4 cups)

**Filling:**
- ⅔ cup apricot preserves
- ¼ cup granulated sugar
- 1 teaspoon vanilla extract
- 2 (8-ounce) blocks ⅓-less-fat cream cheese, softened
- 1 large egg, lightly beaten
- Cooking spray

**Glaze:**
- 1½ cups sifted powdered sugar
- 2 tablespoons fat-free milk
- 1 teaspoon vanilla extract

**1.** To prepare dough, combine first 4 ingredients in a saucepan over medium heat, stirring until sugar dissolves. Remove from heat; cool. Dissolve yeast in warm water in a large bowl; let stand 5 minutes. Stir in sour cream mixture and 2 eggs. Weigh or lightly spoon flour into dry measuring cups; level with a knife. Gradually stir flour into sour cream mixture (dough will be soft and sticky). Cover dough; chill 8 hours or overnight.

**2.** To prepare filling, combine preserves and next 4 ingredients in a medium bowl; beat with a mixer at medium speed until well blended.

**3.** Divide dough into 4 equal portions. Turn each portion out onto a lightly floured surface; knead lightly 4 or 5 times. Roll each portion into a 12 x 8–inch rectangle. Spread one-fourth of filling over each portion, leaving a ¹/₂-inch border. Starting at a long side, carefully roll up each portion jelly-roll fashion; pinch seam and ends to seal.

**4.** Place 2 loaves on each of 2 baking sheets coated with cooking spray. Cut 4 (¹/₄-inch-deep) "X"s in top of each loaf with scissors. Cover and let rise in a warm place (85°), free from drafts, 25 minutes or until doubled in size.

**5.** Preheat oven to 375°.

**6.** Place 1 baking sheet in oven (cover remaining loaves to keep from drying). Bake at 375° for 15 minutes or until lightly browned. Repeat procedure with remaining loaves. Cool loaves slightly.

**7.** To prepare glaze, combine powdered sugar, milk, and 1 teaspoon vanilla, stirring with a whisk. Drizzle warm loaves with glaze. **YIELD:** 4 loaves, 10 slices per loaf (serving size: 1 slice).

CALORIES 145; FAT 5g (sat 3g, mono 1.5g, poly 0.3); PROTEIN 3.3g; CARB 21.6g; FIBER 0.5g; CHOL 30mg; IRON 0.8mg; SODIUM 102mg; CALC 26mg

# Jalapeño, Sausage, Jack, and Egg Breakfast Braid

1 (13.8-ounce) can refrigerated pizza crust dough
Cooking spray
1 tablespoon olive oil
¼ cup chopped onion
4 ounces chicken sausage with jalapeño peppers, chopped

2 large eggs, lightly beaten
½ cup (2 ounces) shredded Monterey Jack cheese
¼ cup shredded cheddar cheese
¼ cup chopped seeded jalapeño peppers
1 large egg white, lightly beaten

**1.** Preheat oven to 425°.
**2.** Unroll dough onto a baking sheet coated with cooking spray; pat into a 15 x 10–inch rectangle.
**3.** Heat oil in a large skillet over medium heat. Add onion and sausage; cook 9 minutes or until lightly browned. Stir in eggs; cook 1½ minutes or until set. Remove from heat.
**4.** Sprinkle Monterey Jack lengthwise down center of dough, leaving about a 2½-inch border on each side. Spoon egg mixture evenly over cheese. Sprinkle cheddar over egg mixture; top with jalapeño peppers.
**5.** Make 2-inch-long diagonal cuts about 1 inch apart on both sides of dough to within ½ inch of filling using a sharp knife or kitchen shears. Arrange strips over filling, alternating strips diagonally over filling. Press ends under to seal. Brush with egg white. Bake at 425° for 15 minutes or until golden brown. Let stand 5 minutes. Cut crosswise into slices. **YIELD:** 6 servings (serving size: 1 slice).

CALORIES 164; FAT 10.4g (sat 4.2g, mono 4.4g, poly 1g); PROTEIN 10.6g; CARB 7.3g; FIBER 0.1g; CHOL 98mg; IRON 0.8mg; SODIUM 344mg; CALC 115mg

## what makes it light
- uses chicken sausage
- uses pizza crust dough, which is lower in fat than crescent roll dough that is used for many breakfast braid recipes

# lunch

"This soup was very rich and flavorful—**hard to believe it's a light** recipe! I will definitely make this one again."

**from cookinglight.com**

# French Onion Soup

2 teaspoons olive oil
4 cups thinly vertically sliced Walla Walla or other sweet onion
4 cups thinly vertically sliced red onion
½ teaspoon sugar
½ teaspoon freshly ground black pepper
¼ teaspoon salt
¼ cup dry white wine

8 cups lower-sodium beef broth
¼ teaspoon chopped fresh thyme
8 (1-ounce) slices French bread, cut into 1-inch cubes
8 (1-ounce) slices reduced-fat, reduced-sodium Swiss cheese (such as Alpine Lace)

**1.** Heat olive oil in a Dutch oven over medium-high heat. Add onions to pan; sauté 5 minutes or until tender. Stir in sugar, pepper, and ¼ teaspoon salt. Reduce heat to medium; cook 20 minutes, stirring frequently. Increase heat to medium-high, and sauté 5 minutes or until onion is golden brown. Stir in wine, and cook 1 minute. Add broth and thyme; bring to a boil. Cover, reduce heat, and simmer 2 hours.

**2.** Preheat broiler.

**3.** Place bread in a single layer on a baking sheet; broil 2 minutes or until toasted, turning after 1 minute.

**4.** Place 8 ovenproof bowls on a jelly-roll pan. Ladle 1 cup soup into each bowl. Divide bread evenly among bowls; top each serving with 1 cheese slice. Broil 3 minutes or until cheese begins to brown. **YIELD:** 8 servings.

CALORIES 290; FAT 9.6g (sat 4.8g, mono 1.9g, poly 0.7g); PROTEIN 16.8g; CARB 33.4g; FIBER 3.1g; CHOL 20mg; IRON 1.6mg; SODIUM 359mg; CALC 317mg

## what makes it light
• uses lower-sodium beef broth
• uses reduced-fat, reduced-sodium Swiss cheese
• uses a minimal amount of oil to caramelize onions

# 5 ways with
# tomato soup

1

## Tomato Alphabet Soup

On chilly autumn afternoons, nothing warms more than a good bowl of creamy tomato soup and a grilled cheese sandwich. Pureed alphabet pasta, instead of cream, thickens the soup in this version.

- 2 tablespoons butter
- 1 cup chopped onion
- 1 cup chopped carrot
- ⅓ cup chopped celery
- 1½ cups vegetable broth
- 1 teaspoon dried basil
- ¼ teaspoon black pepper
- 1 (28-ounce) can diced tomatoes, undrained
- 2 cups cooked alphabet pasta (about 1 cup uncooked pasta), divided
- 1 cup 2% reduced-fat milk

**1.** Melt butter in a saucepan over medium-high heat. Add onion, carrot, and celery; sauté 4 minutes or until tender. Add broth, basil, pepper, and tomatoes, and bring to a boil. Reduce heat; simmer 15 minutes. Stir in ½ cup pasta. Remove from heat; let stand 5 minutes.

**2.** Place half of tomato mixture in a blender, and process until smooth. Pour pureed soup into a large bowl. Repeat procedure with remaining tomato mixture. Return pureed soup to pan; stir in remaining pasta and milk. Cook over medium-high heat 2 minutes or until thoroughly heated, stirring frequently (do not boil). **YIELD:** 6 servings (serving size: about 1 cup).

CALORIES 175; FAT 5.2g (sat 2.9g, mono 1.3g, poly 0.2g); PROTEIN 6.1g; CARB 27.9g; FIBER 4g; CHOL 13mg; IRON 1.3mg; SODIUM 492mg; CALC 93mg

## Creamy Tomato-Balsamic Soup

Cooking the vegetables at the high temperature of 500° caramelizes their natural sugars and deepens their flavor.

    1 cup lower-sodium beef broth, divided
    1 tablespoon brown sugar
    3 tablespoons balsamic vinegar
    1 tablespoon lower-sodium soy sauce
    1 cup coarsely chopped onion
    5 garlic cloves
    2 (28-ounce) cans whole tomatoes,
        drained
    Cooking spray
    ¾ cup half-and-half
    Cracked black pepper (optional)

**1.** Preheat oven to 500°.

**2.** Combine ½ cup broth, sugar, vinegar, and soy sauce in a small bowl. Place onion, garlic, and tomatoes in a 13 x 9–inch baking pan coated with cooking spray. Pour broth mixture over tomato mixture. Bake at 500° for 50 minutes or until vegetables are lightly browned.

**3.** Place tomato mixture in a blender. Add remaining ½ cup broth and half-and-half, and process until smooth. Strain mixture through a sieve into a bowl; discard solids. Garnish with cracked black pepper, if desired. **YIELD:** 4 servings (serving size: about ½ cup).

CALORIES 120; FAT 4.7g (sat 3g, mono 1.5g, poly 0.1g); PROTEIN 3.8g; CARB 14.9g; FIBER 1.7g; CHOL 23mg; IRON 1.7mg; SODIUM 452mg; CALC 120mg

2

## Fresh Tomato Soup ▼

Six tablespoons plain of low-fat yogurt stands in for the half-and-half that's so prevalent in traditional tomato soup recipes. It still offers the creaminess without the fat and calories.

 2 cups fat-free, lower-sodium chicken broth
 1 cup chopped onion
 ¾ cup chopped celery
 1 tablespoon thinly sliced fresh basil
 1 tablespoon tomato paste
 2 pounds plum tomatoes, cut into wedges
 ½ teaspoon salt
 ¼ teaspoon freshly ground black pepper
 6 tablespoons plain low-fat yogurt
 3 tablespoons thinly sliced fresh basil

**1.** Combine first 6 ingredients in a large saucepan; bring to a boil. Reduce heat, and simmer 30 minutes. Place half of tomato mixture in a blender. Remove center piece of blender lid (to allow steam to escape); secure lid on blender. Place a clean towel over opening in blender lid (to avoid splatters). Blend until smooth. Pour into a large bowl. Repeat procedure with remaining tomato mixture. Stir in salt and pepper. Ladle ³⁄₄ cup soup into each of 6 bowls; top each serving with 1 tablespoon yogurt and 1¹⁄₂ teaspoons basil. **YIELD:** 6 servings.

CALORIES 58; FAT 0.8g (sat 0.3g, mono 0.1g, poly 0.2g); PROTEIN 3.1g; CARB 11.3g; FIBER 2.8g; CHOL 1mg; IRON 1.1mg; SODIUM 382mg; CALC 49mg

## Tomato-Basil Soup ▼

Fresh tomato and basil are the stars of this classic summertime tomato soup recipe. Low-fat milk and light cream cheese keep it healthy. Refrigerate soup in an airtight container for up to one week.

 4 cups chopped seeded peeled tomato (about 4 large)
 4 cups lower-sodium tomato juice
 ⅓ cup fresh basil leaves
 1 cup 1% low-fat milk
 ¼ teaspoon salt
 ¼ teaspoon cracked black pepper
 ½ cup (4 ounces) ⅓-less-fat cream cheese, softened
 Basil leaves, thinly sliced (optional)
 8 (½-inch-thick) slices diagonally cut French bread baguette

**1.** Bring tomato and juice to a boil in a large saucepan. Reduce heat; simmer, uncovered, 30 minutes.
**2.** Place tomato mixture and basil in a blender or food processor; process until smooth. Return pureed mixture to pan; stir in milk, salt, and pepper. Add cream cheese, stirring well with a whisk, and cook over medium heat until thick (about 5 minutes). Ladle soup into individual bowls; garnish with sliced basil, if desired. Serve with bread. **YIELD:** 8 servings (serving size: 1 cup soup and 1 bread slice).

CALORIES 133; FAT 4.4g (sat 2.4g, mono 1.3g, poly 0.4g); PROTEIN 5.4g; CARB 18.7g; FIBER 1.9g; CHOL 12mg; IRON 1.5mg; SODIUM 310mg; CALC 77mg

3

4

**5**

## Tomato Garlic Soup with Parmesan Croutons

 4 large tomatoes, cored (about
   2½ pounds)
 2 quarts water
 2 quarts ice water
 1¼ cups uncooked seashell pasta
 4 teaspoons olive oil, divided
 ¾ cup finely chopped red onion
 8 garlic cloves, thinly sliced
 1 cup water
 1 tablespoon chopped fresh flat-leaf
   parsley
 1 tablespoon minced fresh chives
 1 teaspoon minced fresh oregano
 1 teaspoon minced fresh thyme
 2 (14-ounce) cans fat-free, lower-
   sodium chicken broth
 1 tablespoon red wine vinegar
 ½ teaspoon freshly ground black pepper
 8 (½-ounce) slices diagonally cut French
   bread baguette (about 1 inch thick)
 ½ cup (2 ounces) grated fresh Parmesan
   cheese
   Fresh thyme sprigs (optional)

**1.** Score bottom of each tomato with an "X." Bring 2 quarts water to a boil in a Dutch oven. Add tomatoes; cook 30 seconds. Remove tomatoes with a slotted spoon; plunge tomatoes into 2 quarts ice water. Drain and peel. Cut each tomato in half crosswise. Push seeds out of tomato halves using the tip of a knife; discard seeds. Chop tomatoes.

**2.** Cook pasta according to package directions, omitting salt and fat; drain. Toss pasta with 1 teaspoon oil. Cool completely.

**3.** Heat 1 tablespoon oil in Dutch oven over medium-low heat. Add onion; cook 7 minutes, stirring occasionally. Add garlic; cook 3 minutes or until onion is tender, stirring frequently. Stir in tomatoes, 1 cup water, parsley, chives, oregano, thyme, and broth; bring to a boil. Reduce heat, and simmer 20 minutes, stirring occasionally. Add pasta, vinegar, and pepper; cook 1 minute or until thoroughly heated.

**4.** Preheat broiler.

**5.** Place bread slices on a baking sheet, and top each slice with 1 tablespoon cheese. Broil 1½ minutes or until lightly browned. Serve with soup. Garnish with thyme sprigs, if desired. **YIELD:** 4 servings (serving size: 1½ cups soup and 2 croutons).

CALORIES 335; FAT 9.9g (sat 3g, mono 3.8g, poly 1g); PROTEIN 15.3g; CARB 46.6g; FIBER 4.1g; CHOL 11mg; IRON 2.7mg; SODIUM 695mg; CALC 227mg

# broccoli and chicken noodle soup

**The Reader:** Amanda Farmer

**The Story:** A childhood favorite, this creamy soup is a go-to for Amanda. She received the recipe from her mother, Brenda Geiger, and wanted to give it to a friend for a cookbook project. Yet Amanda felt some guilt. "I know it's high in calories and fat, and I want a healthier recipe that's still satisfying," she wrote with her request to *Cooking Light* for an overdue makeover of the recipe.

**The Dilemma:** Several ingredients contributed to the soup's heavy nutritional report card: processed cheese, butter, whole milk, and half-and-half added a hefty amount of fat. Its canned cream of mushroom soup, regular chicken broth, and processed cheese added significant sodium.

**The Solution:** The soup's base warranted the bulk of our attention. We halved the amount of processed cheese and swapped to a lighter version, maintaining a satisfying taste and texture but cutting 79 calories, seven fat grams (five grams of which were saturated), and 286 milligrams of sodium per serving. We made a

white sauce for the soup's base with just three tablespoons of butter and a little flour to thicken low-fat milk; omitting the can of soup cut 25 calories per bowlful. With half the rich half-and-half, we added an extra cup of 1% low-fat milk (instead of the full-fat type) to ensure a silky texture and saved 35 calories, four grams of fat, and two grams of saturated fat. Instead of using one-half cup butter to sauté the onion, we used cooking spray and added fresh mushrooms to enhance the taste. Reducing five tablespoons of butter (three tablespoons are used in the white sauce) shaved 50 calories and six grams of fat (3½ grams saturated) per serving. We switched regular chicken broth for the fat-free, lower-sodium type, and used less to shave 216 milligrams sodium. Since we broke the long noodles, which are easier to eat, we could also halve the amount to eliminate another 40 calories.

|  | BEFORE | AFTER |
|---|---|---|
| Calories per serving | 534 | 317 |
| Fat | 33g | 12.3g |
| Saturated fat | 18.6g | 6.8g |
| Sodium | 1,289mg | 723mg |

**The Feedback:** Amanda and her husband, Lee, commend the revised recipe. **"None of the creaminess is sacrificed,** and the addition of fresh mushrooms enlivens the soup's flavor," she says. Amanda can feel good about preparing—and passing along—this restored childhood favorite.

**If the broccoli florets are large,** break into smaller pieces at the stalk instead of chopping them; they'll cook more quickly. Count on having dinner on the table in about 40 minutes, and serve this soup the moment it's done for the best results. In fact, if you wait, you'll find it gets thicker with time. If you have leftovers, you will want to thin the soup with a little chicken broth or milk to the desired consistency.

# Broccoli and Chicken Noodle Soup

Cooking spray
2 cups chopped onion
1 cup presliced mushrooms
1 garlic clove, minced
3 tablespoons butter
1.1 ounces all-purpose flour (about ¼ cup)
4 cups 1% low-fat milk
1 (14-ounce) can fat-free, lower-sodium chicken broth
4 ounces uncooked vermicelli, broken into 2-inch pieces
2 cups (8 ounces) shredded light processed cheese (such as Velveeta Light)
4 cups (1-inch) cubed cooked chicken breast
3 cups small broccoli florets (8 ounces)
1 cup half-and-half
1 teaspoon freshly ground black pepper
¾ teaspoon salt

**1.** Heat a Dutch oven over medium-high heat. Coat pan with cooking spray. Add onion, mushrooms, and garlic to pan; sauté 5 minutes or until liquid evaporates, stirring occasionally. Reduce heat to medium; add butter to mushroom mixture, stirring until butter melts. Sprinkle mushroom mixture with flour; cook 2 minutes, stirring occasionally. Gradually add milk and broth, stirring constantly with a whisk; bring to a boil. Reduce heat to medium-low; cook 10 minutes or until slightly thick, stirring constantly. Add pasta to pan; cook 10 minutes. Add cheese to pan, and stir until cheese melts. Add chicken and remaining ingredients to pan; cook 5 minutes or until broccoli is tender and soup is thoroughly heated. **YIELD:** 10 servings (serving size: 1 cup).

CALORIES 317; FAT 12.3g (sat 6.8g, mono 2.9g, poly 0.9g); PROTEIN 27.5g; CARB 23.8g; FIBER 1.9g; CHOL 74mg; IRON 1.6mg; SODIUM 723mg; CALC 179mg

30
minutes
or
less

"Comfort food at its best! It's -3°F outside tonight, and this soup hits the spot!

from cookinglight.com

# Broccoli and Cheese Soup

Cooking spray
1 cup chopped onion
2 garlic cloves, minced
3 cups fat-free, lower-sodium chicken broth
1 (12-ounce) package broccoli florets

1.5 ounces all-purpose flour (about ⅓ cup)
2½ cups 2% reduced-fat milk
¼ teaspoon black pepper
8 ounces light processed cheese, cubed (such as Velveeta Light)

**1.** Heat a large nonstick saucepan over medium-high heat. Coat pan with cooking spray. Add onion and garlic; sauté 3 minutes or until tender. Add broth and broccoli. Bring broccoli mixture to a boil over medium-high heat. Reduce heat to medium; cook 10 minutes.

**2.** Weigh or lightly spoon flour into a dry measuring cup. Combine flour and milk, stirring with a whisk until well blended. Add milk mixture to broccoli mixture. Cook 5 minutes or until slightly thick, stirring constantly. Stir in pepper. Remove from heat; add cheese, stirring until cheese melts.

**3.** Place one-third of soup in a blender or food processor, and process until smooth. Return pureed soup mixture to pan. **YIELD**: 6 servings (serving size: $1^{1}/_{3}$ cups).

CALORIES 203; FAT 6.3g (sat 4g, mono 1.8g, poly 0.4g); PROTEIN 15.6g; CARB 21.7g; FIBER 2.9g; CHOL 24mg; IRON 1.2mg; SODIUM 897mg; CALC 385mg

## what makes it light

• uses fat-free, lower-sodium chicken broth
• uses reduced-fat milk instead of cream
• uses light processed cheese
• uses cooking spray instead of butter or oil to sauté onion

# beer cheese soup

**The Reader:** Linda Vujnov

**The Story:** This soup became part of the Vujnov family Christmas Eve tradition 31 years ago, when they moved from Oregon back to California, and Linda's mother-in-law prepared a spread of cold cuts, relishes, cheese, breads, and this rich, savory soup. It's satisfying on its own or with a sandwich to take the chill off a winter day, notes Linda, and easy to pull together with a handful of aromatics, seasonings, cheese, and a bottle of beer. However, she said she was "disappointed to discover the nearly one pound of butter that contributed to the flavor." As an avid runner and mother of four children, she wants to choose wholesome foods and prepare them healthfully. She knew this recipe needed lightening to remain in the family's winter menu repertoire.

**The Dilemma:** Linda knew something had to be done about the ¾ pound of butter in the original recipe. The nearly two cups of shredded full-fat cheddar cheese contributed significant calories, cholesterol, and fat, including 31 grams of saturated fat. Chicken stock and a seasoning additive in the original recipe brought a bowl of soup to 1,767 milligrams of sodium.

**The Solution:** By sautéing the aromatics in cooking spray instead of butter, we shaved 300 calories, 34 grams of fat (most of which was saturated), 242 milligrams of sodium, and most of the cholesterol from each serving. To achieve buttery flavor and a smooth texture without butter, we cooked rich Yukon gold potatoes in fat-free, lower-sodium chicken broth, pureed the mixture, and added it back to the soup. The original soup called for flour as a thickening agent; we used the same amount of flour but added 1% low-fat milk for creaminess. Tinkering with the broth and milk in the soup cut 385 milligrams of sodium per portion. Instead of using all fat-free cheeses, which don't tend to melt well, we opted for a mixture of extrasharp reduced-fat cheddar and full-fat sharp cheddar to boost flavor. That cut four more grams of fat and 43 calories per serving. We omitted the artificial seasoning and used dry mustard, freshly ground black pepper, Worcestershire sauce, and a touch of salt to perk up the flavor—and shave another 40 milligrams of sodium per portion.

**The Feedback:** "I thought the blend of flavors was perfect and loved the thick consistency," Linda reports. She also sprinkled on some crushed red pepper for added zing.

| | BEFORE | AFTER |
|---|---|---|
| Calories per serving | 587 | 363 |
| Fat | 50g | 12.2g |
| Percent of total calories | 77% | 30% |

# Beer Cheese Soup

4½ cups fat-free, lower-sodium chicken broth, divided
1¼ cups cubed peeled Yukon gold potato (about 10 ounces)
Cooking spray
½ cup finely diced onion
½ cup finely diced celery
½ cup finely diced carrot
1 teaspoon minced garlic
2.25 ounces all-purpose flour (about ½ cup)
2½ cups 1% low-fat milk
¾ cup (3 ounces) shredded sharp cheddar cheese
½ cup (2 ounces) shredded reduced-fat extrasharp cheddar cheese
½ teaspoon dry mustard
½ teaspoon Worcestershire sauce
¼ teaspoon freshly ground black pepper
⅛ teaspoon salt
1 (12-ounce) can beer
Freshly ground black pepper (optional)

**1.** Simmer 2 cups broth and potato in a small saucepan. Cook 15 minutes or until potato is tender. Transfer potato mixture to a blender. Remove center piece of blender lid (to allow steam to escape); secure blender lid on blender. Place a clean towel over opening in blender lid (to avoid splatters). Blend until smooth. Set mixture aside.

**2.** Heat a large Dutch oven over medium heat. Coat pan with cooking spray. Add onion, celery, and carrot to pan; cook 5 minutes or until tender, stirring occasionally. Add garlic to pan; cook 30 seconds.

**3.** Weigh or lightly spoon flour into a dry measuring cup; level with a knife. Combine flour, remaining 2½ cups broth, and milk in a medium bowl; stir with a whisk. Add flour mixture to pan; bring to a boil. Cook 1 minute or until slightly thick; stir constantly with a whisk. Add potato mixture, sharp cheddar cheese, and next 5 ingredients to pan; cook 1 minute or until cheese melts, stirring constantly. Add beer to pan; bring to a simmer. Cook 15 minutes or until thoroughly heated. Garnish with black pepper, if desired. **YIELD:** 4 servings (serving size: 2 cups).

CALORIES 363; FAT 12.2g (sat 7.7g, mono 3.5g, poly 0.6g); PROTEIN 20.7g; CARB 41.8g; FIBER 3.4g; CHOL 39mg; IRON 2.1mg; SODIUM 884mg; CALC 480mg

LUNCH

## Chicken and Dumplings

This generous serving of soup is chock-full of vegetables and is hearty enough to pass as a complete meal.

**Broth:**

- 12 cups cold water
- 1 tablespoon whole black peppercorns
- 4 chicken leg quarters, skinned
- 3 celery stalks, sliced
- 2 medium carrots, peeled and sliced
- 2 bay leaves
- 1 large onion, peeled and cut into 8 wedges

**Dumplings:**

- 4.5 ounces all-purpose flour (about 1 cup), divided
- 1 teaspoon baking powder
- ¼ teaspoon salt
- ¼ cup chilled butter, cut into small pieces
- 3 tablespoons buttermilk

**Remaining Ingredients:**

- Cooking spray
- 1½ cups chopped onion
- 1 cup thinly sliced celery
- ¾ cup (¼-inch-thick) slices carrot
- ¾ teaspoon salt
- 1 tablespoon all-purpose flour
- 2 tablespoons finely chopped fresh chives

**1.** To prepare broth, combine first 7 ingredients in a large stockpot; bring to a boil. Reduce heat to medium-low, and simmer 2 hours, skimming as necessary. Remove chicken from broth; cool. Remove meat from bones. Shred meat; set aside. Discard bones. Strain broth through a sieve over a bowl; discard solids. Place broth in a large saucepan; bring to a boil. Cook until reduced to 6 cups (about 8 minutes).

**2.** To prepare dumplings, weigh or lightly spoon 4.5 ounces (about 1 cup) flour into a dry measuring cup; level with a knife. Combine 3.4 ounces (¾ cup) flour, baking powder, and ¼ teaspoon salt; stir with a whisk. Cut in butter with a pastry blender or 2 knives until mixture resembles coarse meal. Add buttermilk; stir to combine. Turn dough out onto a lightly floured surface; knead 5 times, adding remaining 1.1 ounces (¼ cup) flour as needed. Divide mixture into 24 equal portions.

**3.** Heat a large Dutch oven over medium-high heat. Coat pan with cooking spray. Add chopped onion, 1 cup celery, and ¾ cup carrot to pan; sauté 4 minutes, stirring occasionally. Add broth and ¾ teaspoon salt; bring to a boil. Reduce heat, and simmer 20 minutes or until vegetables are tender. Drop dumplings into pan; cover and cook 10 minutes or until dumplings are done, stirring occasionally. Remove ¼ cup liquid from pan; stir in 1 tablespoon flour. Return chicken to pan. Add flour mixture to pan; bring to a boil. Cook 1 minute or until slightly thick, stirring occasionally. Remove from heat; stir in chives. **YIELD:** 4 servings (serving size: about 2 cups).

CALORIES 457; FAT 19.7g (sat 9.6g, mono 5.7g, poly 2.4g); PROTEIN 31.8g; CARB 37.1g; FIBER 3.5g; CHOL 129mg; IRON 3.5mg; SODIUM 906mg; CALC 142mg

# Chicken and Rosemary Dumplings

## Soup:

- 4 cups fat-free, lower-sodium chicken broth
- 3 cups water
- 1 pound chicken drumsticks, skinned
- 1 pound skinless, boneless chicken breast halves
- 2 fresh thyme sprigs
- 2 teaspoons olive oil
- 1½ cups diced carrots
- 1½ cups chopped celery
- 1 cup diced onion
- 2 garlic cloves, minced
- ½ teaspoon salt

## Dumplings:

- 5.6 ounces all-purpose flour (about 1¼ cups)
- 1 tablespoon chopped fresh or ½ teaspoon dried rosemary
- 2 teaspoons baking powder
- ¼ teaspoon salt
- 2 tablespoons butter, softened
- ½ cup low-fat buttermilk
- 1 large egg
- 1.1 ounces all-purpose flour (about ¼ cup)
- ¼ cup water

## Remaining Ingredient:

Freshly ground black pepper

**1.** To prepare soup, combine first 5 ingredients in a large Dutch oven over medium-high heat; bring to a boil. Reduce heat, and simmer, uncovered, 15 minutes or until chicken is done. Remove pan from heat. Remove chicken pieces from broth; cool slightly. Strain broth through a sieve into a large bowl; discard solids. Remove chicken from bones. Discard bones; chop chicken into bite-sized pieces. Set chicken aside.

**2.** Heat oil in pan over medium-high heat. Add carrots, celery, onion, and garlic; sauté 6 minutes or until onion is tender. Add reserved broth mixture and ½ teaspoon salt; simmer 10 minutes. Keep warm.

**3.** To prepare dumplings, lightly spoon flour into dry measuring cups; level with a knife. Combine 5.6 ounces (1¼ cups) flour and next 3 ingredients in a large bowl. Cut in butter with a pastry blender or 2 knives until mixture resembles coarse meal. Combine buttermilk and egg, stirring with a whisk. Add buttermilk mixture to flour mixture, stirring just until combined.

**4.** Return chopped chicken to broth mixture; bring to a simmer over medium-high heat. Combine 1.1 ounces (¼ cup) flour and water, stirring with a whisk until well blended to form a slurry. Add flour mixture to pan; simmer 3 minutes. Drop dumpling dough, 1 tablespoon per dumpling, onto chicken mixture to form 12 dumplings. Cover and cook 7 minutes (do not boil). Sprinkle with pepper. **YIELD:** 6 servings (serving size: 2 dumplings and 1⅓ cups soup).

CALORIES 366; FAT 9.7g (sat 3.8g, mono 3.5g, poly 1.3g); PROTEIN 32.5g; CARB 35.1g; FIBER 2.9g; CHOL 115mg; IRON 3.3mg; SODIUM 936mg; CALC 169mg

3

## Quick Chicken and Dumplings

In this recipe, flour tortillas stand in for the traditional biscuit dough. To quickly thaw frozen mixed vegetables, place them in a colander and rinse with warm water for about a minute.

 1 tablespoon butter
 ½ cup prechopped onion
 2 cups chopped roasted skinless, boneless chicken breast
 1 (10-ounce) box frozen mixed vegetables, thawed
1½ cups water
 1 tablespoon all-purpose flour
 1 (14-ounce) can fat-free, lower-sodium chicken broth
 ¼ teaspoon salt
 ¼ teaspoon black pepper
 1 bay leaf
 8 (6-inch) flour tortillas, cut into ½-inch strips
 1 tablespoon chopped fresh parsley

**1.** Melt butter in a large saucepan over medium-high heat. Add onion; sauté 5 minutes or until tender. Stir in chicken and vegetables; cook 3 minutes or until thoroughly heated, stirring constantly.

**2.** While chicken mixture cooks, combine water, flour, and broth. Gradually stir broth mixture into chicken mixture. Stir in salt, pepper, and bay leaf; bring to a boil. Reduce heat, and simmer 3 minutes. Stir in tortilla strips, and cook 2 minutes or until tortilla strips soften. Remove from heat; stir in parsley. Discard bay leaf. Serve immediately. **YIELD:** 4 servings (serving size: about $1^1/_2$ cups).

CALORIES 366; FAT 9.3g (sat 3.1g, mono 3.9g, poly 1.4g); PROTEIN 29.8g; CARB 40.3g; FIBER 5.3g; CHOL 67mg; IRON 3.4mg; SODIUM 652mg; CALC 104mg

# Chicken and Dumplings from Scratch

**Stew:**

- 1 (4-pound) whole chicken
- 3 quarts water
- 3 cups chopped onion
- 1 cup chopped celery
- 1 cup chopped carrot
- 1 teaspoon salt
- ¼ teaspoon freshly ground black pepper
- 10 garlic cloves, peeled
- 4 fresh thyme sprigs
- 2 bay leaves
- 1.1 ounces all-purpose flour (about ¼ cup)
- 2 teaspoons cornstarch
- 3 tablespoons heavy cream

**Dumplings:**

- ¾ cup 1% low-fat milk
- 1 large egg
- 6.75 ounces all-purpose flour (about 1½ cups)
- 1 tablespoon baking powder
- 1 tablespoon cornmeal
- ½ teaspoon salt

**Remaining Ingredients:**

- 1 tablespoon chopped fresh parsley
- Freshly ground black pepper

**1.** To prepare stew, remove and discard giblets and neck. Rinse chicken with cold water, and place in an 8-quart stockpot. Add water and next 8 ingredients; bring to a simmer. Reduce heat, and simmer 45 minutes; skim surface occasionally, discarding solids. Remove chicken from pot; cool. Strain stock through a sieve into a large bowl; discard solids. Remove skin from chicken. Remove meat from bones; tear meat into 2-inch pieces, and store in refrigerator. Let stock cool to room temperature.

**2.** Pour stock into two zip-top plastic bags. Let stand 15 minutes. Working with one bag at a time, snip off a corner of bag; drain liquid into stockpot, stopping before fat layer reaches opening. Discard fat. Repeat procedure with remaining bag. Bring stock to a boil over medium-high heat; reduce heat, and simmer until reduced to 8 cups (about 15 minutes).

**3.** Heat a cast-iron skillet over medium-high heat. Lightly spoon 1.1 ounces (¼ cup) flour into a dry measuring cup; level with a knife. Add flour to pan; cook 1 minute or until lightly browned, stirring constantly. Combine browned flour and cornstarch in a large bowl; add ⅔ cup stock, stirring with a whisk until smooth. Add flour mixture to remaining stock in pan; bring to a boil over medium-high heat. Cook 2 minutes or until slightly thickened. Reduce heat; stir in cream. Add chicken; keep warm over low heat.

**4.** To prepare dumplings, combine milk and egg in a medium bowl. Lightly spoon 6.75 ounces (1½ cups) flour into dry measuring cups, and level with a knife. Combine flour and next 3 ingredients. Add flour mixture to milk mixture; stir with a fork until dry ingredients are moist.

**5.** Drop one-third of dumpling batter by 8 heaping teaspoonfuls onto chicken mixture. Cover and cook 3 minutes or until dumplings are done (do not allow chicken mixture to boil). Remove dumplings with a slotted spoon; place in a bowl or on a platter; keep warm. Repeat twice with remaining dumpling batter.

**6.** Remove pan from heat; slowly pour stew over dumplings. Sprinkle with parsley and pepper. Serve immediately. **YIELD:** 6 servings (serving size: 1⅓ cups stew and 4 dumplings).

CALORIES 334; FAT 7.9g (sat 3.2g, mono 2.4g, poly 1.2g); PROTEIN 31.4g; CARB 32.2g; FIBER 1.2g; CHOL 130mg; IRON 3.3mg; SODIUM 755mg; CALC 211mg

## 5

## Herbed Chicken and Dumplings

Fluffy herb-flecked dumplings, tender vegetables, and rich dark-meat chicken combine in this soul-satisfying classic. Garnish with parsley sprigs, if desired.

Cooking spray
- 8 ounces skinless, boneless chicken thighs, cut into bite-sized pieces
- ¾ cup (¼-inch) diagonally cut celery
- ½ cup (¼-inch) diagonally cut carrot
- ½ cup chopped onion
- ⅛ teaspoon dried thyme
- 3 fresh parsley sprigs
- 1 bay leaf
- 3 cups fat-free, lower-sodium chicken broth
- 2.25 ounces all-purpose flour (about ½ cup)
- 1 tablespoon chopped fresh parsley
- ¼ teaspoon baking powder
- ¼ teaspoon salt
- ¼ cup 1% low-fat milk

**1.** Heat a large saucepan over medium-high heat. Coat pan with cooking spray. Add chicken to pan; cook 4 minutes, browning on all sides. Remove chicken from pan; keep warm. Add celery and next 5 ingredients to pan; sauté 5 minutes or until onion is tender. Return chicken to pan; cook 1 minute. Add broth to pan; bring mixture to a boil. Cover, reduce heat, and simmer 30 minutes.

**2.** Weigh or lightly spoon 2.25 ounces (about $1/2$ cup) flour into a dry measuring cup; level with a knife. Combine flour, chopped parsley, baking powder, and salt in a medium bowl. Add milk, stirring just until moist. Spoon by heaping teaspoonfuls into broth mixture; cover and simmer 10 minutes or until dumplings are done. Discard parsley sprigs and bay leaf. **YIELD:** 2 servings (serving size: 2 cups).

CALORIES 285; FAT 5.2g (sat 1.5g, mono 1.9g, poly 1.2g); PROTEIN 25g; CARB 35.2g; FIBER 3.1g; CHOL 55mg; IRON 3.4mg; SODIUM 596mg; CALC 133mg

# Simple Clam Chowder

2 bacon slices
2 cups chopped onion
1¼ cups chopped celery
½ teaspoon salt
½ teaspoon dried thyme
2 garlic cloves, minced
6 (6½-ounce) cans chopped clams, undrained
5 cups diced peeled baking potato (about 1 pound)
4 (8-ounce) bottles clam juice
1 bay leaf
2.25 ounces all-purpose flour (about ½ cup)
3 cups fat-free milk
Thyme sprig (optional)

**1.** Cook bacon in a large Dutch oven over medium heat until crisp. Remove bacon from pan, reserving 1 teaspoon drippings in pan. Crumble bacon; set aside. Add onion, celery, salt, dried thyme, and garlic to drippings in pan; cook 4 minutes or until vegetables are tender.
**2.** Drain clams, reserving liquid. Add clam liquid, potato, clam juice, and bay leaf to pan; bring to a boil. Reduce heat, and simmer 15 minutes or until potato is tender. Discard bay leaf.
**3.** Weigh or lightly spoon flour into a dry measuring cup. Combine 2.25 ounces (about ½ cup) flour and milk, stirring with a whisk until smooth. Add flour mixture to pan; bring to a boil. Cook 12 minutes or until thick, stirring constantly. Add clams; cook 2 minutes. Sprinkle with bacon. Garnish with thyme, if desired. **YIELD**: 12 servings (serving size: 1 cup).

CALORIES 257; FAT 2.9g (sat 0.6g, mono 0.6g, poly 0.7g); PROTEIN 28.5g; CARB 27.9g; FIBER 2g; CHOL 67mg; IRON 26.6mg; SODIUM 475mg; CALC 242mg

**what makes it light**
- doesn't use the traditional heavy cream
- uses fat-free milk
- uses minimal amount of bacon drippings for flavor

# recipe makeover
# scallop clam chowder

**The Reader:** Patty Garcia

**The Story:** Patty clipped the original version of this recipe from a newspaper. She and her husband liked the idea of fresh thyme and Pernod (licorice-flavored liqueur) in a creamy, scallop-studded soup. However, since her husband had heart surgery, they have both altered their eating habits to focus on low-fat, low-cholesterol foods. So Patty sent the recipe to *Cooking Light* for a healthful makeover.

**The Dilemma:** The original recipe's six cups of heavy cream produced a velvety broth, and the fat balanced assertive flavors from black pepper, Pernod, and fresh thyme. The cream, however, also contributed an astounding 615 calories, 66 grams of fat, and 245 milligrams of cholesterol per serving. A serving of soup contained twice the daily recommendation for saturated fat intake and nearly all the daily allotment of dietary cholesterol.

**The Solution:** To cut calories and fat from the chowder's base, we used 2% reduced-fat milk and clam juice thickened with a little flour to offer creaminess at a fraction of the fat. Finishing the soup with 1½ cups of half-and-half imparts enough richness to round out the flavors. These changes slashed 502 calories, 60 grams of fat, and most of the cholesterol per serving. We used Yukon gold potatoes, which have a buttery flavor; the potatoes' starch also thickens the chowder. With the fat drastically reduced, we added a little garlic and celery to the onion, and sautéed them in a prudent pat of butter to add flavor to the soup. Also, we reduced the amount of Pernod because, with less fat to temper its assertive flavor, a tablespoon of the liqueur was plenty. To manage sodium, we chose flavorful kosher salt and used a bit less.

**The Feedback:** Patty prepared the newly lightened chowder for a dinner party. "Everyone wanted the recipe—it was a great success."

|  | BEFORE | AFTER |
|---|---|---|
| Calories per serving | 909 | 349 |
| Fat | 70.1g | 8.1g |
| Percent of total calories | 69% | 21% |

**We liked the flavor of the clam juice in this soup,** but you could substitute fat-free, lower-sodium chicken broth. If you don't have Pernod on hand, or prefer to omit the alcohol, substitute one teaspoon anise extract or finely ground aniseed. Serve with crackers.

# Scallop Clam Chowder

2 teaspoons butter
Cooking spray
1½ cups chopped onion (about 1 medium)
¼ cup chopped celery
1 teaspoon minced garlic
4½ cups (½-inch) cubed peeled Yukon gold or red potato (about 1½ pounds)
1¼ teaspoons kosher salt, divided
1 teaspoon freshly ground black pepper, divided

1.1 ounces all-purpose flour (about ¼ cup)
2½ cups clam juice
2½ cups 2% reduced-fat milk
1 tablespoon Pernod (licorice-flavored liqueur)
1½ teaspoons chopped fresh thyme
1½ pounds sea scallops, cut into 1-inch chunks
1½ cups half-and-half
¼ cup chopped fresh chives

**1.** Melt 2 teaspoons butter in a Dutch oven coated with cooking spray over medium-high heat. Add chopped onion and celery; sauté 5 minutes or until tender. Add 1 teaspoon garlic, and sauté 1 minute. Add potato, 1 teaspoon salt, and $^3/_4$ teaspoon pepper; cook 2 minutes. Weigh or lightly spoon 1.1 ounces (about $^1/_4$ cup) flour into a dry measuring cup; level with a knife. Sprinkle flour over potato mixture, and cook 1 minute, stirring frequently. Add clam juice and milk; bring to a boil, stirring constantly. Cover, reduce heat, and simmer 20 minutes or until potato is tender. Partially mash potato using a potato masher. Stir in remaining $^1/_4$ teaspoon salt, remaining $^1/_4$ teaspoon pepper, Pernod, and thyme; simmer 10 minutes. Add scallops and half-and-half; cook 5 minutes or until scallops are done. Sprinkle with chives. **YIELD:** 8 servings (serving size: about $1^1/_4$ cups chowder and $1^1/_2$ teaspoons chives).

CALORIES 349; FAT 8.1g (sat 4.6g, mono 2.2g, poly 0.2g); PROTEIN 33.8g; CARB 32.7g; FIBER 2.1g; CHOL 94mg; IRON 1.3mg; SODIUM 842mg; CALC 220mg

# 5 ways with

# chili

1

## White Bean and Turkey Chili

1 tablespoon canola oil

2 cups diced yellow onion (about 2 medium)

1½ tablespoons chili powder

1 tablespoon minced garlic

1½ teaspoons ground cumin

1 teaspoon dried oregano

3 (15.8-ounce) cans Great Northern beans, rinsed and drained

4 cups fat-free, lower-sodium chicken broth

3 cups chopped cooked turkey

½ cup diced seeded plum tomato (about 1)

⅓ cup chopped fresh cilantro

2 tablespoons fresh lime juice

½ teaspoon salt

½ teaspoon freshly ground black pepper

8 lime wedges (optional)

**1.** Heat oil in a large Dutch oven over medium-high heat. Add onion; sauté 10 minutes or until tender and golden. Add chili powder, garlic, and cumin; sauté 2 minutes. Add oregano and beans; cook 30 seconds. Add broth; bring to a simmer. Cook 20 minutes.

**2.** Place 2 cups bean mixture in a blender or food processor, and process until smooth. Return pureed mixture to pan. Add turkey, and cook 5 minutes or until thoroughly heated. Remove from heat. Add diced tomato, chopped cilantro, lime juice, salt, and pepper, stirring well. Garnish with lime wedges, if desired.

**YIELD:** 8 servings (serving size: about 1 cup).

CALORIES 286; FAT 6g (sat 1.2g, mono 2.1g, poly 1.6g); PROTEIN 32.4g; CARB 24.3g; FIBER 5.5g; CHOL 85mg; IRON 4.8mg; SODIUM 435mg; CALC 105mg

## All-American Chili

- 6 ounces hot turkey Italian sausage
- 2 cups chopped onion
- 1 cup chopped green bell pepper
- 8 garlic cloves, minced
- 1 pound ground sirloin
- 1 jalapeño pepper, chopped
- 2 tablespoons chili powder
- 2 tablespoons brown sugar
- 1 tablespoon ground cumin
- 3 tablespoons tomato paste
- 1 teaspoon dried oregano
- ½ teaspoon freshly ground black pepper
- ¼ teaspoon salt
- 2 bay leaves
- 1¼ cups Merlot or other fruity red wine
- 2 (28-ounce) cans whole tomatoes, undrained and coarsely chopped
- 2 (15-ounce) cans kidney beans, drained
- ½ cup (2 ounces) shredded reduced-fat sharp cheddar cheese

**1.** Heat a large Dutch oven over medium-high heat. Remove casings from sausage. Add sausage, onion, and next 4 ingredients to pan; cook 8 minutes or until sausage and beef are browned, stirring to crumble.

**2.** Add chili powder and next 7 ingredients, and cook 1 minute, stirring constantly. Stir in wine, tomatoes, and kidney beans; bring to a boil. Cover, reduce heat, and simmer 1 hour, stirring occasionally.

**3.** Uncover and cook 30 minutes, stirring occasionally. Discard bay leaves. Sprinkle each serving with cheddar cheese. **YIELD**: 8 servings (serving size: 1¼ cups chili and 1 tablespoon cheese).

CALORIES 375; FAT 12g (sat 4.6g, mono 4.1g, poly 1.1g); PROTEIN 28.9g; CARB 33.7g; FIBER 8.2g; CHOL 59mg; IRON 5mg; SODIUM 969mg; CALC 165mg

2

## Chunky Vegetarian Chili ▼

This vegetarian chili recipe is a great way to get kids to eat fiber-rich foods. It can be taken on camping trips and in school lunches in a thermos.

- 1 tablespoon vegetable oil
- 2 cups chopped onion
- ½ cup chopped yellow bell pepper
- ½ cup chopped green bell pepper
- 2 garlic cloves, minced
- 1 tablespoon brown sugar
- 1½ tablespoons chili powder
- 1 teaspoon ground cumin
- 1 teaspoon dried oregano
- ½ teaspoon salt
- ½ teaspoon black pepper
- 2 (14.5-ounce) cans stewed tomatoes, undrained
- 2 (15-ounce) cans black beans, rinsed and drained
- 1 (15-ounce) can kidney beans, rinsed and drained
- 1 (16-ounce) can pinto beans, rinsed and drained

**1.** Heat oil in a Dutch oven over medium-high heat. Add onion, bell peppers, and garlic; sauté 5 minutes or until tender. Add sugar and remaining ingredients, and bring to a boil. Reduce heat, and simmer 30 minutes. **YIELD:** 8 servings (serving size: 1 cup).

CALORIES 257; FAT 2.7 g (sat 0.3g; mono 0.5g, poly 1.2g); PROTEIN 12.8g; CARB 48.8g; FIBER 14.2g; CHOL 0mg; IRON 4.5mg; SODIUM 876mg; CALC 150mg

## Cincinnati Turkey Chili ▼

- 4 ounces uncooked spaghetti
- Cooking spray
- 8 ounces lean ground turkey
- 1½ cups prechopped onion, divided
- 1 cup chopped green bell pepper
- 1 tablespoon bottled minced garlic
- 1 tablespoon chili powder
- 2 tablespoons tomato paste
- 1 teaspoon ground cumin
- 1 teaspoon dried oregano
- ¼ teaspoon ground cinnamon
- ⅛ teaspoon ground allspice
- ½ cup fat-free, lower-sodium chicken broth
- 1 (15-ounce) can kidney beans, rinsed and drained
- 1 (14.5-ounce) can diced tomatoes, undrained
- 2½ tablespoons chopped semisweet chocolate
- ¼ teaspoon salt
- ¾ cup (3 ounces) shredded sharp cheddar cheese

**1.** Cook pasta according to package directions, omitting salt and fat. Drain; set aside.
**2.** Heat a Dutch oven over medium-high heat. Coat pan with cooking spray. Add turkey; cook 3 minutes, stirring to crumble. Add 1 cup onion, bell pepper, and garlic; sauté 3 minutes. Stir in chili powder and next 5 ingredients; cook 1 minute. Add broth, beans, and tomatoes;

3 4

bring to a boil. Cover, reduce heat, and simmer 20 minutes, stirring occasionally. Remove from heat; stir in chocolate and salt. Serve chili over spaghetti; top with remaining $^1/_2$ cup onion and cheese. **YIELD**: 4 servings (serving size: about $^1/_2$ cup spaghetti, $1^1/_2$ cups chili, 2 tablespoons onion, and 3 tablespoons cheese).

CALORIES 408; FAT 13.8g (sat 6.6g, mono 4.3g, poly 1.7g); PROTEIN 24.5g; CARB 47.4g; FIBER 7.9g; CHOL 67mg; IRON 3.7mg; SODIUM 765mg; CALC 237mg

## Mexican Black Bean Sausage Chili ▶

5

**Sausage:**

- 1½ tablespoons Hungarian sweet paprika
- 2 tablespoons minced garlic
- 3 tablespoons dry red wine
- 2 tablespoons sherry vinegar
- 2 teaspoons ancho chili powder
- 1 teaspoon ground cumin
- ½ teaspoon dried oregano
- ½ teaspoon ground coriander
- ½ teaspoon black pepper
- Dash of kosher salt
- ¾ pound lean ground pork
- ¾ pound ground turkey breast

**Chili:**

- 2 tablespoons olive oil
- 2 cups diced onion (about 2 medium)
- 1 tablespoon ground cumin
- 1 tablespoon finely minced garlic
- 2 teaspoons dried oregano
- 3 canned chipotle chiles in adobo sauce, minced
- 4 (15-ounce) cans black beans, rinsed and drained, divided
- 3 cups fat-free, lower-sodium chicken broth, divided
- 3 cups water
- 2 (14.5-ounce) cans no salt-added diced tomatoes, drained
- ¼ cup freshly squeezed lime juice
- ¼ cup very finely chopped cilantro
- Low-fat sour cream (optional)
- Sliced green onions (optional)

**1.** To prepare sausage, combine first 12 ingredients in a large bowl. Cover and refrigerate overnight.

**2.** To prepare chili, heat oil in a large saucepan over medium-high heat. Add sausage mixture; cook 7 minutes or until browned, stirring to crumble. Add onion, 1 tablespoon cumin, 1 tablespoon garlic, 2 teaspoons oregano, and chiles; cook 4 minutes or until onion is tender. Place $1^1/_2$ cups black beans and 1 cup broth in a food processor; process until smooth. Add pureed beans, remaining beans, remaining 2 cups broth, water, and tomatoes to pan; bring to a boil. Reduce heat, and simmer, partially covered, 45 minutes or until slightly thick. Stir in juice and cilantro. Ladle about $1^3/_4$ cups chili into each of 6 bowls. Garnish each serving with sour cream and sliced green onions, if desired. **YIELD**: 6 servings.

CALORIES 395; FAT 11g (sat 2.9g, mono 6g, poly 2.1g); PROTEIN 35.3g; CARB 40.4g; FIBER 13.7g; CHOL 78mg; IRON 6mg; SODIUM 989mg; CALC 128mg

**Bacon, blue cheese, avocado, and chicken** are all ingredients in the classic Cobb salad. Serve with a chilled summer soup or a sandwich for a light and refreshing meal.

# Chicken Cobb Salad

Cooking spray
1½ pounds skinless, boneless chicken
      breast cutlets
¼ teaspoon salt
¼ teaspoon black pepper
8 cups mixed greens

1 cup cherry tomatoes, halved
⅓ cup diced peeled avocado
2 tablespoons sliced green onions
⅓ cup fat-free Italian dressing
2 tablespoons crumbled blue cheese
1 bacon slice, cooked and crumbled

**1.** Heat a large nonstick skillet over medium-high heat. Coat pan with cooking spray. Sprinkle chicken with salt and pepper. Add chicken to pan; cook 5 minutes on each side or until done. Cut into ¹/₂-inch slices.

**2.** Combine greens, tomatoes, avocado, and onions in a large bowl. Drizzle greens mixture with dressing; toss gently to coat. Arrange about 2 cups greens mixture on each of 4 salad plates. Top each serving with 4 ounces chicken, 1¹/₂ teaspoons cheese, and about ¹/₂ teaspoon bacon. **YIELD**: 4 servings.

CALORIES 263; FAT 8g (sat 2.4g, mono 3.2g, poly 1.4g); PROTEIN 37.9g; CARB 8.9g; FIBER 3.7g; CHOL 99mg; IRON 2.6mg; SODIUM 606mg; CALC 89mg

## what makes it light

- uses skinless chicken breast cutlets
- uses fat-free Italian dressing instead of traditional creamy ranch-style or blue cheese dressing
- uses less of the traditional ingredients that are high in calories
- doesn't use boiled eggs

30
minutes
or
less

30
minutes
or
less

"This is my absolute favorite **Cooking Light** recipe. Be sure and use real maple syrup, as pancake syrup will not do this recipe justice. Guests are wowed by it. It is all I can do not to lick the dressing left over on my plate."

**from cookinglight.com**

# Spinach Salad with Maple-Dijon Vinaigrette

¼ cup maple syrup
3 tablespoons minced shallots (about 1 medium)
2 tablespoons red wine vinegar
1 tablespoon canola oil
1 tablespoon country-style Dijon mustard
¼ teaspoon salt

¼ teaspoon freshly ground black pepper
1 garlic clove, minced
1 cup sliced mushrooms
½ cup vertically sliced red onion
½ cup chopped Braeburn apple
4 bacon slices, cooked and crumbled
1 (10-ounce) package fresh spinach

**1.** Combine first 8 ingredients in a large bowl, stirring with a whisk. Add mushrooms and remaining ingredients; toss well to coat. **YIELD**: 8 servings (serving size: about 1½ cups).

CALORIES 80; FAT 3.3g (sat 0.6g, mono 1.6g, poly 0.7g); PROTEIN 2.6g; CARB 11.1g; FIBER 1.2g; CHOL 3mg; IRON 1.2mg; SODIUM 219mg; CALC 43mg

## what makes it light

- uses less canola oil than a traditional vinaigrette
- uses only ½ slice bacon per serving
- doesn't use boiled eggs
- uses chopped apple to boost fiber and flavor without fat

**This fun, kid-friendly indulgence** was a hit at taste testing and received our highest rating. The recipe can easily be multiplied to make as many sandwiches as you need.

# Grilled Peanut Butter and Banana Split Sandwich

2 (1-ounce) slices firm white sandwich bread, divided
1 teaspoon butter, softened
1 tablespoon creamy peanut butter
2 teaspoons honey
½ teaspoon semisweet chocolate minichips

1 large strawberry, thinly sliced
½ small banana, cut lengthwise into 3 slices (about 2 ounces)
1 tablespoon pineapple jam

**1.** Spread one side of each white bread slice with $^1/_2$ teaspoon butter. Combine peanut butter and honey; spread over plain side of 1 bread slice. Sprinkle with chocolate chips; top evenly with strawberry slices and banana slices.

**2.** Spread pineapple jam over plain side of remaining bread slice. Carefully assemble sandwich.

**3.** Heat a small nonstick skillet over medium-high heat. Add sandwich; cook 2 minutes on each side or until lightly browned. **YIELD:** 1 serving (serving size: 1 sandwich).

CALORIES 436; FAT 14.5g (sat 4.2g, mono 6g, poly 3.2g); PROTEIN 9.4g; CARB 72g; FIBER 4.6g; CHOL 10mg; IRON 3mg; SODIUM 497mg; CALC 100mg

## what makes it light

- uses a combination of peanut butter and honey to reduce calories and fat
- uses fresh fruit instead of jelly

1

## All-American Grilled Cheese with a Twist

- 8 (1-ounce) slices country white bread
- 2 cups (4 ounces) shredded sharp cheddar cheese
- 12 (¼-inch-thick) slices plum tomato (about 3 tomatoes)
- ¼ cup thinly sliced fresh basil
- Cooking spray

**1.** Place 4 bread slices on a work surface; arrange ½ cup cheddar cheese on each slice. Top each slice with 3 tomato slices and 1 tablespoon basil. Top with remaining 4 bread slices.

**2.** Heat a large nonstick skillet over medium heat. Coat pan with cooking spray. Add sandwiches to pan; cook 4 minutes or until lightly browned. Turn sandwiches over; cover and cook 2 minutes or until cheese melts.

**YIELD:** 4 servings (serving size: 1 sandwich).

CALORIES 247; FAT 10.5g (sat 6.3g, mono 3.4g, poly 0.6g); PROTEIN 11.6g; CARB 30g; FIBER 3.2g; CHOL 30mg; IRON 1.1mg; SODIUM 464mg; CALC 233mg

## Grilled Tomato and Brie Sandwiches ▼

- 8 (1-ounce) slices 100% whole-grain bread (about ¼ inch thick)
- 1 teaspoon olive oil
- 1 garlic clove, halved
- 2 teaspoons country-style Dijon mustard
- 4 ounces Brie cheese, thinly sliced
- 1⅓ cups packaged baby arugula and spinach greens (such as Dole)
- 8 (¼-inch-thick) slices beefsteak tomato
- Cooking spray

**1.** Preheat grill to high heat.
**2.** Brush one side of each bread slice with oil; rub cut sides of garlic over oil. Spread ½ teaspoon mustard on each of 4 bread slices, oil side down. Top each bread slice with 1 ounce cheese, ⅓ cup greens, and 2 tomato slices. Top each with remaining 4 bread slices, oil side up.
**3.** Place sandwiches on grill rack coated with cooking spray; grill 2 minutes on each side or until lightly toasted and cheese melts. **YIELD:** 4 servings (serving size: 1 sandwich).

CALORIES 234; FAT 10.1g (sat 5.1g, mono 3.1g, poly 1g); PROTEIN 11g; CARB 26.9g; FIBER 6.5g; CHOL 28mg; IRON 1.8mg; SODIUM 445mg; CALC 210mg

## Grilled Tomato, Smoked Turkey, and Muenster Sandwiches ▼

- 1 tablespoon minced red onion
- 3 tablespoons fat-free sour cream
- 1 tablespoon Dijon mustard
- 1 teaspoon chopped fresh or ¼ teaspoon dried thyme
- 4 teaspoons butter, softened
- 4 (1½-ounce) slices sourdough bread
- 6 (1-ounce) slices fat-free, honey-roasted smoked turkey breast
- 4 (½-inch-thick) slices tomato
- 2 (½-ounce) slices Muenster cheese

**1.** Combine first 4 ingredients in a bowl. Spread 1 teaspoon butter on one side of each bread slice. Spread 2 tablespoons mustard mixture over unbuttered side of each of 2 bread slices; top each with 3 turkey slices, 2 tomato slices, 1 cheese slice, and 1 bread slice (with buttered side up).
**2.** Heat a large nonstick skillet over medium heat until hot. Add sandwiches; cover and cook 3 minutes on each side or until golden brown.
**YIELD:** 2 sandwiches (serving size: 1 sandwich).

CALORIES 451; FAT 14.2g (sat 8g, mono 4.5g, poly 0.9g); PROTEIN 27.9g; CARB 48.7g; FIBER 1.8g; CHOL 65mg; IRON 2.4mg; SODIUM 913mg; CALC 238mg

## Tomato-Provolone Sandwiches with Pesto Mayo

- 3 tablespoons organic canola mayonnaise (such as Spectrum)
- 5 teaspoons refrigerated pesto
- 8 (1½-ounce) slices sourdough bread
- 4 (½-ounce) slices provolone cheese
- 1 cup arugula leaves
- 8 (¼-inch-thick) slices tomato
- ¼ teaspoon freshly ground black pepper
- ⅛ teaspoon salt

**1.** Preheat broiler.

**2.** Combine mayonnaise and pesto in a bowl, stirring well.

**3.** Arrange bread in a single layer on a baking sheet. Broil bread 2 minutes or until toasted. Turn bread over; place 1 cheese slice on each of 4 bread slices. Broil 1 minute or until cheese is bubbly. Spread about 2 teaspoons pesto mixture over each cheese-topped bread slice. Arrange ¼ cup arugula and 2 tomato slices over pesto mixture; sprinkle tomato slices evenly with pepper and salt. Spread about $1^{1}/_{2}$ teaspoons remaining pesto mixture evenly over one side of each remaining 4 bread slices; place 1 slice, pesto-side down, on top of each sandwich.

**YIELD:** 4 servings (serving size: 1 sandwich).

CALORIES 329; FAT 16.7g (sat 3.4g, mono 5.8g, poly 6.3g); PROTEIN 11g; CARB 35.7g; FIBER 2.9g; CHOL 16mg; IRON 3.3mg; SODIUM 630mg; CALC 194mg

4

# 5

## Grown-Up Grilled Cheese Sandwiches

A new take on a familiar favorite pairs grilled cheese with a BLT for a luscious veggie-packed sandwich that feels like an indulgence. Serve with zesty dill pickle spears. If you have extra room in your budget, pair with a sweet-tart hard cider.

    Cooking spray
  1 cup vertically sliced red onion
  1 large garlic clove, minced
  1 cup (4 ounces) shredded reduced-fat sharp white cheddar cheese (such as Cracker Barrel)
  8 (1½-ounce) slices hearty white bread (such as Pepperidge Farm)
  2 cups fresh spinach leaves
  8 (¼-inch-thick) slices tomato
  6 center-cut bacon slices, cooked

**1.** Heat a large nonstick skillet over medium-low heat. Coat pan with cooking spray. Add 1 cup onion and garlic; cook 10 minutes or until tender and golden brown, stirring occasionally.

**2.** Sprinkle 2 tablespoons cheese over each of 4 bread slices. Top each slice with ½ cup spinach, 2 tomato slices, 2 tablespoons onion mixture, and 1½ bacon slices. Sprinkle each with 2 tablespoons cheese; top with remaining 4 bread slices.

**3.** Heat skillet over medium heat. Coat pan with cooking spray. Place sandwiches in pan, and cook 3 minutes on each side or until golden brown and cheese melts. **YIELD:** 4 servings (serving size: 1 sandwich).

CALORIES 376; FAT 11g (sat 5.3g, mono 4.8g, poly 0.6g); PROTEIN 20.2g; CARB 50.3g; FIBER 3.3g; CHOL 24mg; IRON 2.9mg; SODIUM 876mg; CALC 308mg

# Pimiento Cheese Sandwiches

2 tablespoons block-style fat-free cream cheese, softened
¼ cup reduced-fat mayonnaise
¼ teaspoon finely grated onion
⅛ teaspoon Worcestershire sauce
⅛ teaspoon salt
Dash of ground red pepper
1 cup (4 ounces) shredded reduced-fat extrasharp cheddar cheese
1 tablespoon chopped pecans, toasted
½ (2-ounce) jar diced pimiento, undrained
⅛ teaspoon smoked paprika (optional)
8 (1-ounce) slices white bread

**1.** Beat together cream cheese and next 5 ingredients. Stir in cheese, pecans, pimiento, and smoked paprika, if desired. Cover and chill up to 3 hours.

**2.** Spread $1/4$ cup cheese mixture over 4 bread slices. Top with remaining 4 bread slices. **YIELD**: 4 servings (serving size: 1 sandwich).

CALORIES 296; FAT 14g (sat 5.3g, mono 1.1g, poly 1.1g); PROTEIN 12.2g; CARB 29.1g; FIBER 1.7g; CHOL 26mg; IRON 2.2mg; SODIUM 819mg; CALC 301mg

## what makes it light

- uses fat-free cream cheese
- uses reduced-fat mayonnaise
- uses reduced-fat extrasharp cheddar cheese

"This was a big hit, which is saying a lot in my family. **My son wanted seconds, which is rare for anything he thinks is healthy**.

**from cookinglight.com**"

# Tuna Melts

3 tablespoons finely chopped red onion
3 tablespoons organic canola mayonnaise
1 teaspoon grated lemon rind
¼ teaspoon fennel seeds, crushed
¼ teaspoon freshly ground black pepper
3 center-cut bacon slices, cooked and crumbled
2 (5-ounce) cans albacore tuna in water, drained and flaked
8 (1½-ounce) slices sourdough bread
4 (½-ounce) slices provolone cheese
Cooking spray

**1.** Combine first 7 ingredients in a medium bowl, stirring well to coat. Place 4 bread slices on a flat surface; top each bread slice with 1 cheese slice. Divide tuna mixture evenly among bread slices; top each serving with 1 remaining bread slice.

**2.** Heat a large skillet over medium heat. Lightly coat sandwiches with cooking spray. Place sandwiches in pan; top with another heavy skillet. Cook 3 minutes on each side or until lightly browned (leave skillet on sandwiches as they cook). **YIELD**: 4 servings (serving size: 1 sandwich).

CALORIES 405; FAT 17.7g (sat 4g, mono 5.1g, poly 6.9g); PROTEIN 28.3g; CARB 33.3g; FIBER 2.3g; CHOL 49mg; IRON 3.6mg; SODIUM 872mg; CALC 182mg

## what makes it light

- uses canola mayonnaise, which is healthier than regular mayonnaise
- uses less mayonnaise than traditional recipes
- uses center-cut bacon instead of regular bacon
- uses cooking spray instead of butter or oil to cook sandwiches

**Fish tacos with a Baja flair** are flavorful partners to the cabbage slaw, which adds crunch and a peppery bite.

# Baja Fish Tacos

2 tablespoons taco seasoning
1 tablespoon fresh lime juice
1 tablespoon fresh orange juice
1 pound mahimahi or other firm
   white fish fillets, cut into bite-sized
   pieces
1 tablespoon vegetable oil

2 cups presliced green cabbage
½ cup chopped green onions
½ cup reduced-fat sour cream
8 (6-inch) corn tortillas
8 lime wedges (optional)
Cilantro sprigs (optional)

**1.** Combine first 3 ingredients in a medium bowl. Add fish; toss to coat.
**2.** Heat oil in a large nonstick skillet over medium-high heat. Add fish; sauté 5 minutes or until fish is done.
**3.** Combine cabbage, onions, and sour cream in a medium bowl.
**4.** Warm tortillas according to package directions. Spoon about $^1/_4$ cup cabbage mixture down center of each tortilla. Divide fish evenly among tortillas; fold in half. Serve with lime wedges and cilantro, if desired. **YIELD**: 4 servings (serving size: 2 fish tacos and 2 lime wedges).

CALORIES 327; FAT 9.4g (sat 3.3g, mono 1.3g, poly 2.8g); PROTEIN 26g; CARB 35.8g; FIBER 4.6g; CHOL 98mg; IRON 2.4mg; SODIUM 624mg; CALC 182mg

## what makes it light

- uses reduced-fat sour cream
- fish isn't battered and deep-fried
- uses a minimal amount of oil to sauté fish

30
minutes
or
less

30 minutes or less

**A New Orleans specialty,** this sandwich is often made with deep-fried shrimp. Broiling the shrimp, which are coated in garlicky breadcrumbs, delivers big flavor without the fat.

# Shrimp Po'Boys with Spicy Ketchup

| | |
|---|---|
| 3 tablespoons dry breadcrumbs | 1½ teaspoons fresh lemon juice |
| ¼ teaspoon salt | ½ teaspoon Worcestershire sauce |
| ¼ teaspoon black pepper | ¼ teaspoon chili powder |
| 1 garlic clove, minced | ¼ teaspoon hot sauce |
| 1 tablespoon olive oil | 2 (10-inch) submarine rolls, split |
| 1 pound large shrimp, peeled and deveined | 2 cups torn curly leaf lettuce |
| ¼ cup ketchup | ½ cup thinly sliced red onion |

**1.** Preheat broiler.

**2.** Line a baking sheet with heavy-duty aluminum foil. Combine breadcrumbs, salt, pepper, and garlic in a medium bowl, stirring with a fork. Combine oil and shrimp; toss well. Place half of shrimp in breadcrumb mixture; toss well to coat. Place breaded shrimp in a single layer on prepared baking sheet. Repeat procedure with remaining shrimp and breadcrumb mixture. Broil 4 minutes or until shrimp are done.

**3.** Combine ketchup, juice, Worcestershire, chili powder, and hot sauce in a small bowl, stirring with a whisk.

**4.** Spread 2 tablespoons ketchup mixture over cut sides of each roll half. Place 1 cup lettuce over bottom half of each roll; top with ¼ cup onion. Arrange 1 cup shrimp on each roll half; top with remaining roll half. Cut sandwiches in half. **YIELD:** 4 servings (serving size: 1 sandwich half).

CALORIES 401; FAT 9.1g (sat 1.7g, mono 4.6g, poly 1.7g); PROTEIN 30g; CARB 48.9g; FIBER 3g; CHOL 172mg; IRON 5.3mg; SODIUM 864mg; CALC 183mg

## what makes it light

- shrimp are broiled, not deep-fried
- uses a lower-calorie spicy ketchup instead of a mayonnaise-laden tartar sauce

**Bright citrus and licorice notes from the fennel** complement the sweet, tarragon-flecked lobster meat. We use New England–style hot dog buns, which are top-split and have an open crumb on the sides.

# Lobster Salad Rolls with Shaved Fennel and Citrus

3 cups coarsely chopped cooked lobster meat (about 3 [1¼-pound] lobsters)

3 tablespoons canola mayonnaise

2 teaspoons chopped fresh tarragon

½ teaspoon kosher salt, divided

2 cups thinly sliced fennel bulb (about 1 medium)

½ teaspoon grated orange rind

1 tablespoon fresh orange juice

1 tablespoon fresh lemon juice

1 tablespoon rice wine vinegar

2 teaspoons extra-virgin olive oil

¼ teaspoon freshly ground black pepper

Cooking spray

6 (1½-ounce) hot dog buns

Lemon wedges (optional)

**1.** Combine lobster, mayonnaise, 2 teaspoons tarragon, and ¼ teaspoon salt; cover and refrigerate.

**2.** Combine fennel, remaining ¼ teaspoon salt, orange rind, and next 5 ingredients.

**3.** Heat a large nonstick skillet over medium heat. Coat pan with cooking spray. Add buns to pan; cook 2 minutes on each side or until lightly browned. Place ⅓ cup fennel salad in each bun. Top each serving with ½ cup lobster salad. Serve with lemon wedges, if desired. **YIELD:** 6 servings (serving size: 1 lobster roll).

CALORIES 238; FAT 6.2g (sat 0.8g, mono 3g, poly 1.9g); PROTEIN 19.4g; CARB 24.9g; FIBER 1.9g; CHOL 52mg; IRON 1.9mg; SODIUM 699mg; CALC 120mg

## what makes it light

- uses less mayonnaise than traditional recipes
- doesn't call for a buttered, toasted bun like most traditional recipes

**This is also called a patty melt:** ground meat and cheese nestled between slices of bread (any kind will do) and grilled. Prewrapped slices of processed cheddar cheese are the only way to go, as they melt better. We do it here far lighter than you're likely to find it on the road.

# Grilled Sourdough Cheddar Melts

| | |
|---|---|
| 2 teaspoons butter, divided | ⅛ teaspoon salt |
| Cooking spray | 4 (¾-ounce) slices 2% reduced-fat |
| 2 cups coarsely chopped onion | processed sharp cheddar cheese |
| 1 pound ground round | 8 (1½-ounce) slices sourdough or white |
| ¼ teaspoon freshly ground black pepper | bread |

**1.** Melt 1 teaspoon butter in a large nonstick skillet coated with cooking spray over medium-high heat. Add onion, and cook 4 minutes or until golden brown, stirring frequently. Reduce heat; cook 10 minutes or until tender, stirring occasionally. Set aside.

**2.** Preheat broiler.

**3.** Combine beef, pepper, and salt in a medium bowl. Divide beef mixture into 4 equal portions, shaping each into a $1/4$-inch-thick oval patty. Place patties on a broiler pan coated with cooking spray; broil 4 minutes on each side or until done.

**4.** Place 1 cheese slice over each of 4 bread slices; top each slice with 1 patty and 3 tablespoons onion mixture. Cover with remaining bread slices. Melt $1/2$ teaspoon butter in pan coated with cooking spray over medium heat; add 2 sandwiches to pan. Cook 4 minutes on each side until browned and cheese melts. Repeat procedure with $1/2$ teaspoon butter and remaining sandwiches. **YIELD:** 4 servings (serving size: 1 sandwich).

CALORIES 462; FAT 11.5g (sat 5.3g, mono 3.1g, poly 0.9g); PROTEIN 38.5g; CARB 49.3g; FIBER 3g; CHOL 80mg; IRON 5.2mg; SODIUM 909mg; CALC 357mg

## what makes it light

- uses ground round
- uses reduced-fat cheese
- uses a minimal amount of butter to grill sandwiches

## Stilton Burgers

2 teaspoons olive oil
4 cups sliced onion (about 12 ounces)
½ teaspoon salt, divided
1 pound ground sirloin
2 tablespoons grated onion
2 tablespoons Worcestershire sauce
⅛ teaspoon ground black pepper
2 garlic cloves, minced
Cooking spray
¼ cup crumbled Stilton cheese
4 (2-ounce) French hamburger rolls, split
4 green leaf lettuce leaves
4 (¼-inch-thick) slices tomato

**1.** Preheat grill to medium-high heat.
**2.** Heat a large skillet over medium heat. Add oil to pan. Add sliced onion and ¼ teaspoon salt; cook 18 minutes or until golden, stirring occasionally.

**3.** Combine ¼ teaspoon salt, beef, and next 4 ingredients; toss gently. Divide mixture into 4 equal portions, shaping each into a ½-inch-thick patty.
**4.** Place patties on grill rack lightly coated with cooking spray; grill 4 minutes on each side or until desired degree of doneness. Top each patty with 1 tablespoon cheese during last 2 minutes of cooking.
**5.** Place cut sides of rolls on grill rack; grill 1 minute. Place bottom halves of rolls on 4 plates; top each serving with 1 lettuce leaf, 1 tomato slice, 1 patty, ¼ cup onion mixture, and 1 roll top. **YIELD:** 4 servings (serving size: 1 burger).

CALORIES 393; FAT 15g (sat 6.3g, mono 6g, poly 0.6g); PROTEIN 28.3g; CARB 35.3g; FIBER 2.1g; CHOL 75mg; IRON 5.1mg; SODIUM 849mg; CALC 142mg

## Southwestern Turkey-Cheddar Burgers with Grilled Onions

Wheat germ adds a nuttiness that complements the turkey and spices. For more spicy heat, use Monterey Jack cheese with jalapeño peppers.

    ¾ cup finely chopped Maui or other
        sweet onion
    ⅓ cup wheat germ
    1½ teaspoons ancho chile powder
    ¾ teaspoon ground cumin
    ½ teaspoon salt
    ¼ teaspoon ground red pepper
    1½ pounds ground turkey breast
    Cooking spray
    4 ounces extrasharp cheddar cheese,
        thinly sliced
    6 (½-inch-thick) slices Maui or other
        sweet onion
    6 (2-ounce) Kaiser rolls, split
    6 tablespoons Chipotle-Poblano
        Ketchup

**1.** Prepare grill.
**2.** Combine first 7 ingredients in a large bowl. Divide mixture into 6 equal portions, shaping each into a ½-inch-thick patty.
**3.** Place patties on grill rack coated with cooking spray; grill 5 minutes. Turn patties over; grill 2 minutes. Divide cheese evenly over patties; grill an additional 5 minutes or until a thermometer registers 165°. Remove from grill; let stand 5 minutes.
**4.** Place onion slices on grill rack coated with cooking spray; grill 4 minutes on each side or until browned and tender.
**5.** Place rolls, cut sides down, on grill rack; grill 1 minute or until toasted. Place 1 patty on bottom half of each roll; top each serving with 1 onion slice, 1 tablespoon Chipotle-Poblano Ketchup, and top half of roll. **YIELD:** 6 servings (serving size: 1 burger).

CALORIES 395; FAT 10.7g (sat 4.8g, mono 2.5g, poly 1.6g); PROTEIN 32.8g; CARB 42.6g; FIBER 3.3g; CHOL 54mg; IRON 3.4mg; SODIUM 853mg; CALC 211mg

## Chipotle-Poblano Ketchup

    1 poblano chile (about 5 ounces)
    1 cup ketchup
    2 tablespoons minced seeded chipotle
        chiles, canned in adobo sauce (about
        2 chiles)
    ½ teaspoon ground cumin

**1.** Preheat broiler.
**2.** Pierce poblano two times with the tip of a knife. Place poblano on a foil-lined baking sheet; broil 10 minutes or until blackened, turning occasionally. Place in a zip-top plastic bag; seal. Let stand 15 minutes. Peel and discard skins. Cut a lengthwise slit in poblano; discard seeds and stem. Finely chop poblano.
**3.** Combine poblano and remaining ingredients. Refrigerate in an airtight container for up to 2 weeks. **YIELD:** $1^{1}/_{4}$ cups (serving size: 1 tablespoon).

CALORIES 15; FAT 0.2g (sat 0g, mono 0g, poly 0.1g); PROTEIN 0.3g; CARB 3.6g; FIBER 0.4g; CHOL 0mg; IRON 0.2mg; SODIUM 150mg; CALC 3mg

## Italian Meatball Burgers ▼

- 8 ounces sweet turkey Italian sausage
- 1 teaspoon dried oregano
- 1 teaspoon dried basil
- ½ teaspoon salt
- ½ teaspoon fennel seeds, crushed
- ⅛ teaspoon garlic powder
- 1 pound ground sirloin
  Cooking spray
- 2 ounces fresh mozzarella cheese, thinly sliced
- 6 (2-ounce) Italian bread rolls, split
- ¾ cup fat-free tomato-basil pasta sauce (such as Muir Glen)

**1.** Prepare grill.
**2.** Remove casings from sausage. Combine sausage, oregano, basil, salt, fennel seeds, garlic powder, and ground sirloin. Divide beef mixture into 6 equal portions, shaping each into a ¹/₂-inch-thick patty.
**3.** Place patties on grill rack coated with cooking spray; grill 5 minutes. Turn patties over; grill 2 minutes. Divide fresh mozzarella cheese evenly over patties, and grill an additional 5 minutes or until a thermometer registers 165°. Remove from grill; let stand 5 minutes.
**4.** Place rolls, cut sides down, on grill rack; grill 1 minute or until toasted. Place 1 patty on bottom half of each roll; top each serving with 2 tablespoons sauce and top half of roll. **YIELD:** 6 servings (serving size: 1 burger).

CALORIES 375; FAT 13.9g (sat 5.3g, mono 4.4g, poly 1.7g); PROTEIN 28.1g; CARB 32.7g; FIBER 1.8g; CHOL 80mg; IRON 4.5mg; SODIUM 894mg; CALC 130mg

## Portobello Burgers ▼

- ¼ cup lower-sodium soy sauce
- ¼ cup balsamic vinegar
- 2 tablespoons olive oil
- 3 garlic cloves, minced
- 4 (4-inch) portobello mushroom caps
- 1 small red bell pepper
  Cooking spray
- ¼ cup reduced-fat mayonnaise
- ½ teaspoon olive oil
- ⅛ teaspoon ground red pepper
- 4 (2-ounce) onion sandwich buns
- 4 (¼-inch-thick) slices tomato
- 4 curly leaf lettuce leaves

**1.** Combine first 4 ingredients in a large zip-top plastic bag; add mushrooms to bag. Seal and marinate at room temperature 2 hours, turning bag occasionally. Remove mushrooms from bag; discard marinade.
**2.** Prepare grill to medium heat.
**3.** Cut bell pepper in half lengthwise; discard

**3**

**4**

seeds and membranes. Place pepper halves on grill rack coated with cooking spray; grill 15 minutes or until blackened, turning occasionally. Place in a zip-top plastic bag; seal. Let stand 10 minutes. Peel. Reserve 1 pepper half for another use. Finely chop 1 pepper half; place in a small bowl. Add mayonnaise, $1/2$ teaspoon oil, and ground red pepper; stir well.

**4.** Place mushrooms, gill sides down, on grill rack coated with cooking spray; grill 4 minutes on each side. Place buns, cut sides down, on grill rack coated with cooking spray; grill 30 seconds on each side or until toasted. Spread 2 tablespoons mayonnaise mixture on top half of each bun. Place 1 mushroom on bottom half of each bun. Top each mushroom with 1 tomato slice and 1 lettuce leaf; cover with top halves of buns. **YIELD:** 4 servings (serving size: 1 burger).

CALORIES 251; FAT 8.4g (sat 2.3g, mono 3.7g, poly 2.1g); PROTEIN 7.3g; CARB 37.9g; FIBER 2.4g; CHOL 0mg; IRON 2.2mg; SODIUM 739mg; CALC 81mg

## Chipotle Salmon Burgers ▲

**Mayonnaise:**

> 1 tablespoon chopped fresh cilantro
> 3 tablespoons light mayonnaise
> 2 tablespoons finely chopped fresh mango
> 1 tablespoon finely chopped fresh pineapple
> $1/8$ teaspoon finely grated lime rind

**Burgers:**

> $1/3$ cup chopped green onions
> $1/4$ cup chopped fresh cilantro
> 1 tablespoon finely chopped chipotle chile, canned in adobo sauce
> 2 teaspoons fresh lime juice
> $1/4$ teaspoon salt
> 1 (1$1/4$-pound) salmon fillet, skinned and cut into 1-inch pieces
> Cooking spray
> 4 English muffins
> 4 butter lettuce leaves

**1.** To prepare mayonnaise, place first 5 ingredients in a food processor or blender; process until smooth. Transfer to a bowl; cover and chill.

**2.** To prepare burgers, place onions, $1/4$ cup cilantro, chile, and juice in a food processor; process until finely chopped. Add salt and salmon; pulse 4 times or until salmon is coarsely ground and mixture is well blended.

**3.** Divide salmon mixture into 4 equal portions; shape each portion into a (1-inch-thick) patty. Cover and chill 30 minutes.

**4.** Heat a grill pan over medium-high heat. Coat pan with cooking spray. Add patties to pan; cook 6 minutes on each side or until desired degree of doneness.

**5.** Wipe skillet with paper towels; recoat with cooking spray. Place 2 muffins, cut sides down, in pan; cook 2 minutes or until lightly toasted. Repeat procedure with cooking spray and remaining muffins.

**6.** Place 1 muffin bottom on each of 4 plates; top each serving with 1 lettuce leaf and 1 patty. Spread about 1 tablespoon mayonnaise mixture over each patty; place 1 muffin top on each serving. **YIELD:** 4 servings (serving size: 1 burger).

CALORIES 408; FAT 15g (sat 2.6g, mono 4.5g, poly 6.6g); PROTEIN 37.4g; CARB 28.9g; FIBER 2.9g; CHOL 94mg; IRON 3.8mg; SODIUM 595mg; CALC 124mg

30
minutes
or
less

# Spicy Bistro Steak Subs

1 tablespoon butter
2 garlic cloves, minced
1 pound thinly sliced lean deli
  roast beef
2 tablespoons ketchup
4 teaspoons Worcestershire sauce

½ teaspoon dried basil
½ teaspoon dried oregano
¼ teaspoon ground red pepper
1 (12-ounce) can dark beer
6 (2½-ounce) hoagie rolls with sesame
  seeds, cut in half lengthwise

**1.** Melt butter in a large nonstick skillet over medium-high heat. Add minced garlic, and sauté 2 minutes. Add roast beef and next 6 ingredients, and bring to a boil. Reduce heat, and simmer 2 minutes, stirring frequently. Drain roast beef in a colander over a bowl, reserving sauce. Divide roast beef evenly among roll bottoms, and top with roll tops. Serve sandwiches with reserved sauce. **YIELD**: 6 servings (serving size: 1 sandwich and 3 tablespoons sauce).

CALORIES 345; FAT 10.6g (sat 3.4g, mono 4.5g, poly 1.6g); PROTEIN 21.4g; CARB 40.6g; FIBER 1.6g; CHOL 2mg; IRON 3.8mg; SODIUM 938mg; CALC 67mg

## what makes it light

- uses lean deli roast beef instead of prime rib
- doesn't include cheese like many traditional recipes

# Memphis Pork Sandwiches

**Pork:**
- 8 hickory wood chunks (about 4 pounds)
- 2 tablespoons paprika
- 1 tablespoon freshly ground black pepper
- 1 tablespoon turbinado sugar
- 1½ teaspoons kosher salt
- 1½ teaspoons garlic powder
- 1½ teaspoons onion powder
- 1½ teaspoons dry mustard
- 1 (5-pound) bone-in pork shoulder (Boston butt)
- ⅓ cup white vinegar
- 1 tablespoon Worcestershire sauce
- 1 teaspoon canola oil
- 1 (12-ounce) can beer
- 2 cups water
- Cooking spray

**Slaw:**
- ¼ cup finely chopped onion
- 1½ tablespoons prepared mustard
- 1½ tablespoons white vinegar
- 1 tablespoon reduced-fat mayonnaise
- 1½ teaspoons granulated sugar
- ¼ teaspoon salt
- 6 cups chopped green cabbage

**Remaining Ingredients:**
- 13 hamburger buns
- 1⅔ cups Memphis Barbecue Sauce

**1.** To prepare pork, soak wood chunks in water about 16 hours; drain.

**2.** Combine paprika and next 6 ingredients; reserve 1 tablespoon paprika mixture. Rub half of remaining paprika mixture onto pork. Place in a large zip-top plastic bag; seal and refrigerate overnight.

**3.** Remove pork from refrigerator; let stand at room temperature 30 minutes. Rub remaining half of paprika mixture onto pork.

**4.** Combine reserved 1 tablespoon paprika mixture, ⅓ cup vinegar, Worcestershire, oil, and beer in a small saucepan; cook over low heat 5 minutes or until warm.

**5.** Remove grill rack; set aside. Prepare grill for indirect grilling, heating one side to medium-low and leaving one side with no heat. Maintain temperature at 225°. Pierce bottom of a disposable aluminum foil pan several times with the tip of a knife. Place pan on heated side of grill; add half of wood chunks to pan. Place another disposable aluminum foil pan (do not pierce pan) on unheated side of grill. Pour 2 cups water in pan. Coat grill rack with cooking spray; place grill rack on grill.

**6.** Place pork on grill rack over foil pan on unheated side. Close lid; cook 4½ hours or until a thermometer registers 170°, gently brushing pork with beer mixture every hour (avoid brushing off sugar mixture). Add additional wood chunks halfway during cooking time. Discard any remaining beer mixture.

**7.** Preheat oven to 250°.

**8.** Remove pork from grill. Wrap pork in several layers of aluminum foil, and place in a baking pan. Bake at 250° for 2 hours or until a thermometer registers 195°. Remove from oven. Let stand, still wrapped, 1 hour or until pork easily pulls apart. Unwrap pork; trim and discard fat. Shred pork with 2 forks.

**9.** While pork bakes and rests, prepare slaw. Combine onion and next 5 ingredients in a large bowl. Add cabbage, and toss to coat. Cover and chill 3 hours before serving. Serve pork and slaw on buns with Memphis Barbecue Sauce. **YIELD:** 13 servings (serving size: 1 bun, 3 ounces pork, about ⅓ cup slaw, and about 1½ tablespoons sauce).

CALORIES 387; FAT 15.2g (sat 5.1g, mono 6.3g, poly 2.2g); PROTEIN 26.6g; CARB 33.7g; FIBER 2.3g; CHOL 74mg; IRON 3.5mg; SODIUM 843mg; CALC 120mg

# Memphis Barbecue Sauce

1 cup ketchup
¾ cup white vinegar
2 tablespoons brown sugar
1 tablespoon onion powder
2 tablespoons Worcestershire sauce

2 tablespoons prepared mustard
½ teaspoon freshly ground black pepper
¼ teaspoon salt
⅛ teaspoon ground red pepper

**1.** Combine all ingredients in a medium saucepan; bring to a simmer. Cook 5 minutes; serve warm. **YIELD**: 2 cups (serving size: 2 tablespoons).

CALORIES 25; FAT 0.1g (sat 0g, mono 0.1g, poly 0g); PROTEIN 0.4g; CARB 6.4g; FIBER 0.2g; CHOL 0mg; IRON 0.3mg; SODIUM 247mg; CALC 10mg

## what makes it light

- uses reduced-fat mayonnaise
- fat is trimmed from pork before it's shredded unlike many restaurant recipes
- uses a minimal amount of mayonnaise in slaw

30
minutes
or
less

# Grilled Cuban Sandwiches

2 tablespoons Dijon mustard
1 (8-ounce) loaf French bread, cut in half horizontally
6 ounces reduced-fat Swiss cheese, thinly sliced (such as Alpine Lace)

6 ounces deli-sliced ham (such as Hillshire Farms)
8 sandwich-sliced dill pickles
Cooking spray
Sandwich-sliced dill pickles (optional)

**1.** Spread mustard evenly over cut sides of bread. Arrange half of cheese and half of ham on bottom half of loaf; top with pickle slices. Repeat layer with remaining cheese and ham; cover with top half of loaf. Cut into quarters.

**2.** Heat a large, heavy skillet over medium-high heat. Coat pan with cooking spray. Add sandwiches; press with a heavy skillet (such as cast-iron). Cook 2 minutes on each side. Garnish with dill pickles, if desired. **YIELD**: 4 servings (serving size: 1 sandwich).

CALORIES 335; FAT 11g (sat 5.3g, mono 2.1g, poly 0.9g); PROTEIN 23.1g; CARB 36g; FIBER 3g; CHOL 43mg; IRON 2.8mg; SODIUM 1,301mg; CALC 318mg

## what makes it light

- uses reduced-fat Swiss cheese
- not grilled with oil or butter
- uses less amounts of traditional high-fat ingredients

**Double-breading the tomato slices** gives them a crunchy coating. Soaking the tomatoes in hot water draws out their moisture, which helps keep them crisp when cooked. On their own, the fried green tomatoes in this recipe are a classic Southern side dish.

# Open-Faced Bacon, Lettuce, and Fried Green Tomato Sandwiches

2 medium green tomatoes, cut into 12 (¼-inch-thick) slices (about 1 pound)
2 tablespoons fat-free milk
4 large egg whites, lightly beaten
1½ cups yellow cornmeal
¾ teaspoon salt
¼ teaspoon freshly ground black pepper

2 tablespoons olive oil, divided
5 tablespoons light mayonnaise
1 teaspoon fresh lemon juice
¼ teaspoon hot sauce
6 (1½-ounce) slices white bread, toasted
6 Bibb lettuce leaves
9 bacon slices, cooked and cut in half
2 tablespoons fresh chives

**1.** Place tomato slices in a large bowl; cover with hot water. Let stand 15 minutes. Drain and pat dry with paper towels. Combine milk and egg whites, stirring with a whisk. Combine cornmeal, salt, and pepper in a shallow dish, stirring with a whisk. Dip each tomato slice in milk mixture; dredge in cornmeal mixture. Return tomato slices, one at a time, to milk mixture; dredge in cornmeal mixture.

**2.** Heat 1 tablespoon oil in a large nonstick skillet over medium-high heat. Add half of tomato slices; cook 4 minutes on each side or until crisp and golden. Repeat procedure with remaining oil and tomato slices.

**3.** Combine mayonnaise, juice, and hot sauce, stirring with a whisk. Spread about 1 tablespoon mayonnaise mixture onto each bread slice; top with 1 lettuce leaf, 3 bacon pieces, and 2 tomato slices. Sprinkle each sandwich with 1 teaspoon chives. Serve immediately. **YIELD:** 6 servings (serving size: 1 sandwich).

CALORIES 386; FAT 12.8g (sat 2.8g, mono 4.5g, poly 2.6g); PROTEIN 12.2g; CARB 56.2g; FIBER 3.9g; CHOL 16mg; IRON 2.2mg; SODIUM 834mg; CALC 44mg

**? what makes it light**
- uses fat-free milk
- uses egg whites
- pan-fried, not deep-fried, in a minimal amount of olive oil
- uses olive oil
- uses light mayonnaise

# Pork and Pinto Bean Nachos

Meat:

- 1 (1-pound) pork tenderloin, trimmed
- 2 tablespoons olive oil, divided
- ½ teaspoon salt, divided
- ¼ teaspoon black pepper
- Cooking spray
- 2 tablespoons fresh lime juice
- 1 teaspoon minced garlic

Beans:

- 1 can chipotle chiles in adobo sauce
- 2 tablespoons water
- 2 teaspoons fresh lime juice
- 1 teaspoon chili powder
- ¼ teaspoon salt
- 2 (15-ounce) cans pinto beans, rinsed and drained
- 4 applewood-smoked bacon slices, cooked and crumbled

Topping:

- 1½ cups chopped plum tomato
- 1 cup diced avocado
- ½ cup chopped jícama
- ⅓ cup chopped onion
- 2 tablespoons fresh lime juice
- 1 tablespoon olive oil
- ¼ teaspoon salt

Remaining Ingredients:

- 6 ounces sturdy tortilla chips (8 cups)
- 1¼ cups (5 ounces) shredded reduced-fat Colby and Monterey Jack cheese blend
- ¼ cup chopped fresh cilantro
- 1 jalapeño pepper, thinly sliced

**1.** Preheat oven to 500°.

**2.** To prepare meat, rub pork with 1 tablespoon oil, ¼ teaspoon salt, and black pepper. Place pork in a shallow roasting pan coated with cooking spray. Bake at 500° for 23 minutes or until a thermometer registers 160°. Remove from pan; cool 10 minutes. Shred pork with 2 forks to measure 2 cups; place in a small bowl. Stir in remaining 1 tablespoon oil, remaining ¼ teaspoon salt, 2 tablespoons juice, and garlic.

**3.** To prepare beans, remove 2 chipotle chiles and 1 teaspoon adobo sauce from can; reserve remaining chiles and sauce for another use. Drop chiles through food chute with food processor on; pulse 3 times or until coarsely chopped. Add adobo sauce, water, and next 4 ingredients; process 5 seconds or until smooth. Stir in bacon.

**4.** Preheat broiler.

**5.** To prepare topping, combine plum tomato and next 6 ingredients; toss well to coat.

**6.** Arrange tortilla chips in a single layer on a large rimmed baking sheet. Top evenly with bean mixture; top with meat mixture, and sprinkle with cheese. Broil 4 minutes or until cheese melts. Top evenly with topping, cilantro, and jalapeño. Serve immediately. **YIELD:** 6 servings (serving size: 1 ounce chips, ½ cup beans, ⅓ cup pork, and ½ cup topping).

CALORIES 517; FAT 26.9g (sat 6.8g, mono 12.4g, poly 3.3g); PROTEIN 31.4g; CARB 38.4g; FIBER 8.9g; CHOL 66mg; IRON 3.3mg; SODIUM 991mg; CALC 248mg

## what makes it light

- uses lean pork tenderloin
- uses reduced-fat cheese
- smaller portion size than traditional recipes

# Muffuletta

**Grilled Vegetables:**
- ¼ cup reduced-fat Italian dressing
- 8 (½-inch-thick) slices eggplant (about 1 pound)
- 2 (½-inch-thick) slices Vidalia or other sweet onion
- 1 medium yellow squash, thinly sliced
- 1 medium red bell pepper, cut into 4 wedges
- Cooking spray

**Olive Salad:**
- 1 cup chopped tomato or quartered cherry tomatoes
- ⅓ cup chopped pepperoncini peppers
- ¼ cup sliced pimiento-stuffed olives
- 2 tablespoons pepperoncini juice
- ½ teaspoon dried thyme
- ½ teaspoon cracked black pepper

**Remaining Ingredients:**
- 1 (16-ounce) loaf French bread, cut in half horizontally
- 2 ounces thinly sliced provolone cheese
- 2 ounces thinly sliced reduced-fat hard salami (such as Franklin)

**1.** To prepare grilled vegetables, combine first 5 ingredients in a zip-top plastic bag; seal and marinate in refrigerator 2 hours, turning bag occasionally.

**2.** Prepare grill.

**3.** Remove vegetables from plastic bag; place vegetables on grill rack coated with cooking spray. Grill 5 minutes on each side or until vegetables are tender.

**4.** To prepare olive salad, combine tomato and next 5 ingredients.

**5.** Hollow out bottom half of bread, leaving a 1-inch-thick shell; reserve torn bread for another use. Arrange cheese in bottom half of the bread. Top with salami, grilled vegetables, olive salad, and top half of bread. Wrap loaf with plastic wrap; refrigerate up to 24 hours. Cut into 4 pieces just before serving. **YIELD:** 4 servings (serving size: 1 piece).

CALORIES 384; FAT 11.9g (sat 4.3g, mono 3.4g, poly 1.9g); PROTEIN 16.3g; CARB 55.1g; FIBER 7.9g; CHOL 23mg; IRON 3.4mg; SODIUM 1,313mg; CALC 204mg

## what makes it light
- uses reduced-fat Italian dressing
- uses reduced-fat hard salami
- grilled vegetables replace the bulk of meat that's in a traditional muffuletta
- doesn't use oil in the olive salad like traditional recipes

"Yummy, yummy. **Best egg salad I've ever eaten, and adding it to BLT is just genius.** Can't wait for my leftovers today at lunch. My husband is not a big fan of egg salad, but he loved it, too. We will definitely make this again."

**from cookinglight.com**

# Egg Salad BLTs

¼ cup fat-free mayonnaise
3 tablespoons thinly sliced green onions
3 tablespoons reduced-fat sour cream
2 teaspoons whole-grain Dijon mustard
½ teaspoon freshly ground black pepper
¼ teaspoon grated lemon rind
8 hard-cooked large eggs

8 (1½-ounce) slices peasant bread or firm sandwich bread, toasted
4 center-cut bacon slices, cooked and cut in half crosswise
8 (¼-inch-thick) slices tomato
4 large Boston lettuce leaves

**1.** Combine first 6 ingredients in a medium bowl, stirring well.
**2.** Cut 2 eggs in half lengthwise; reserve 2 yolks for another use. Coarsely chop remaining egg whites and whole eggs. Add eggs to mayonnaise mixture; stir gently to combine.
**3.** Arrange 4 bread slices on a cutting board or work surface. Top each bread slice with $1/2$ cup egg mixture, 2 bacon pieces, 2 tomato slices, 1 lettuce leaf, and 1 bread slice. Serve sandwich immediately. **YIELD**: 4 servings (serving size: 1 sandwich).

CALORIES 371; FAT 11.7g (sat 4.1g, mono 4.4g, poly 1.4g); PROTEIN 21.9g; CARB 44g; FIBER 2.4g; CHOL 329mg; IRON 4mg; SODIUM 892mg; CALC 70mg

## what makes it light

- uses fat-free mayonnaise
- uses reduced-fat sour cream
- uses fewer egg yolks than traditional recipes
- uses center-cut bacon, which is lower in fat than regular bacon

30
minutes
or
less

**This hearty sandwich** is a filling lunch option. Prepare the chicken salad at home the night before, and then assemble the sandwich at work the next day. Substitute baguettes for focaccia if you want.

# Pesto Chicken Salad Sandwiches

½ cup reduced-fat mayonnaise
⅓ cup plain fat-free yogurt
⅓ cup commercial pesto (such as Buitoni)
1½ tablespoons fresh lemon juice
½ teaspoon salt
½ teaspoon black pepper
4 cups cubed skinless, boneless rotisserie chicken breast
1 cup diced celery
⅓ cup chopped walnuts, toasted
1 (1-pound) focaccia bread, cut in half horizontally, toasted, and cut into 20 slices
1 (12-ounce) bottle roasted red bell peppers, drained and chopped
10 romaine lettuce leaves

**1.** Combine first 6 ingredients in a large bowl, stirring with a whisk. Stir in chicken, celery, and walnuts.

**2.** Spread $1/2$ cup salad onto each of 10 bread slices. Top each slice with about 2 tablespoons bell pepper, 1 lettuce leaf, and 1 bread slice. **YIELD:** 10 servings (serving size: 1 sandwich).

CALORIES 324; FAT 10g (sat 1.2g, mono 0.6g, poly 2.2g); PROTEIN 26.4g; CARB 31.6g; FIBER 1.6g; CHOL 55mg; IRON 2.3mg; SODIUM 725mg; CALC 39mg

## what makes it light

• uses low-fat mayonnaise
• uses fat-free yogurt

"Wow! These were delicious! My son and husband love Reuben sandwiches, and I was happy to find a way to make these a healthier choice."

from cookinglight.com

# Turkey Reuben Panini

8 (½-ounce) slices thin-slice rye bread
¼ cup fat-free Thousand Island dressing
8 (½-ounce) thin slices reduced-fat Swiss cheese
¼ cup refrigerated sauerkraut, rinsed and drained

8 ounces low-sodium deli turkey breast (such as Boar's Head)
Cooking spray

**1.** Spread one side of each bread slice evenly with $1^{1}/_{2}$ teaspoons dressing. Place 1 cheese slice on dressed side of each of 4 bread slices; top each with 1 tablespoon sauerkraut and 2 ounces turkey. Top each sandwich with 1 cheese slice and 1 bread slice, dressed side down. Coat outside of each sandwich (top and bottom) with cooking spray. Heat a large skillet over medium-high heat. Add sandwiches to pan. Place a cast-iron or other heavy skillet on top of sandwiches; press gently to flatten sandwiches (leave cast-iron skillet on sandwiches while they cook). Cook 2 minutes on each side or until browned and cheese melts. **YIELD:** 4 servings (serving size: 1 sandwich).

CALORIES 268; FAT 7.5g (sat 3g, mono 0.6g, poly 0.4g); PROTEIN 25.2g; CARB 25.7g; FIBER 3.1g; CHOL 35mg; IRON 1.7mg; SODIUM 819mg; CALC 304mg

## what makes it light

- uses fat-free Thousand Island dressing
- uses reduced-fat Swiss cheese
- uses turkey, which is lower in sodium and fat than the traditional corned beef or pastrami

# spinach-cheese bake

**The Reader:** Joyce Keil

**The Story:** Joyce's sister-in-law, Judy Wipf, gave her this egg, cheese, and spinach casserole recipe 30 years ago, and it has been a family favorite since. However, Joyce eats more healthfully these days by preparing *Cooking Light* recipes and eating plenty of fruits and vegetables. While she enjoyed the dish's rich cheese and spinach combination, she knew the recipe needed to be revamped. "You can see the fat glistening" on the baked casserole, she wrote to us.

**The Dilemma:** This original recipe's short ingredient list belied its heavy nutrition profile. One pound of cheese, one-quarter cup of butter, three eggs, and a cup of whole milk contributed a hefty amount of fat and most of the dish's calories. One serving contained more than half of a day's worth of saturated fat, as well as one-third of the dietary cholesterol for someone on a 2,000-calorie diet.

**The Solution:** We reduced the butter to one table-spoon, which was melted and used to grease the pan and maintain the casserole's buttery back note. And we reduced the total amount of cheese and substituted a lower-fat yet tasty cheese to keep fat in check: We combined ¾ cup Monterey Jack cheese with 1¼ cups of more assertive-tasting reduced-fat sharp cheddar cheese. These changes cut more than 13 grams of fat (nearly 9 grams saturated) and 135 calories per portion. The butter, cheese, and eggs contributed most of the original's cholesterol count, but by using less butter, mostly reduced-fat cheese, and 1 cup of fat-free and cholesterol-free egg substitute (in place of the original's three whole eggs), we slashed 89 milligrams of cholesterol per serving. Adding a bit more spinach improved the fiber and iron content. And to compensate for this addition, we increased the flour-milk mixture with minimal extra calories by using fat-free milk instead of whole. Adding a little mustard and a few spices further boosted the savory quality of the casserole.

**The Feedback:** When Joyce prepared the recipe for her daughter, she feared reducing the butter so drastically wouldn't work. But her daughter was "pleased and frankly amazed" by the trimmed-down recipe and deemed the lightened casserole's texture and taste comparable to the original.

|  | BEFORE | AFTER |
|---|---|---|
| Calories per serving | 286 | 157 |
| Fat | 21.2g | 6g |
| Percent of total calories | 34% | 67% |

**You can assemble the casserole in less than 10 minutes** by using preshredded cheeses. Pair this dish with a fresh berry salad and mini muffins for a lovely Mother's Day or graduation brunch.

# Spinach-Cheese Bake

| | |
|---|---|
| 1 tablespoon butter, melted | 1½ cups fat-free milk |
| Cooking spray | 1 cup egg substitute |
| 2 (6-ounce) packages fresh baby spinach | 1 teaspoon salt |
| 1¼ cups (5 ounces) shredded reduced-fat sharp cheddar cheese | 1 teaspoon baking powder |
| | 2 teaspoons Dijon mustard |
| ¾ cup (3 ounces) shredded Monterey Jack cheese | ¼ teaspoon freshly ground black pepper |
| | ⅛ teaspoon ground nutmeg |
| 6 ounces all-purpose flour (about 1⅓ cups) | ⅛ teaspoon ground red pepper |

**1.** Preheat oven to 350°.

**2.** Pour butter into bottom of a 13 x 9–inch baking dish coated with cooking spray; tilt dish to coat. Place spinach evenly in bottom of dish; sprinkle evenly with cheeses.

**3.** Weigh or lightly spoon 6 ounces (about $1^1/3$ cups) flour into dry measuring cups; level with a knife. Combine flour and remaining ingredients in a medium bowl; stir with a whisk until blended. Pour milk mixture over cheese. Bake at 350° for 40 minutes or until lightly browned. Serve immediately. **YIELD**: 12 servings.

CALORIES 157; FAT 6g (sat 3.7g, mono 1.7g, poly 0.4g); PROTEIN 10.8g; CARB 15.1g; FIBER 1.6g; CHOL 18mg; IRON 2.6mg; SODIUM 494mg; CALC 263mg

# dinner

This is one of my favorite **Cooking Light** recipes of all time! It has outstanding texture and flavor for a lightened soup! Truly delicious! **This soup actually won a "cook off" contest at work,** and when I told everyone it was from **Cooking Light** they couldn't believe it!!

**from cookinglight.com**

# Baked Potato Soup

4 baking potatoes (about 2½ pounds)
3 ounces all-purpose flour (about ⅔ cup)
6 cups 2% reduced-fat milk
1 cup (4 ounces) reduced-fat shredded extrasharp cheddar cheese, divided
1 teaspoon salt
½ teaspoon freshly ground black pepper
1 cup reduced-fat sour cream
¾ cup chopped green onions, divided
6 bacon slices, cooked and crumbled
Cracked black pepper (optional)

**1.** Preheat oven to 400°.

**2.** Pierce potatoes with a fork; bake at 400° for 1 hour or until tender. Cool. Peel potatoes; coarsely mash.

**3.** Weigh or lightly spoon flour into a dry measuring cup; level with a knife. Place flour in a large Dutch oven; gradually add milk, stirring with a whisk until blended. Cook over medium heat until thick and bubbly (about 8 minutes). Add mashed potatoes, $3/4$ cup cheese, salt, and $1/2$ teaspoon pepper, stirring until cheese melts. Remove from heat.

**4.** Stir in sour cream and $1/2$ cup onions. Cook over low heat 10 minutes or until thoroughly heated (do not boil). Ladle $1^1/2$ cups soup into each of 8 bowls. Sprinkle each serving with $1^1/2$ teaspoons cheese, $1^1/2$ teaspoons onions, and about 1 tablespoon bacon. Garnish with cracked pepper, if desired. **YIELD:** 8 servings (serving size: about $1^1/2$ cups soup, $1^1/2$ teaspoons cheese, $1^1/2$ teaspoons onions, and about 1 tablespoon bacon).

CALORIES 329; FAT 10.8g (sat 5.9g, mono 3.5g, poly 0.7g); PROTEIN 13.6g; CARB 44.5g; FIBER 2.8g; CHOL 38mg; IRON 1.1mg; SODIUM 587mg; CALC 407mg

## what makes it light

- uses reduced-fat milk rather than cream for the base
- uses extrasharp reduced-fat cheese for maximum flavor
- uses reduced-fat sour cream

# 5 ways with

# pizza

## Chicago Deep-Dish Pizza

2 teaspoons sugar
1 package dry yeast (about 2¼ teaspoons)
1 cup warm water (100° to 110°)
1 tablespoon extra-virgin olive oil
12.38 ounces all-purpose flour (about 2¾ cups), divided
¼ cup yellow cornmeal
½ teaspoon salt
Cooking spray
2 cups (8 ounces) shredded part-skim mozzarella cheese, divided
2 precooked mild Italian chicken sausages (about 6 ounces), casings removed, chopped
1 (28-ounce) can whole tomatoes, drained
1½ teaspoons chopped fresh oregano
1½ teaspoons chopped fresh basil
2 cups thinly sliced mushrooms (about 6 ounces)
¾ cup chopped green bell pepper
¾ cup chopped red bell pepper

**1.** Dissolve sugar and yeast in warm water in a large bowl; let stand 5 minutes. Stir in olive oil.
**2.** Weigh or lightly spoon flour into dry measuring cups; level with a knife. Combine 11.25 ounces (about 2½ cups) flour, cornmeal, and salt in a bowl. Stir flour mixture into yeast mixture until dough forms a ball. Turn dough out onto a lightly floured surface. Knead until smooth and elastic (about 5 minutes); add enough of remaining flour, 1 tablespoon at a time, to prevent dough from sticking to hands (dough will feel sticky).
**3.** Place dough in a large bowl coated with cooking spray, turning to coat top. Cover and let rise in a warm place (85°), free from drafts, 45 minutes or until doubled in size. (Gently press two fingers into dough. If indentation remains, dough has risen enough.) Punch dough down; cover and let rest 5 minutes. Roll dough into an 11 x 15–inch rectangle on a lightly floured surface. Place dough in a 13 x 9–inch baking dish coated with cooking spray; press dough up sides of dish. Spread 1½ cups cheese evenly over dough. Arrange chopped sausage evenly over cheese.
**4.** Preheat oven to 400°.
**5.** Chop tomatoes; place in a sieve. Stir in oregano and basil; drain tomato mixture 10 minutes.
**6.** Heat a large nonstick skillet over medium heat. Coat pan with cooking spray. Add mushrooms to pan; cook 5 minutes, stirring occasionally. Stir in peppers; cook 8 minutes or until tender, stirring occasionally. Arrange vegetables over sausage; spoon tomato mixture evenly over vegetables and sausage. Sprinkle evenly with remaining ½ cup cheese. Bake at 400° for 25 minutes or until crust browns and cheese bubbles. Cool 5 minutes before cutting. **YIELD:** 8 servings (serving size: 1 piece).

CALORIES 330; FAT 9.2g (sat 4.6g, mono 3.2g, poly 1g); PROTEIN 17.8g; CARB 44g; FIBER 3.2g; CHOL 31mg; IRON 3.9mg; SODIUM 365mg; CALC 244mg

## Pizza Margherita

Because this classic Neapolitan-style pizza is so simple, it depends on quality ingredients. Use the best fresh mozzarella and basil you can find.

- 1 cup warm water (100° to 110°), divided
- 10 ounces bread flour (about 2 cups plus 2 tablespoons)
- 1 package dry yeast (about 2¼ teaspoons)
- 4 teaspoons olive oil
- ¾ teaspoon kosher salt, divided
- Cooking spray
- 1 tablespoon yellow cornmeal
- ¾ cup Pizza Sauce
- 1¼ cups (5 ounces) thinly sliced fresh mozzarella cheese
- ⅓ cup small fresh basil leaves

**1.** Pour ¾ cup warm water in the bowl of a stand mixer with dough hook attached. Weigh or lightly spoon flour into dry measuring cups and spoons; level with a knife. Add flour to ¾ cup water; mix until combined. Cover; let stand 20 minutes. Combine remaining ¼ cup water and yeast in a small bowl; let stand 5 minutes or until bubbly. Add yeast mixture, oil, and ½ teaspoon salt to flour mixture; mix 5 minutes or until a soft dough forms. Place dough in a large bowl coated with cooking spray; cover surface of dough with plastic wrap lightly coated with cooking spray. Refrigerate 24 hours.

**2.** Remove dough from refrigerator. Let stand, covered, 1 hour or until dough comes to room temperature. Punch dough down. Press dough out to a 12-inch circle on a lightly floured baking sheet, without raised sides, sprinkled with cornmeal. Crimp edges to form a ½-inch border. Cover dough loosely with plastic wrap.

**3.** Position an oven rack in the lowest setting. Place a pizza stone on lowest rack. Preheat oven to 500°. Preheat pizza stone for 30 minutes before baking dough.

**4.** Remove plastic wrap from dough. Sprinkle dough with remaining ¼ teaspoon salt. Spread Pizza Sauce evenly over dough, leaving a ½-inch border. Arrange cheese slices evenly over pizza.

Slide pizza onto preheated pizza stone, using a spatula as a guide. Bake at 500° for 15 minutes or until crust is golden. Cut pizza into 10 wedges, and sprinkle evenly with basil. **YIELD:** 5 servings (serving size: 2 wedges).

CALORIES 421; FAT 10.9g (sat 4.7g, mono 4.7g, poly 1g); PROTEIN 16.9g; CARB 62.8g; FIBER 6.5g; CHOL 22mg; IRON 4.4mg; SODIUM 754mg; CALC 267mg

## Pizza Sauce

- 2 tablespoons extra-virgin olive oil
- 5 garlic cloves, minced
- 1 (28-ounce) can San Marzano tomatoes
- ½ teaspoon kosher salt
- ½ teaspoon dried oregano

**1.** Heat oil in a medium saucepan over medium heat. Add garlic to pan; cook 1 minute, stirring frequently. Remove tomatoes from can using a slotted spoon, reserving juices. Crush tomatoes. Stir tomatoes, juices, salt, and oregano into garlic mixture; bring to a boil. Reduce heat, and simmer 30 minutes, stirring occasionally. **YIELD:** 6 servings (serving size: about ⅓ cup).

CALORIES 66; FAT 4.7g (sat 0.7g, mono 3.3g, poly 0.6g); PROTEIN 1.2g; CARB 6.2g; FIBER 1.4g; CHOL 0mg; IRON 1.4mg; SODIUM 175mg; CALC 48mg

## Pepperoni Pizza

Cooking spray
2 cups thinly sliced cremini mushrooms
  (about 4 ounces)
Basic Pizza Dough
2 teaspoons olive oil
Basic Pizza Sauce (recipe on page 169)
1½ cups (6 ounces) shredded part-skim
  mozzarella cheese
2 tablespoons grated fresh Parmesan
  cheese
2 ounces sliced turkey pepperoni
  (such as Hormel)

**1.** Position one oven rack in the middle setting. Position another rack in the lowest setting, and place a rimless baking sheet on the bottom rack. Preheat oven to 500°.
**2.** Heat a large nonstick skillet over medium-high heat. Coat pan with cooking spray. Add sliced mushrooms to pan, and sauté 5 minutes or until moisture evaporates.
**3.** Remove plastic wrap from Basic Pizza Dough; discard. Brush oil over dough. Remove preheated baking sheet from oven; close oven door. Slide dough onto preheated baking sheet, using a spatula as a guide. Bake on lowest oven rack at 500° for 8 minutes. Remove from oven.
**4.** Spread Basic Pizza Sauce in an even layer over crust, leaving a ¼-inch border. Top sauce with mushrooms. Sprinkle mushrooms evenly with mozzarella and Parmesan. Arrange pepperoni on top of cheese. Bake on middle rack an additional 10 minutes or until crust is golden brown and cheese melts. Cut into 12 wedges.
**YIELD:** 6 servings (serving size: 2 wedges).

CALORIES 346; FAT 8.2g (sat 3.8g, mono 3g, poly 0.8g); PROTEIN 18.1g; CARB 49.5g; FIBER 3.6g; CHOL 29mg; IRON 4mg; SODIUM 692mg; CALC 249mg

## Basic Pizza Dough

2 teaspoons honey
1 package active dry yeast (about
  2¼ teaspoons)
¾ cup warm water (100° to 110°)
10 ounces all-purpose flour (about
  2¼ cups), divided
½ teaspoon salt
Cooking spray
2 tablespoons stone-ground yellow
  cornmeal

**1.** Dissolve honey and yeast in ³/₄ cup warm water in a large bowl. Let stand 5 minutes or until bubbly. Weigh or lightly spoon flour into dry measuring cups; level with a knife. Add 2 cups flour and salt to yeast mixture; stir until a soft dough forms. Turn dough out onto a lightly floured surface. Knead until smooth

3

and elastic (about 6 minutes); add enough of remaining flour, 1 tablespoon at a time, to prevent dough from sticking to hands (dough will feel slightly sticky).

**2.** Place dough in a large bowl coated with cooking spray, turning to coat top. Cover and let rise in a warm place (85°), free from drafts, 30 minutes or until doubled in size. (Gently press two fingers into dough. If indentation remains, dough has risen enough.)

**3.** Roll dough into a 12-inch circle (about ¼ inch thick) on a lightly floured surface. Place dough on a rimless baking sheet sprinkled with cornmeal. Crimp edges of dough with fingers to form a rim. Lightly spray surface of dough with cooking spray, and cover with plastic wrap. Place dough in refrigerator up to 30 minutes. Bake according to recipe directions. **YIELD:** 1 (12-inch) crust.

CALORIES 1,155; FAT 3.4g (sat 0.6g, mono 0.5g, poly 1.3g); PROTEIN 33.8g; CARB 242.5g; FIBER 10.8g; CHOL 0mg; IRON 14.3mg; SODIUM 1,195mg; CALC 49mg

## Basic Pizza Sauce

Cooking spray
- ¼ cup finely chopped onion
- 1 garlic clove, minced
- ¼ cup white wine
- 2 tablespoons tomato paste
- 1 teaspoon dried oregano
- ⅛ teaspoon freshly ground black pepper
- 1 (14.5-ounce) can crushed tomatoes, undrained
- 1 tablespoon chopped fresh basil
- ½ teaspoon balsamic vinegar

**1.** Heat a large saucepan over medium-high heat. Coat pan with cooking spray. Add onion to pan; sauté 3 minutes or until tender. Add garlic to pan; sauté 30 seconds. Stir in wine; cook 30 seconds. Add tomato paste, oregano, pepper, and tomatoes. Reduce heat, and simmer 20 minutes or until thick. Remove from heat; stir in basil and vinegar. Cool. **YIELD:** 1⅓ cups.

CALORIES 203; FAT 0.3g (sat 0.1g, mono 0.1g, poly 0.1g); PROTEIN 9.6g; CARB 42.2g; FIBER 10.1g; CHOL 0mg; IRON 7.3mg; SODIUM 953mg; CALC 201mg

4

## Chicken, Red Grape, and Pesto Pizza ▲

- 1 (11-ounce) can refrigerated thin-crust pizza dough
Cooking spray
- ⅓ cup refrigerated pesto
- 1½ cups seedless red grapes, halved
- 8 ounces shredded skinless, boneless rotisserie chicken breast
- 3 garlic cloves, thinly sliced
- 4 ounces fresh mozzarella cheese, thinly sliced
- 3 tablespoons grated Romano cheese
- ¼ teaspoon black pepper
- ¼ cup sliced green onions

**1.** Preheat oven to 425°.

**2.** On a lightly floured surface, pat dough into a 12-inch circle; place dough on a pizza pan coated with cooking spray. Spread pesto evenly over dough, leaving a ½-inch border around edges. Arrange grapes evenly over dough; top with chicken. Top with garlic and mozzarella; sprinkle with Romano and pepper. Bake at 425° for 20 minutes or until crust is golden brown. Sprinkle with onions. Cut into 12 wedges. **YIELD:** 6 servings (serving size: 2 wedges).

CALORIES 364; FAT 14.4g (sat 4.8g, mono 6.3g, poly 1.4g); PROTEIN 22.6g; CARB 34.6g; FIBER 1.7g; CHOL 55mg; IRON 2.5mg; SODIUM 562mg; CALC 191mg

## Herbed Cheese Pizza

**Dough:**

- 9.5 ounces bread flour (about 2 cups), divided
- 2 cups warm water (100° to 110°), divided
- 1 teaspoon sugar
- 2 packages dry yeast (about 4½ teaspoons)
- 14.6 ounces all-purpose flour (about 3¼ cups), divided
- 1 teaspoon salt
- 2 teaspoons olive oil
- Cooking spray

**Topping:**

- 2 teaspoons dried oregano
- 2 teaspoons ground cumin
- 1 teaspoon hot paprika
- ¾ teaspoon coarsely ground black pepper, divided
- 1 teaspoon olive oil
- 1 cup finely chopped onion
- ½ teaspoon salt
- 5 garlic cloves, minced
- 1 bay leaf
- 1 (28-ounce) can diced tomatoes
- 10 ounces sliced kasseri cheese
- 3 tablespoons minced fresh parsley

**1.** To prepare dough, weigh or lightly spoon bread flour into dry measuring cups; level with a knife. Combine 4.75 ounces (about 1 cup) bread flour, 1 cup warm water, sugar, and yeast in a bowl; let stand 15 minutes.

**2.** Weigh or lightly spoon all-purpose flour into dry measuring cups; level with a knife. Combine 13.5 ounces (about 3 cups) all-purpose flour, remaining 4.75 ounces (about 1 cup) bread flour, and 1 teaspoon salt in a large bowl; make a well in center. Add yeast mixture, remaining 1 cup warm water, and 2 teaspoons oil to flour mixture; stir well. Turn dough out onto a floured surface. Knead until smooth and elastic (about 10 minutes); add enough of remaining flour, 1 tablespoon at a time, to prevent dough from sticking to hands.

**3.** Place dough in a large bowl coated with cooking spray, turning to coat top. Cover and let rise in a warm place (85°), free from drafts, 45 minutes or until doubled in size. (Press two fingers into dough. If indentation remains, dough has risen enough.) Punch dough down; divide dough into 8 equal portions. Cover and let rest 20 minutes.

**4.** To prepare topping, combine oregano, cumin, paprika, and ½ teaspoon black pepper. Heat a large skillet over medium-high heat. Add olive oil to pan. Add onion; sauté 3 minutes. Add salt, remaining ¼ teaspoon black pepper, garlic, bay leaf, and tomatoes; bring to a boil. Reduce heat, and simmer 15 minutes or until thick. Remove from heat; discard bay leaf.

**5.** Preheat oven to 450°.

**6.** Working with one dough portion at a time (cover remaining dough to keep from drying), roll each portion into a 6-inch circle on a lightly floured surface; place circle on a baking sheet coated with cooking spray. Repeat procedure with remaining dough portions. Top each crust with ¼ cup tomato mixture, 1¼ ounces cheese, and ½ teaspoon oregano mixture. Bake at 450° for 12 minutes or until crusts are lightly browned. Sprinkle evenly with parsley.

**YIELD:** 8 servings (serving size: 1 pizza).

CALORIES 493; FAT 13.7g (sat 7.9g, mono 1.4g, poly 0.4g); PROTEIN 19.4g; CARB 73.9g; FIBER 5.1g; CHOL 38mg; IRON 5.2mg; SODIUM 917mg; CALC 296mg

# Easy Meatless Manicotti

2 cups (8 ounces) shredded part-skim
  mozzarella cheese, divided
1 (16-ounce) carton fat-free cottage
  cheese
1 (10-ounce) package frozen chopped
  spinach, thawed, drained, and
  squeezed dry
¼ cup (1 ounce) grated fresh Parmesan
  cheese

1½ teaspoons dried oregano
¼ teaspoon salt
¼ teaspoon black pepper
1 (8-ounce) package manicotti (14 shells)
1 (26-ounce) jar fat-free tomato-basil
  pasta sauce
Cooking spray
1 cup water

**1.** Preheat oven to 375°.

**2.** Combine $1^{1}/_{2}$ cups mozzarella, cottage cheese, and next 5 ingredients in a medium bowl. Spoon about 3 tablespoons cheese mixture into each uncooked manicotti. Pour half of tomato-basil pasta sauce into a 13 x 9–inch baking dish coated with cooking spray. Arrange stuffed shells in a single layer over sauce, and top with remaining sauce. Pour 1 cup water into dish. Sprinkle remaining $^{1}/_{2}$ cup mozzarella evenly over sauce. Cover tightly with foil. Bake at 375° for 1 hour or until shells are tender. Let stand 10 minutes before serving. **YIELD:** 7 servings (serving size: 2 manicotti).

CALORIES 328; FAT 9g (sat 4.8g, mono 2.2g, poly 0.5g); PROTEIN 23.8g; CARB 38.3g; FIBER 3.9g; CHOL 23mg; IRON 3mg; SODIUM 891mg; CALC 451mg

## spinach fettuccine

DINNER

**The Reader:** Kathy Gordon

**The Story:** The spinach, bacon, and Parmesan pasta recipe was a family favorite Kathy inherited about 15 years ago from her mom, Sharon, who clipped it from a newspaper. "My mom prepared it when we had company, and it was a big hit because it's so delicious," recalls Kathy. But she stopped making the dish about 10 years ago, when she and her husband, Mike, started eating more healthfully.

**The Dilemma:** "This recipe is easy and delicious but so full of fat," she says. The original butter-, cream-, and bacon-laden dish was as heavy on the palate as the waistline. A single serving contributed nearly a full day's worth of sodium, a whopping 27 grams of saturated fat, and more than half the suggested daily cholesterol intake.

**The Solution:** We modified several components yet still created a rich, creamy, and bacon-crisped result. The original sauce included one egg, 1 1/2 cups heavy cream, 1/2 cup butter, and 2 cups Parmesan cheese, which contributed a total of 34 grams of fat per serving.

Sodium was another concern with the original recipe. Almost half the dish's sodium and one-third of its fat came from a pound of bacon. We were able to keep about 1/2 pound by switching to leaner center-cut bacon, which shaved 194 calories, 15 grams of fat, and 823 milligrams of sodium per portion. To keep the lightened recipe's sodium level in check, we halved the amount of salt added to the final product and omitted salt from the pasta cooking water, shaving an additional 325 milligrams of sodium per serving. A few small but significant adjustments enhanced the taste of the lighter version. For example, a minced garlic clove and additional freshly ground black pepper boosted the flavor.

**The Feedback:** "I like the lighter version better," says Kathy. One big difference, she notes, is that "you can actually taste the spinach and bacon now," whereas before, the fat masked other flavors in the dish. And what did Mom—who clipped the recipe to begin with—think? "She approved of the lightened version," says Kathy, remarking that there were no leftovers.

| | BEFORE | AFTER |
|---|---|---|
| Calories per serving | 800 | 365 |
| Fat | 53.2g | 12.2g |
| Percent of total calories | 60% | 30% |

**You can use Asiago cheese** for a slightly sweeter flavor, or Parmigiano-Reggiano for a sharper flavor than the pecorino Romano.

# Spinach Fettuccine

1 pound uncooked fettuccine
1 tablespoon butter
1 garlic clove, minced
¼ cup (2 ounces) ⅓-less-fat cream cheese
¾ cup fat-free, lower-sodium chicken broth
3 tablespoons all-purpose flour
¾ cup (3 ounces) grated fresh pecorino Romano cheese

¾ cup half-and-half
1 teaspoon salt
½ teaspoon freshly ground black pepper
1 (10-ounce) package frozen chopped spinach, thawed, drained, and squeezed dry
10 center-cut bacon slices, cooked and crumbled (about 1¼ cups)
Parsley sprigs (optional)

**1.** Cook pasta according to package instructions, omitting salt and fat. Drain pasta, reserving $1/2$ cup pasta water.

**2.** Melt butter in a large nonstick skillet over medium-high heat. Add garlic; sauté 30 seconds. Add reserved pasta water and cream cheese, stirring with a whisk until smooth.

**3.** Combine broth and flour in a small bowl, stirring with a whisk until smooth. Add flour mixture to pan, stirring with a whisk to combine; bring to a boil. Cook 2 minutes or until mixture thickens, stirring constantly. Remove from heat; add pecorino Romano, stirring until smooth. Add half-and-half, salt, and pepper. Stir in spinach. Combine cheese mixture and pasta in a large bowl, tossing to coat. Place about 1 cup pasta mixture in each of 8 bowls; top each serving with $2^1/2$ tablespoons bacon. Garnish with parsley, if desired. **YIELD:** 8 servings.

CALORIES 365; FAT 12.2g (sat 6.3g, mono 3.3g, poly 0.6g); PROTEIN 15.9g; CARB 46.6g; FIBER 2.3g; CHOL 34mg; IRON 1.8mg; SODIUM 681mg; CALC 188mg

# 5 ways with
# mac and cheese

1

## Bacon, Ranch, and Chicken Mac and Cheese

- 8 ounces uncooked elbow macaroni
- 1 applewood-smoked bacon slice
- 8 ounces skinless, boneless chicken breast, cut into ½-inch pieces
- 1 tablespoon butter
- 1 tablespoon all-purpose flour
- 1½ cups fat-free milk
- ⅓ cup condensed 45% reduced-sodium 98% fat-free cream of mushroom soup, undiluted
- ¾ cup (3 ounces) shredded six-cheese Italian blend (such as Sargento)
- ½ teaspoon onion powder
- ½ teaspoon garlic powder
- ½ teaspoon chopped fresh dill
- ½ teaspoon salt
- Cooking spray
- ½ cup (2 ounces) shredded colby-Jack cheese

**1.** Cook pasta according to package directions, omitting salt and fat; drain.

**2.** Cook bacon in a large nonstick skillet over medium heat until crisp. Remove bacon from pan, reserving drippings in pan. Finely chop bacon; set aside. Increase heat to medium-high. Add chicken to drippings in pan; sauté 6 minutes or until done.

**3.** Melt butter in a large saucepan over medium heat; sprinkle flour evenly into pan. Cook 2 minutes, stirring constantly with a whisk. Combine milk and soup, stirring with a whisk; gradually add milk mixture to saucepan, stirring with a whisk. Bring to a boil; cook 2 minutes or until thick. Remove from heat; let stand 4 minutes or until sauce cools to 155°. Add Italian cheese blend, onion powder, garlic powder, dill, and salt, stirring until cheese melts. Stir in pasta and chicken.

**4.** Preheat broiler. Spoon mixture into an 8-inch square baking dish coated with cooking spray. Sprinkle evenly with reserved bacon and colby-Jack cheese. Broil 3 minutes or until cheese melts. **YIELD:** 4 servings (serving size: about 2 cups).

CALORIES 497; FAT 17g (sat 9.2g, mono 4.7g, poly 1.4g); PROTEIN 33.3g; CARB 51.7g; FIBER 2g; CHOL 74mg; IRON 2.4mg; SODIUM 767mg; CALC 368mg

## Macaroni and Cheese with Roasted Tomatoes ▼

   3 cups halved cherry tomatoes
Cooking spray
   ¼ teaspoon black pepper
   3 ounces sourdough bread, torn into
     pieces
   1 teaspoon butter, melted
  12 ounces uncooked large elbow macaroni
   2 cups (8 ounces) shredded extrasharp
     cheddar cheese
   ¼ cup egg substitute
  1½ teaspoons kosher salt
   ¼ teaspoon ground red pepper
   1 (12-ounce) can evaporated low-fat milk

**1.** Preheat oven to 375°.
**2.** Place tomatoes in a 13 x 9-inch baking dish
coated with cooking spray. Sprinkle with black
pepper. Bake at 375° for 30 minutes or until
browned, stirring occasionally.
**3.** While tomatoes cook, place bread in a food
processor; pulse 2 times or until crumbly. Toss
crumbs with melted butter. Sprinkle the crumbs
on a baking sheet, and bake at 375° for 12
minutes or until golden, stirring frequently.
**4.** Cook macaroni in boiling water 7 minutes;
drain. Return macaroni to pan; place over
medium-low heat. Add cheese and remaining
ingredients; cook 4 minutes or until cheese melts,
stirring constantly. Stir in tomatoes. Sprinkle
each serving with about 3 tablespoons breadcrumbs. **YIELD:** 8 servings (serving size: 1 cup).

CALORIES 357; FAT 11.4g (sat 6.6g, mono 3.1g, poly 0.8g);
PROTEIN 18.1g; CARB 45.2g; FIBER 2g; CHOL 33mg;
IRON 2.7mg; SODIUM 669mg; CALC 350mg

## Sausage Mac and Cheese ▲

   4 ounces chicken and sun-dried
     tomato sausage (such as Gerhard's),
     chopped
  1¼ cups fat-free milk
   2 tablespoons all-purpose flour
   ¾ cup (3 ounces) shredded reduced-
     fat sharp cheddar cheese
   ⅓ cup (about 1⅓ ounces) shredded
     Monterey Jack cheese
   ¼ cup (2 ounces) ⅓-less-fat cream
     cheese
   ½ teaspoon onion powder
   ¼ teaspoon garlic salt
   5 cups hot cooked elbow macaroni
     (about 8 ounces uncooked pasta)
Chopped fresh parsley (optional)

**1.** Heat a large nonstick saucepan over medium-
high heat. Add sausage; sauté 4 minutes or until
browned. Combine milk and flour in a small
bowl, stirring well with a whisk. Add milk
mixture to pan; bring to a boil, stirring constantly. Reduce heat to medium. Stir in cheeses,
onion powder, and garlic salt; cook 3 minutes
or until cheeses melt, stirring constantly. Stir
in pasta. Garnish with parsley, if desired. Serve
immediately. **YIELD:** 4 servings (serving size:
about 1¼ cups).

CALORIES 433; FAT 13.9g (sat 7.8g, mono 3.8g, poly 0.9g);
PROTEIN 23.6g; CARB 53.1g; FIBER 2.7g; CHOL 56mg;
IRON 2.4mg; SODIUM 538mg; CALC 340mg

4

## Chipotle Macaroni and Cheese

This macaroni and cheese is a favorite of ours because it is incredibly tasty and easy to prepare. You don't even have to make a white sauce for this creamy dish. The acidic tomatoes counter the richness of the cheeses.

1 (7-ounce) can chipotle chiles in adobo sauce
1 tablespoon butter
½ cup finely chopped onion
½ cup finely chopped green bell pepper
1 garlic clove, minced
2 tablespoons all-purpose flour
1 (14½-ounce) can diced tomatoes and green chiles, undrained
4 cups hot cooked elbow macaroni (about 2 cups uncooked)
2 cups (8 ounces) shredded reduced-fat sharp cheddar cheese
1 cup 1% low-fat cottage cheese
1 cup 2% reduced-fat milk
¼ cup (1 ounce) grated fresh Parmesan cheese
1 large egg, lightly beaten
Cooking spray
3 tablespoons dry breadcrumbs

**1.** Preheat oven to 350°.
**2.** Remove 1 teaspoon adobo sauce from can; set aside. Remove 2 chipotle chiles from can; finely chop to measure 1 tablespoon. Reserve remaining chiles and adobo sauce for another use.
**3.** Melt butter in a Dutch oven over medium-high heat. Add chopped chiles, onion, bell pepper, and garlic; cook 4 minutes or until onion is tender, stirring frequently. Sprinkle with flour; cook 30 seconds, stirring constantly. Reduce heat to medium; add tomatoes. Cook 3 minutes or until thickened. Add reserved 1 teaspoon adobo sauce, pasta, cheddar cheese, cottage cheese, milk, Parmesan, and egg; stir to combine. Spoon pasta mixture into a 2-quart baking dish coated with cooking spray; top with breadcrumbs. Bake at 350° for 30 minutes or until bubbly. **YIELD:** 6 servings (serving size: about 1 cup).

CALORIES 324; FAT 8.5g (sat 4.6g, mono 2.4g, poly 0.6g); PROTEIN 34.2g; CARB 39.6g; FIBER 2g; CHOL 56mg; IRON 2.4mg; SODIUM 756mg; CALC 307mg

## Three-Cheese Macaroni and Cheese

Try this rich and creamy three-cheese macaroni and cheese for the ultimate feel-good meal. "If I go more than a day or two without pasta, watch out, because I get nasty," jokes one cookinglight.com user. Other users admit hankering for high-quality cheese. Keep a close eye on the flour while it cooks so it doesn't burn.

- 1 teaspoon olive oil
- 1 cup finely chopped onion (about 1 medium)
- 2 tablespoons all-purpose flour
- 1 garlic clove, minced
- 1½ cups 1% low-fat milk
- 1 bay leaf
- ½ cup (2 ounces) crumbled Gorgonzola cheese
- ¾ cup (3 ounces) grated Parmigiano-Reggiano cheese, divided
- ¼ teaspoon salt
- 2 cups uncooked elbow macaroni (about 8 ounces)
- Cooking spray
- ⅔ cup (about 2½ ounces) shredded part-skim mozzarella cheese
- ⅔ cup panko (Japanese breadcrumbs)
- ⅛ teaspoon freshly ground black pepper

**1.** Heat oil in a medium saucepan over medium heat. Add onion to pan; cook 8 minutes or until tender, stirring occasionally. Add flour and garlic; cook 1 minute, stirring constantly. Stir in milk and bay leaf; bring to a boil. Cook 2 minutes or until thick, stirring constantly with a whisk. Add Gorgonzola, $^{1}/_{2}$ cup Parmigiano-Reggiano, and salt; stir until cheeses melt. Discard bay leaf.

**2.** Preheat oven to 375°.

**3.** Cook pasta in boiling water 5 minutes or until almost tender, omitting salt and fat; drain well. Add pasta to cheese mixture, stirring well. Place about $^{1}/_{2}$ cup pasta mixture into each of 6 (1-cup) ramekins coated with cooking spray. Sprinkle evenly with mozzarella. Top evenly with remaining pasta mixture. Combine

remaining $^{1}/_{4}$ cup Parmigiano-Reggiano and panko; sprinkle evenly over pasta mixture. Spray lightly with cooking spray; sprinkle with black pepper. Bake at 375° for 25 minutes or until heated. **YIELD:** 6 servings (serving size: about 1 ramekin).

CALORIES 321; FAT 9.9g (sat 5.6g, mono 2.3g, poly 0.9g); PROTEIN 17.4g; CARB 40.8g; FIBER 2.4g; CHOL 26mg; IRON 1.5mg; SODIUM 487mg; CALC 332mg

5

30
minutes
or
less

"Very tasty. Reminds me of my dad's fried catfish, but much less mess and fat! We enjoyed it with creamy coleslaw, which was the first coleslaw I've made in years. I chose to serve both with plain roasted green beans. Awesome nostalgia. Definitely to be repeated!

**from cookinglight.com**

# Cornmeal-Crusted Catfish

3 bacon slices
⅓ cup yellow cornmeal
2 teaspoons salt-free Cajun seasoning
½ teaspoon salt
4 (6-ounce) catfish fillets

**1.** Cook bacon in a large nonstick skillet over medium heat until crisp. Remove bacon from pan; reserve 2 teaspoons drippings in pan. Crumble bacon; reserve for another use.

**2.** Combine cornmeal, seasoning, and salt in a shallow dish. Dredge fillets in cornmeal mixture, shaking off excess.

**3.** Heat reserved drippings in pan over medium-high heat. Add fillets; cook 5 minutes on each side or until fish flakes easily when tested with a fork or until desired degree of doneness.

**YIELD:** 4 servings (serving size: 1 fillet).

CALORIES 277; FAT 13.7g (sat 3.4g, mono 6.9g, poly 2.3g); PROTEIN 27.5g; CARB 8.9g; FIBER 0.9g; CHOL 93mg; IRON 1.6mg; SODIUM 412mg; CALC 13mg

## what makes it light

- uses salt-free Cajun seasoning
- pan-seared, not deep-fried
- uses minimal amount of bacon drippings

"My fish was crisp on the outside and flaky in the middle. My husband is a fried catfish fiend, and he loved this. **Next time I will make more hush puppies, because we were fighting over them they were so good.**

**from cookinglight.com**

# Fried Catfish with Hush Puppies and Tartar Sauce

Tartar Sauce:
- ¼ cup organic canola mayonnaise (such as Spectrum)
- 1 tablespoon dill pickle relish
- 1 tablespoon chopped fresh flat-leaf parsley
- 1 teaspoon prepared horseradish
- ¾ teaspoon fresh lemon juice
- ⅛ teaspoon salt

Catfish:
- 8 cups peanut oil
- 6 (6-ounce) catfish fillets
- ½ teaspoon salt
- 9 ounces all-purpose flour (about 2 cups), divided

- 1¼ cups cornmeal
- 1 teaspoon freshly ground black pepper
- 2 cups buttermilk
- 2 large eggs, lightly beaten

Hush Puppies:
- 3.4 ounces all-purpose flour (about ¾ cup)
- ⅓ cup cornmeal
- ⅓ cup buttermilk
- 3 tablespoons grated onion
- 1 teaspoon baking powder
- ¼ teaspoon salt
- ¼ teaspoon ground red pepper
- 1 large egg, lightly beaten

**1.** To prepare tartar sauce, combine first 6 ingredients. Cover and chill.

**2.** To prepare catfish, clip a candy/fry thermometer to a Dutch oven; add oil to pan. Heat oil to 385°.

**3.** Sprinkle fillets evenly with ¹/₂ teaspoon salt. Place 4.5 ounces (1 cup) flour in a shallow dish. Combine remaining 4.5 ounces (1 cup) flour, cornmeal, and black pepper in a shallow dish. Combine 2 cups buttermilk and 2 eggs in a shallow dish. Dredge fillets in flour; dip in buttermilk mixture. Dredge in cornmeal mixture; shake off excess breading. Place 2 fillets in hot oil; cook 5 minutes or until done, turning occasionally. Make sure oil temperature does not drop below 375°. Remove fillets from pan using a slotted spoon; drain on paper towels. Return oil temperature to 385°. Repeat procedure twice with remaining fillets.

**4.** To prepare hush puppies, weigh or lightly spoon 3.4 ounces (³/₄ cup) flour into a dry measuring cups; level with a knife. Combine 3.4 ounces flour and remaining ingredients. Drop batter 1 tablespoonful at a time into pan; fry at 375° for 5 minutes or until browned, turning frequently. Remove hush puppies from pan using a slotted spoon; drain on paper towels. **YIELD**: 6 servings (serving size: 1 fillet, 2 hush puppies, and 4 teaspoons tartar sauce).

CALORIES 507; FAT 23.8g (sat 4.1g, mono 8.4g, poly 9.4g); PROTEIN 29.4g; CARB 43g; FIBER 2.6g; CHOL 153mg; IRON 3.6mg; SODIUM 846mg; CALC 171mg

"I grew up eating tuna noodle casserole and had to beg my husband to try it when I made this recipe. He was hooked after one bite. **I stuck to the recipe, and it came out delicious.** Overall, a keeper for a weeknight dinner."

**from cookinglight.com**

# Tuna Noodle Casserole

8 ounces uncooked wide egg noodles
2 tablespoons olive oil
½ cup chopped yellow onion
⅓ cup chopped carrot
2 tablespoons all-purpose flour
2¾ cups fat-free milk
½ cup (4 ounces) ⅓-less-fat cream cheese, softened
2 tablespoons Dijon mustard

½ teaspoon salt
½ teaspoon freshly ground black pepper
1 cup frozen peas, thawed
½ cup (2 ounces) grated Parmigiano-Reggiano cheese, divided
2 (5-ounce) cans albacore tuna in water, drained and flaked
Cooking spray

**1.** Preheat broiler.
**2.** Cook noodles according to package directions, omitting salt and fat. Drain. Heat a large skillet over medium heat. Add oil to pan; swirl to coat. Add onion and carrot; cook 6 minutes or until carrot is almost tender, stirring occasionally. Sprinkle with flour; cook 1 minute, stirring constantly. Gradually stir in milk; cook 5 minutes, stirring constantly with a whisk until slightly thick. Stir in cream cheese, mustard, salt, and pepper; cook 2 minutes, stirring constantly.
**3.** Remove pan from heat. Stir in noodles, peas, ¼ cup Parmigiano-Reggiano cheese, and tuna. Spoon mixture into a shallow broiler-safe 2-quart baking dish coated with cooking spray; top with remaining ¼ cup Parmigiano-Reggiano cheese. Broil 3 minutes or until golden and bubbly. Let stand 5 minutes before serving. **YIELD:** 6 servings (serving size: $1^1/3$ cups).

CALORIES 422; FAT 16.5g (sat 7.1g, mono 6.3g, poly 1.8g); PROTEIN 27.4g; CARB 40.6g; FIBER 3g; CHOL 88mg; IRON 2.4mg; SODIUM 756mg; CALC 293mg

## what makes it light

- uses fat-free milk
- uses ⅓-less-fat cream cheese
- uses only a small amount of Parmigiano-Reggiano cheese, which is a more flavorful option than regular Parmesan or cheddar cheese that's used in traditional recipes

"I have made this several times—as little appetizers and as a full entrée. **Everyone—I mean everyone—I make this for says they're the best crab cakes they have ever eaten.** If you want to win over the crowd, this recipe is a slam dunk."

**from cookinglight.com**

# Louisiana Crab Cakes with Creole Tartar Sauce

Tartar Sauce:
- ½ cup reduced-fat mayonnaise
- 3 tablespoons sweet pickle relish
- 2 tablespoons capers, drained and rinsed
- 1 teaspoon Creole mustard
- ¼ teaspoon salt-free Cajun-Creole seasoning (such as The Spice Hunter)
- ¼ teaspoon hot pepper sauce (such as Tabasco)

Crab Cakes:
- 4 (1-ounce) slices white bread
- ¼ cup finely chopped onion
- ¼ cup finely chopped red bell pepper
- 1 tablespoon chopped fresh parsley
- 1 tablespoon fresh lemon juice
- 1 tablespoon hot pepper sauce (such as Tabasco)
- ¼ teaspoon freshly ground black pepper
- 1 pound lump crabmeat, shell pieces removed
- 1 large egg, lightly beaten
- 1 large egg white, lightly beaten
- 4 teaspoons vegetable oil, divided

Parsley sprigs (optional)
Lemon wedges (optional)

**1.** To prepare tartar sauce, combine first 6 ingredients, stirring with a whisk. Let stand 10 minutes.
**2.** To prepare crab cakes, place bread in a food processor; pulse 10 times or until coarse crumbs measure 2 cups. Combine 1 cup breadcrumbs, onion, and next 8 ingredients; mix well. Divide crab mixture into 8 equal portions. Form each portion into a ½-inch-thick patty. Place 1 cup breadcrumbs in a shallow dish. Dredge patties, one at a time, in breadcrumbs.
**3.** Heat 2 teaspoons oil in a large nonstick skillet over medium-high heat. Add 4 patties; cook 3 minutes on each side or until golden brown. Repeat procedure with remaining oil and patties. Serve with tartar sauce. Garnish with parsley sprigs and lemon wedges, if desired. **YIELD:** 4 servings (serving size: 2 crab cakes and 2 tablespoons tartar sauce).

CALORIES 331; FAT 11g (sat 1.8g, mono 2.6g, poly 5.3g); PROTEIN 28.2g; CARB 29.1g; FIBER 1.4g; CHOL 167mg; IRON 2.5mg; SODIUM 992mg; CALC 163mg

## what makes it light
- uses reduced-fat mayonnaise
- uses salt-free Cajun-Creole seasoning
- uses minimal amount of oil to sauté crab cakes

30
minutes
or
less

**One (8-ounce) container select oysters**, undrained, can be substituted for crawfish, if desired.

# Gulf of Mexico Gumbo

4.5 ounces all-purpose flour (about 1 cup)
1 teaspoon canola oil
2 cups chopped onion
1 cup chopped green bell pepper
½ cup chopped celery
4 garlic cloves, minced
1 cup sliced okra
1 cup chopped tomato
1½ cups water
1 teaspoon Cajun-Creole Seasoning
4 (8-ounce) bottles clam juice

2 bay leaves
½ pound skinned red snapper or other firm white fish fillet, cut into 1-inch pieces
¼ cup thinly sliced green onions
¾ pound crawfish, peeled
¼ pound medium shrimp, peeled and deveined
½ teaspoon hot sauce
4½ cups hot cooked long-grain rice

**1.** Place flour in a 9-inch cast-iron skillet; cook over medium heat 20 minutes or until browned, stirring constantly with a whisk. (If flour browns too fast, remove it from heat, and stir until it cools down.) Remove from heat; set aside.

**2.** Heat oil in a large Dutch oven over medium heat. Add onion, bell pepper, celery, and garlic; sauté 8 minutes or until vegetables are tender. Add okra and tomato; cover and cook 5 minutes, stirring occasionally. Add 1½ cups water, Cajun-Creole Seasoning, clam juice, and bay leaves, and bring to a boil. Gradually add browned flour, stirring with a whisk. Reduce heat; simmer, uncovered, 45 minutes, stirring occasionally.

**3.** Add snapper; cook 5 minutes. Add green onions, crawfish, and shrimp; cook 10 minutes or until seafood is done. Stir in hot sauce; discard bay leaves. Serve gumbo over rice. **YIELD**: 9 servings (serving size: 1 cup gumbo and ½ cup rice).

CALORIES 254; FAT 1.8g (sat 0.3g, mono 0.3g, poly 0.7g); PROTEIN 16.8g; CARB 41.8g; FIBER 2.4g; CHOL 59mg; IRON 3.1mg; SODIUM 447mg; CALC 73mg

## Cajun-Creole Seasoning

1 tablespoon salt
¾ teaspoon ground red pepper

½ teaspoon garlic powder
½ teaspoon black pepper

**1.** Combine all ingredients in a bowl; stir well. **YIELD:** about 1½ tablespoons.

CALORIES 0; FAT 0g (sat 0g, mono 0g, poly 0g); PROTEIN 0g; CARB 0g; FIBER 0g; CHOL 0mg; IRON 0mg; SODIUM 97mg; CALC 0mg

## what makes it light
- uses a minimal amount of oil compared to traditional recipes
- doesn't use oil to brown the flour like a traditional roux

# recipe makeover
## shrimp étouffée

**The Reader:** Katharine O'Hara McIntyre

**The Story:** Katharine began dating her Louisiana-native husband, Charles Aaron, while attending law school in New Orleans. He introduced her to "some wonderful foods," including shrimp étouffée, a spicy Cajun classic made with a rich, nutty roux. After much trial and error, Katharine perfected a recipe for the dish that easily adjusts to accommodate a dinner for two or a hungry crowd of 10. Unfortunately, the expansion of her culinary repertoire with such indulgent dishes, combined with the stresses of a recent move to Maryland and intense study for the bar exam, began to stretch the couple's waistlines, as well. They have since adopted more healthful cooking habits, but Katharine would like to treat Charles to his beloved Louisiana fare on a more regular basis.

**The Dilemma:** *Étouffée* is the French word for "smothered," and this dish swims in two sticks of butter and sodium-laden ingredients. With 32 grams total fat and 1,200 milligrams of sodium per serving, the original contains nearly half the recommended daily intakes of both.

**The Solution:** We trimmed the ¾ cup butter originally used in the roux to ¼ cup, shaving 134 calories, 15 grams of total fat, and 12 grams of saturated fat per serving. Since we used less butter, we also cut down on the flour so the roux achieved an appropriately thick, nutty consistency that contributes to a pleasing, silky étouffée. To further reduce fat, we sautéed what Louisianans call "the trinity of aromatics" (bell pepper, onion, and celery) in just one tablespoon of butter to stretch the rich flavor and add body to the finished dish. This change trimmed another five grams of fat (three grams of it saturated) and another 50 calories per portion.

**The Feedback:** Katharine is pleased with our improvements. In fact, except for the addition of the red bell pepper, the couple **"couldn't tell the difference between the regular and the lightened version,"** says Katharine. They're delighted to re-introduce this much-loved taste of home to their dinner table.

| | BEFORE | AFTER |
|---|---|---|
| Calories per serving | 623 | 395 |
| Fat | 32.5g | 12.2g |
| Percent of total calories | 47% | 28% |

# Shrimp Étouffée

4 cups fat-free, less-sodium chicken broth
1 teaspoon dried thyme
1 teaspoon dried basil
1 bay leaf
$^{1}/_{3}$ cup butter, divided
1/2 cup all-purpose flour (about $2^{1}/_{4}$ ounces)
Cooking spray
$1^{1}/_{2}$ cups chopped onion
$^{2}/_{3}$ cup diced celery
$^{1}/_{2}$ cup chopped red bell pepper
$^{1}/_{2}$ cup chopped green bell pepper
$^{3}/_{4}$ cup water

$^{1}/_{4}$ cup tomato paste
1 tablespoon salt-free Cajun seasoning
$1^{1}/_{2}$ teaspoons minced garlic
$^{1}/_{4}$ teaspoon salt
$^{1}/_{4}$ teaspoon black pepper
$^{1}/_{4}$ teaspoon ground red pepper
1 teaspoon Worcestershire sauce
$^{1}/_{2}$ cup chopped green onions
$^{1}/_{2}$ cup chopped fresh flat-leaf parsley, divided
1 pound medium shrimp, peeled and deveined (about 30 shrimp)
4 cups hot cooked long-grain rice

**1.** Combine first 4 ingredients in a small saucepan over medium heat; bring to a simmer. Cover and remove from heat.

**2.** Melt $^{1}/_{4}$ cup butter in a medium saucepan over medium heat. Lightly spoon flour into a dry measuring cup; level with a knife. Add flour to pan; cook 8 minutes or until very brown, stirring constantly with a whisk. Remove from heat. Add 1 cup broth mixture to pan; stir with a whisk until smooth. Add remaining 3 cups broth mixture, stirring with a whisk until smooth; set aside.

**3.** Melt remaining 1 tablespoon plus 1 teaspoon butter in a large Dutch oven coated with cooking spray over medium-high heat. Add $1^{1}/_{2}$ cups onion, celery, and bell peppers to pan; cook 10 minutes or until vegetables are tender and onion is golden brown, stirring occasionally. Stir in $^{3}/_{4}$ cup water, scraping pan to loosen browned bits. Add tomato paste, Cajun seasoning, garlic, salt, black pepper, and red pepper to onion mixture; cook 1 minute, stirring constantly. Add reserved broth-flour mixture and Worcestershire sauce to pan, stirring well to combine; bring to a simmer. Cook 10 minutes, stirring occasionally. Add green onions, $^{1}/_{4}$ cup parsley, and shrimp; cook 3 minutes or until shrimp are done. Discard bay leaf. Serve over rice. Sprinkle each serving with 2 teaspoons remaining parsley, if desired. **YIELD:** 6 servings (serving size: about $1^{1}/_{4}$ cups étouffée and $^{2}/_{3}$ cup rice).

CALORIES 395; FAT 12.2g (sat 6.9g, mono 3g, poly 1.1g); PROTEIN 22.6g; CARB 47.9g; FIBER 3.6g; CHOL 142mg; IRON 4.9mg; SODIUM 655mg; CALC 102mg

**Using both andouille sausage and juicy pink shrimp,** jambalaya is like a spicy surf-and-turf. To save time, buy frozen peeled shrimp and thaw in the refrigerator or under cold, running water.

# Jambalaya with Shrimp and Andouille Sausage

1 tablespoon olive oil
1 cup chopped onion
1 cup chopped red bell pepper
1 tablespoon minced garlic
6 ounces andouille sausage, sliced
1 cup uncooked long-grain white rice
1 teaspoon paprika
1 teaspoon freshly ground black pepper
1 teaspoon dried oregano
½ teaspoon onion powder
½ teaspoon dried thyme
¼ teaspoon garlic salt

1 bay leaf
2 cups fat-free, lower-sodium chicken broth
¾ cup water
1 tablespoon tomato paste
½ teaspoon hot pepper sauce
1 (14.5-ounce) can no-salt-added diced tomatoes, undrained
½ pound peeled and deveined medium shrimp
2 tablespoons chopped fresh parsley

**1.** Heat olive oil in a large Dutch oven over medium-high heat. Add chopped onion, chopped bell pepper, minced garlic, and sausage; sauté 5 minutes or until vegetables are tender.
**2.** Add rice and next 7 ingredients; cook 2 minutes. Add broth, water, tomato paste, hot pepper sauce, and diced tomatoes; bring to a boil. Cover, reduce heat, and simmer 20 minutes. Add shrimp; cook 5 minutes. Let stand 5 minutes. Discard bay leaf. Stir in parsley. **YIELD:** 4 servings (serving size: 1½ cups).

CALORIES 426; FAT 12.7g (sat 3.9g, mono 2.8g, poly 1g); PROTEIN 25g; CARB 52.7g; FIBER 4.9g; CHOL 117mg; IRON 5.1mg; SODIUM 763mg; CALC 99mg

**? what makes it light**
• uses a smaller amount of andouille sausage than traditional recipes

## 1

## Italian Meat Loaf with Fresh Basil and Provolone

In addition to providing the lift in cakes, egg whites act as a binder for dishes such as crab cakes, salmon patties, and meat loaf. Serve this dish with your favorite mashed potato recipe.

- 1 cup boiling water
- ½ cup sun-dried tomatoes, packed without oil
- ½ cup ketchup
- 1 cup seasoned breadcrumbs
- ¾ cup finely chopped onion
- ¾ cup chopped fresh basil
- ½ cup (2 ounces) shredded sharp provolone cheese
- 2 large egg whites
- 2 garlic cloves, minced
- 1 pound ground round
- Cooking spray
- ⅓ cup ketchup

**1.** Combine boiling water and tomatoes in a bowl; let stand 30 minutes or until soft. Drain tomatoes; finely chop.

**2.** Preheat oven to 350°.

**3.** Combine ½ cup ketchup, breadcrumbs, and next 6 ingredients in a large bowl. Add tomatoes to meat mixture. Shape meat mixture into a 9 x 5–inch loaf on a broiler pan coated with cooking spray. Spread ⅓ cup ketchup over meat loaf. Bake at 350° for 1 hour or until a thermometer registers 160°. Let stand 10 minutes before slicing. Cut into 12 slices. **YIELD:** 6 servings (serving size: 2 slices).

CALORIES 294; FAT 8.7g (sat 3.6g, mono 3.2g, poly 0.7g); PROTEIN 24.3g; CARB 30.8g; FIBER 2.5g; CHOL 53mg; IRON 3.9mg; SODIUM 893mg; CALC 149mg

## Classic Meat Loaf

Combining three types of ground meat lends more depth to the overall flavor of this meat loaf recipe. Serve with roasted carrots and onions.

- 1 (1½-ounce) slice white bread
- 2 tablespoons fat-free milk
- ½ cup ketchup, divided
- ⅔ pound ground beef, extra lean (raw)
- ½ pound lean ground veal
- 6 ounces lean ground pork
- ½ cup chopped onion
- ⅓ cup chopped fresh parsley
- 1 tablespoon Dijon mustard
- 1 teaspoon dried basil
- ¾ teaspoon salt
- ¼ teaspoon black pepper
- 2 large egg whites

Cooking spray

**1.** Preheat oven to 350°.

**2.** Place bread in a food processor; pulse 10 times or until coarse breadcrumbs measure 1½ cups.

**3.** Combine breadcrumbs and milk in a large bowl; let stand 5 minutes. Add 2 tablespoons ketchup and remaining ingredients except cooking spray.

**4.** Shape meat mixture into a 9 x 5–inch loaf on a broiler pan coated with cooking spray. Spread remaining 6 tablespoons ketchup over top of meat loaf. Bake at 350° for 1 hour or until a thermometer registers 160°. Let stand 10 minutes. Cut loaf into 12 slices. **YIELD:** 6 servings (serving size: 2 slices).

CALORIES 231; FAT 7.9g (sat 3.1g, mono 3.2g, poly 0.8g); PROTEIN 26.7g; CARB 13.2g; FIBER 0.9g; CHOL 79mg; IRON 2.3mg; SODIUM 764mg; CALC 49mg

## Barbecue Meat Loaf ▼

This easy meat loaf recipe gets its great flavor from barbecue sauce.

1½ pounds ground beef, extra lean (raw)
½ cup dry breadcrumbs
½ cup chopped onion
⅓ cup barbecue sauce, divided
1 tablespoon prepared mustard
1½ teaspoons chili powder
1 teaspoon garlic powder
½ teaspoon salt
½ teaspoon freshly ground black pepper
2 large egg whites
Cooking spray

**1.** Preheat oven to 350°.
**2.** Combine beef, breadcrumbs, onion, 1 tablespoon barbecue sauce, and remaining ingredients except cooking spray in a large bowl.
**3.** Shape meat mixture into a 9 x 5–inch loaf on a broiler pan coated with cooking spray. Spread remaining barbecue sauce over top of meat loaf. Bake at 350° for 1 hour or until a thermometer registers 160°. Let stand 10 minutes. Cut loaf into 12 slices. **YIELD:** 6 servings (serving size: 2 slices).

CALORIES 203; FAT 5.4g (sat 2.2g, mono 2.2g, poly 0.5g); PROTEIN 27.3g; CARB 10.5g; FIBER 1.1g; CHOL 61mg; IRON 3.2mg; SODIUM 517mg; CALC 26mg

## Mini Meat Loaves ▼

½ cup ketchup
1½ tablespoons Dijon mustard
1 pound ground sirloin
¾ cup finely chopped onion
¼ cup seasoned breadcrumbs
½ teaspoon salt
½ teaspoon dried oregano
⅛ teaspoon black pepper
1 large egg, lightly beaten
Cooking spray

**1.** Preheat oven to 400°.
**2.** Combine ketchup and mustard, stirring well with a whisk. Reserve $2^{1}/_{2}$ tablespoons ketchup mixture. Combine remaining ketchup mixture, beef, and next 6 ingredients in a large bowl, stirring to combine.
**3.** Divide beef mixture into 4 equal portions. Shape each portion into a 4 x $2^{1}/_{2}$–inch loaf; place loaves on a jelly-roll pan coated with cooking spray.
**4.** Spread about 2 teaspoons reserved ketchup mixture evenly over each loaf. Bake at 400° for 25 minutes or until done. **YIELD:** 4 servings (serving size: 1 mini loaf).

CALORIES 255; FAT 7.9g (sat 2.8g, mono 3.2g, poly 0.4g); PROTEIN 27.4g; CARB 15.7g; FIBER 0.9g; CHOL 120mg; IRON 2.7mg; SODIUM 944mg; CALC 31mg

3

4

## Diner Meat Loaf Muffins

This delicious mini meat loaf muffin recipe allows you to sit down to a meat loaf in a half hour. Serve with steamed green beans and roasted potato wedges for an at-home version of a blue-plate special.

    1 teaspoon olive oil
    1 cup finely chopped onion
    ½ cup finely chopped carrot
    1 teaspoon dried oregano
    2 garlic cloves, minced
    1 cup ketchup, divided
 1½ pounds ground beef, extra lean (raw)
    1 cup finely crushed fat-free saltine
      crackers (about 20)
    2 tablespoons prepared mustard
    1 teaspoon Worcestershire sauce
    ¼ teaspoon freshly ground black pepper
    2 large eggs
Cooking spray

**1.** Preheat oven to 350°.

**2.** Heat olive oil in a large nonstick skillet over medium-high heat. Add chopped onion, chopped carrot, dried oregano, and minced garlic; sauté 2 minutes. Cool.

**3.** Combine onion mixture, ½ cup ketchup, and remaining ingredients except cooking spray in a large bowl.

**4.** Spoon meat mixture into 12 muffin cups coated with cooking spray. Top each with 2 teaspoons ketchup. Bake at 350° for 25 minutes or until a thermometer registers 160°. Let stand 5 minutes. **YIELD**: 6 servings (serving size: 2 muffins).

CALORIES 276; FAT 8.6g (sat 3g, mono 4g, poly 0.8g); PROTEIN 28.7g; CARB 21.7g; FIBER 1.8g; CHOL 131mg; IRON 3.9mg; SODIUM 759mg; CALC 48mg

> If you like a classic beef stroganoff (and I do) this is perfect! **Whatever is 'missing' to make this light, I didn't miss it!**
>
> **from cookinglight.com**

# Beef Stroganoff

1 pound boneless sirloin steak, trimmed
Cooking spray
3 cups sliced cremini mushrooms
   (about 8 ounces)
½ cup chopped onion
1 tablespoon butter
2 tablespoons all-purpose flour
1 cup fat-free, lower-sodium beef broth
¼ cup dry sherry

½ teaspoon salt
⅛ teaspoon freshly ground black pepper
¾ cup reduced-fat sour cream
4 cups hot cooked egg noodles
   (8 ounces uncooked)
3 tablespoons minced fresh flat-leaf
   parsley
Parsley sprigs (optional)

**1.** Cut beef diagonally across grain into ¼-inch-wide strips; cut strips into 2-inch pieces.

**2.** Heat a large nonstick skillet over medium-high heat. Coat pan with cooking spray. Add beef to pan; sauté 2 minutes or until lightly browned. Remove beef from pan; place in a medium bowl, and keep warm. Add cremini mushrooms and onion to pan; sauté 4 minutes. Add cremini mushroom mixture to beef.

**3.** Melt butter in pan over medium heat. Add flour. Cook 1 minute, stirring with a whisk. Gradually add broth, stirring constantly. Cook 1 minute or until thickened and bubbly, stirring constantly.

**4.** Add beef mixture, sherry, salt, and pepper to pan; bring to a boil. Reduce heat, and simmer 4 minutes. Remove from heat; let stand 30 seconds. Stir in sour cream.

**5.** Combine noodles and minced parsley. Serve beef mixture over noodles. Garnish with parsley sprigs, if desired. **YIELD:** 6 servings (serving size: about ⅔ cup beef mixture and ⅔ cup noodles).

CALORIES 352; FAT 11.7g (sat 5.3g, mono 3.9g, poly 1g); PROTEIN 24.2g; CARB 36g; FIBER 1.8g; CHOL 87mg; IRON 3.1mg; SODIUM 355mg; CALC 40mg

## what makes it light

- uses a minimal amount of butter
- uses fat-free, lower-sodium beef broth
- uses reduced-fat sour cream
- uses a smaller amount of meat than normal for six servings
- uses earthy mushrooms to replace a bulk of the meat

## what makes it light

- uses fat-free milk
- uses egg whites
- uses less oil than traditional recipes

"This has become my go-to recipe. **It satisfies my husband's craving for steak and gravy, and it satisfies my need for lighter fare.** By using a no-salt-added beef broth you can lower the sodium even more. It absolutely has the taste of down-home comfort food, but it only takes minutes to make. I usually have my husband do the potatoes, and I do the steaks. Add a vegetable, and you are done! It's great for company because it's so quick and easy."

**from cookinglight.com**

# Country-Fried Steak with Mushroom Gravy

3 tablespoons fat-free milk
2 large egg whites
1.5 ounces all-purpose flour (about ⅓ cup)
½ teaspoon onion powder
½ teaspoon salt
¼ teaspoon garlic powder
¼ teaspoon black pepper
4 (4-ounce) sirloin cubed steaks

2 teaspoons vegetable oil
2⅔ cups frozen mashed potatoes (such as Ore Ida)
1⅓ cups fat-free milk
2 cups mushrooms, quartered
2½ tablespoons all-purpose flour
¼ teaspoon salt
1 (14.5-ounce) can fat-free, lower-sodium beef broth (such as Swanson)

**1.** Combine 3 tablespoons milk and egg whites in a shallow dish, stirring with a whisk. Combine 1.5 ounces flour and next 4 ingredients in a shallow dish. Working with one steak at a time, dip in egg mixture; dredge in flour mixture. Repeat procedure with remaining steaks, egg mixture, and flour mixture.

**2.** Heat oil in a large nonstick skillet over medium-high heat. Add steaks; cook 3 minutes on each side or until browned. Remove steaks from pan; keep warm.

**3.** While steaks cook, prepare mashed potatoes according to package directions, using $1^1/_3$ cups milk. Keep warm.

**4.** Add mushrooms to pan; sauté 3 minutes. Combine $2^1/_2$ tablespoons flour, $^1/_4$ teaspoon salt, and broth, stirring with a whisk. Add broth mixture to pan. Bring to a boil; cook 1 minute, stirring constantly. Spoon over steaks. Serve with mashed potatoes. **YIELD**: 4 servings (serving size: 1 steak, about $^1/_3$ cup gravy, and about 1 cup mashed potatoes).

CALORIES 436; FAT 14.7g (sat 5.1g, mono 4.8g, poly 2.2g); PROTEIN 38.2g; CARB 34.7g; FIBER 1.9g; CHOL 189mg; IRON 4.6mg; SODIUM 759mg; CALC 147mg

*I am a stew lover, and this one ranks with the best,* even the venerable Julia! I made it for guests, and they all raved about it. The raisins combined with the Guinness provide a subtle hint of sweetness.

**from cookinglight.com**

# Beef and Guinness Stew

2 tablespoons canola oil, divided
1 tablespoon butter, divided
1.1 ounces all-purpose flour (about ¼ cup)
2 pounds boneless chuck roast, trimmed and cut into 1-inch cubes
1 teaspoon salt, divided
5 cups chopped onion (about 3 onions)
1 tablespoon tomato paste
4 cups fat-free, lower-sodium beef broth
1 (11.2-ounce) bottle Guinness Draught

1 tablespoon raisins
1 teaspoon caraway seeds
½ teaspoon black pepper
1½ cups (½-inch-thick) diagonal slices carrot (about 8 ounces)
1½ cups (½-inch-thick) diagonal slices parsnip (about 8 ounces)
1 cup (½-inch) cubed peeled turnip (about 8 ounces)
2 tablespoons finely chopped fresh flat-leaf parsley

**1.** Heat 1 tablespoon oil in a Dutch oven over medium-high heat. Add $1^1/_2$ teaspoons butter to pan. Place flour in a shallow dish. Sprinkle beef with $^1/_2$ teaspoon salt; dredge beef in flour. Add half of beef to pan; cook 5 minutes, turning to brown on all sides. Remove beef from pan with a slotted spoon. Repeat procedure with remaining 1 tablespoon oil, $1^1/_2$ teaspoons butter, and beef.
**2.** Add onion to pan; cook 5 minutes or until tender, stirring occasionally. Stir in tomato paste; cook 1 minute, stirring frequently. Stir in broth and beer, scraping pan to loosen browned bits. Return meat to pan. Stir in remaining $^1/_2$ teaspoon salt, raisins, caraway seeds, and pepper; bring to a boil. Cover, reduce heat, and simmer 1 hour, stirring occasionally. Uncover and bring to a boil. Cook 50 minutes, stirring occasionally. Add carrot, parsnip, and turnip. Cover, reduce heat to low, and simmer 30 minutes, stirring occasionally. Uncover and bring to a boil; cook 10 minutes or until vegetables are tender. Sprinkle with parsley. **YIELD:** 8 servings (serving size: about 1 cup).

CALORIES 365; FAT 19.4g (sat 6.8g, mono 8.6g, poly 1.7g); PROTEIN 25.3g; CARB 18.8g; FIBER 3.6g; CHOL 62mg; IRON 2.6mg; SODIUM 454mg; CALC 52mg

## what makes it light

- uses minimal amount of canola oil and butter to brown two pounds of meat
- lower-sodium broth keeps the sodium lower than most stews

"Are you kidding me? This is unbelievably good! I followed the recipe exactly and was just blown away by the results. The meat was so tender you could cut it with a fork, and the flavor was awesome. Adding cloves took it to a whole other level. I served this with Yorkshire pudding and almost licked my plate. By far, the best **Cooking Light** recipe I've made to date.

**from cookinglight.com**

# Beef Daube Provençal

2 teaspoons olive oil
12 garlic cloves, crushed
1 (2-pound) boneless chuck roast, trimmed and cut into 2-inch cubes
1½ teaspoons salt, divided
½ teaspoon freshly ground black pepper, divided
1 cup red wine
2 cups chopped carrot
1½ cups chopped onion

½ cup lower-sodium beef broth
1 tablespoon tomato paste
1 teaspoon chopped fresh rosemary
1 teaspoon chopped fresh thyme
Dash of ground cloves
1 (14.5-ounce) can diced tomatoes
1 bay leaf
3 cups cooked medium egg noodles (about 4 cups uncooked noodles)

**1.** Preheat oven to 300°.

**2.** Heat oil in a small Dutch oven over low heat. Add garlic; cook 5 minutes or until garlic is fragrant, stirring occasionally. Remove garlic with a slotted spoon, and set aside. Increase heat to medium-high. Add beef to pan; sprinkle with ½ teaspoon salt and ¼ teaspoon pepper. Cook 5 minutes, browning on all sides. Remove beef from pan. Add wine to pan; bring to a boil, scraping pan to loosen browned bits. Add garlic, beef, 1 teaspoon salt, ¼ teaspoon pepper, carrot, and next 8 ingredients, and bring to a boil.

**3.** Cover and bake at 300° for 2½ hours or until beef is tender. Discard bay leaf. Serve over noodles.

**YIELD**: 6 servings (serving size: about ¾ cup stew and ½ cup noodles).

**Note:** To make in a slow cooker, prepare through Step 2. Place beef mixture in an electric slow cooker. Cover and cook on HIGH 5 hours.

CALORIES 367; FAT 12.8g (sat 4.3g, mono 5.8g, poly 0.9g); PROTEIN 29.1g; CARB 33.4g; FIBER 3.9g; CHOL 105mg; IRON 4.3mg; SODIUM 776mg; CALC 76mg

## what makes it light
• uses minimal amount of oil to sauté meat

**what makes it light**

• serving size is smaller than traditional recipes
• uses lower-sodium soy sauce
• no added salt keeps total sodium lower than normal

"This recipe was OUTSTANDING! I have tried making roasts in the slow cooker time and time again and have always failed. Often the meat is so overcooked it is inedible. **This roast is delicious and the meat is super juicy.** The vegetables at the bottom make for a wonderful side. This is a VERY HIGH recommendation and has already become a favorite."

**from cookinglight.com**

# Company Pot Roast

1 (2-pound) boneless chuck roast, trimmed and cut in half
1/4 cup lower-sodium soy sauce
2 garlic cloves, minced
1 cup beef broth
1 (.35-ounce) package dried morel mushrooms
1 tablespoon cracked black pepper
3 tablespoons sun-dried tomato paste
2 medium onions (about 3/4 pound), quartered

1 (16-ounce) package carrots, cut into 2-inch pieces
16 small red potatoes (about 2 pounds), halved
1 tablespoon vegetable oil
1 1/2 tablespoons all-purpose flour
3 tablespoons water
Chopped fresh parsley (optional)

**1.** Combine roast, soy sauce, and garlic in a large zip-top plastic bag; seal bag, and marinate in refrigerator at least 8 hours, turning bag occasionally.

**2.** Bring broth to a boil in a small saucepan; add mushrooms. Remove from heat; cover and let stand 20 minutes. Drain mushrooms through a cheesecloth-lined colander over a bowl, reserving broth mixture.

**3.** Remove roast from bag, reserving marinade. Sprinkle roast with pepper, gently pressing pepper into roast. Combine reserved marinade, mushroom broth mixture, and tomato paste; stir well, and set aside.

**4.** Place mushrooms, onion, carrot, and potato in a 6-quart electric slow cooker; toss gently.

**5.** Heat oil in a large skillet over medium-high heat. Add roast, browning well on all sides. Place roast over vegetables in slow cooker. Pour tomato paste mixture into pan, scraping to loosen browned bits. Pour tomato paste mixture over roast and vegetables. Cover with lid; cook on high-heat setting 1 hour. Reduce to low-heat setting, and cook 8 hours or until roast is tender. Place roast and vegetables on a serving platter; keep warm. Reserve liquid in slow cooker; increase to high-heat setting.

**6.** Place flour in bowl. Gradually add water, stirring with a whisk until well blended. Add flour mixture to liquid in slow cooker. Cook, uncovered, 15 minutes or until slightly thick, stirring frequently. Serve gravy with roast and vegetables. Garnish with parsley, if desired. **YIELD**: 8 servings (serving size: 3 ounces roast, 1 onion wedge, about 3 carrot pieces, 4 potato halves, and about 1/4 cup gravy).

CALORIES 384; FAT 12.5g (sat 4.2g, mono 0g, poly 0g); PROTEIN 27.4g; CARB 40g; FIBER 5.6g; CHOL 76mg; IRON 5mg; SODIUM 488mg; CALC 49mg

**A rich sauce with plenty of meat** feels like the old-world Italian dish but fits in the new-world nutrition sense. A little liquid remaining in the sauce helps coat the pasta.

# Spaghetti with Pork Bolognese

1½ tablespoons extra-virgin olive oil
2 cups finely chopped onion
½ cup finely chopped carrot (about 1 medium)
½ cup finely chopped celery (about 1 stalk)
1½ teaspoons chopped garlic
1 teaspoon kosher salt, divided
1 bay leaf
1 pound ground pork tenderloin
¾ pound ground pork
2 ounces pancetta, finely diced
¼ cup tomato paste
2 cups chopped plum tomato (about ½ pound)
1½ cups organic vegetable broth (such as Swanson)
1 cup dry white wine
1 cup 1% low-fat milk
⅛ teaspoon grated whole nutmeg
1 (2-ounce) piece Parmigiano-Reggiano rind
1 (3-inch) cinnamon stick
½ teaspoon freshly ground black pepper
8 cups hot cooked spaghetti (about 16 ounces uncooked)
½ cup (2 ounces) grated fresh Parmigiano-Reggiano
½ cup chopped fresh parsley

**1.** Heat olive oil in a large Dutch oven over medium heat. Add onion, carrot, celery, garlic, ¼ teaspoon salt, and bay leaf to pan; cook 8 minutes or until vegetables are tender, stirring occasionally. Increase heat to medium-high. Add ground pork tenderloin, ground pork, pancetta, and ¼ teaspoon salt; sauté 8 minutes or until pork loses its pink color. Stir in tomato paste; cook 1 minute. Add tomato and next 5 ingredients; bring to a boil. Reduce heat, and simmer 45 minutes. Add cinnamon; simmer 30 minutes or until most of liquid evaporates. Discard bay leaf, rind, and cinnamon stick; stir in remaining ½ teaspoon salt and pepper. Arrange 1 cup noodles on each of 8 plates; top each with about ¾ cup sauce. Sprinkle each serving with 1 tablespoon grated cheese and 1 tablespoon parsley. **YIELD:** 8 servings.

CALORIES 512; FAT 18g (sat 6.8g, mono 6.8g, poly 1.6g); PROTEIN 34.5g; CARB 51.4g; FIBER 4.5g; CHOL 79mg; IRON 4mg; SODIUM 770mg; CALC 205mg

## what makes it light

- uses low-fat milk
- uses more lean pork tenderloin than ground pork, which cuts down on fat
- uses a small amount of pancetta, which adds big flavor without a lot of fat

30
minutes
or
less

**Excellent!** These were literally the best pork chops I've ever made. I will never buy barbecue sauce again.

from cookinglight.com

# Barbecued Pork Chops

Sauce:

- ¼ cup packed brown sugar
- ¼ cup ketchup
- 1 tablespoon Worcestershire sauce
- 1 tablespoon lower-sodium soy sauce

Remaining Ingredients:

- 6 (6-ounce) bone-in center-cut pork chops (about ½ inch thick)
- 1 teaspoon dried thyme
- 1 teaspoon garlic salt
- ¼ teaspoon ground red pepper

Cooking spray

**1.** Preheat grill or broiler.

**2.** To prepare sauce, combine first 4 ingredients in a small bowl. Place $^1/_4$ cup sauce in a small bowl, and set aside.

**3.** Trim fat from pork. Combine thyme, garlic salt, and pepper; sprinkle over pork. Place pork on grill rack or broiler pan coated with cooking spray; cook 6 minutes on each side, basting with remaining sauce. Serve pork chops with reserved $^1/_4$ cup sauce. **YIELD**: 6 servings (serving size: 1 pork chop and $1^1/_2$ tablespoons sauce).

CALORIES 244; FAT 11.3g (sat 3.9g, mono 5g, poly 1.4g); PROTEIN 24.6g; CARB 9.9g; FIBER 0.2g; CHOL 77mg; IRON 1.5mg; SODIUM 649mg; CALC 22mg

## what makes it light

- uses a homemade sauce, which is lower in calories and sodium than a commerical sauce

"This recipe will definitely be on repeat! Sometimes eating something like lasagna leaves you feeling heavy, but this is a great, lightened version that is just as flavorful.

from cookinglight.com

# Tomato-Basil Lasagna with Prosciutto

5 garlic cloves
1 (16-ounce) carton 1% low-fat cottage cheese
½ cup (4 ounces) block-style fat-free cream cheese
¼ cup (1 ounce) grated fresh Romano cheese, divided
2½ teaspoons dried basil
½ teaspoon crushed red pepper

1 large egg
1 (26-ounce) bottle fat-free tomato-basil pasta sauce (such as Muir Glen)
Cooking spray
12 cooked lasagna noodles
1 cup (4 ounces) chopped prosciutto or ham
1 cup (4 ounces) shredded part-skim mozzarella cheese

**1.** Preheat oven to 375°.

**2.** Drop garlic through food chute with food processor on, and process until minced. Add cottage cheese; process 2 minutes or until smooth. Add cream cheese, 2 tablespoons Romano, basil, pepper, and egg; process until well blended.

**3.** Spread $^1/_2$ cup pasta sauce in bottom of a 13 x 9–inch baking dish coated with cooking spray. Arrange 3 noodles over pasta sauce; top with 1 cup cheese mixture, $^1/_3$ cup prosciutto, and $^3/_4$ cup pasta sauce. Repeat layers two times, ending with noodles. Spread remaining pasta sauce over noodles. Sprinkle with 2 tablespoons Romano and mozzarella.

**4.** Cover and bake at 375° for 45 minutes or until sauce is bubbly. Uncover and bake an additional 15 minutes. Let lasagna stand 5 minutes. **YIELD:** 9 servings.

CALORIES 272; FAT 5.6g (sat 2.8g, mono 1.8g, poly 0.6g); PROTEIN 20.8g; CARB 33g; FIBER 2.1g; CHOL 47mg; IRON 2.3mg; SODIUM 775mg; CALC 213mg

## what makes it light

- uses fat-free tomato-basil pasta sauce
- uses part-skim mozzarella
- uses low-fat cottage cheese and fat-free cream cheese to replace full-fat ricotta used in traditional recipes

"This was a deliciously salty-and-sweet dish that was a huge hit at my house! My husband was skeptical and wanted to stick with traditional meat and spaghetti for dinner but was impressed with the end result. **The pasta was creamy and rich like a homemade mac 'n' cheese,** and the bacon added an incredible flavor to the otherwise overly indulgent dish.

**from cookinglight.com**

# Roasted Butternut Squash and Bacon Pasta

¾ teaspoon salt, divided
½ teaspoon dried rosemary
¼ teaspoon freshly ground black pepper
3 cups (1-inch) cubed peeled butternut squash
Cooking spray
6 sweet hickory-smoked bacon slices (raw)
1 cup thinly sliced shallots

8 ounces uncooked mini penne (tube-shaped pasta)
1.1 ounces all-purpose flour (about ¼ cup)
2 cups 2% reduced-fat milk
¾ cup (3 ounces) shredded sharp provolone cheese
⅓ cup (1½ ounces) grated fresh Parmesan cheese

**1.** Preheat oven to 425°.

**2.** Combine ¼ teaspoon salt, rosemary, and pepper. Place squash on a foil-lined baking sheet coated with cooking spray; sprinkle with salt mixture. Bake at 425° for 45 minutes or until tender and lightly browned. Increase oven temperature to 450°.

**3.** Cook bacon in a large nonstick skillet over medium heat until crisp. Remove bacon from pan, reserving 1½ teaspoons drippings in pan; crumble bacon. Increase heat to medium-high. Add shallots to pan; sauté 8 minutes or until tender. Combine squash mixture, bacon, and shallots; set aside.

**4.** Cook pasta according to package directions, omitting salt and fat. Drain well.

**5.** Combine flour and ½ teaspoon salt in a Dutch oven over medium-high heat. Gradually add milk, stirring constantly with a whisk; bring to a boil. Cook 1 minute or until slightly thick, stirring constantly. Remove from heat. Add provolone, stirring until cheese melts. Add pasta to cheese mixture, tossing well to combine. Spoon pasta mixture into an 11 x 7–inch baking dish lightly coated with cooking spray; top with squash mixture. Sprinkle evenly with Parmesan cheese. Bake at 450° for 10 minutes or until cheese melts and begins to brown. **YIELD**: 5 servings.

CALORIES 469; FAT 14.4g (sat 7.3g, mono 4.4g, poly 0.9g); PROTEIN 22.1g; CARB 66.6g; FIBER 6.8g; CHOL 40mg; IRON 3.5mg; SODIUM 849mg; CALC 443mg

## what makes it light

- uses reduced-fat milk
- uses cooking spray instead of oil to roast squash
- uses a minimal amount of reserved bacon drippings to sauté shallots
- uses sharp provolone for big flavor impact

**The luxurious, velvety texture** of a good pasta carbonara is ephemeral at best, so you must enjoy it right away. Tempering the egg with hot pasta water keeps the sauce creamy by preventing it from curdling. For a smoky taste, use bacon in place of pancetta.

# Linguine Carbonara

4 ounces uncooked linguine
½ cup 1% low-fat milk
3 tablespoons grated fresh Parmesan cheese
1 tablespoon chopped fresh parsley
⅛ teaspoon salt
⅛ teaspoon freshly ground black pepper

Cooking spray
⅓ cup chopped pancetta (about 1½ ounces)
¼ cup finely chopped onion
1 garlic clove, minced
1 large egg

**1.** Cook pasta according to package directions, omitting salt and fat. Drain pasta in a colander over a bowl, reserving $^{1}/_{4}$ cup cooking liquid.

**2.** Combine milk and next 4 ingredients in a small bowl; set milk mixture aside.

**3.** Heat a medium nonstick skillet over medium-high heat. Coat pan with cooking spray. Add pancetta to pan; sauté 3 minutes or until lightly browned. Add onion and garlic to pan; sauté 3 minutes or until onion is lightly browned. Reduce heat to medium-low. Add milk mixture and pasta to pan; toss gently to coat.

**4.** Place egg in a small bowl; stir with a whisk. Gradually add $^{1}/_{4}$ cup reserved hot cooking liquid, stirring constantly with a whisk. Gradually add egg mixture to pan, stirring constantly; cook 4 minutes or until sauce is thick and creamy. **YIELD:** 2 servings (serving size: about $1^{1}/_{4}$ cups).

CALORIES 387; FAT 13g (sat 5.8g, mono 4.5g, poly 1.3g); PROTEIN 19.2g; CARB 48.2g; FIBER 2.3g; CHOL 130mg; IRON 2.6mg; SODIUM 682mg; CALC 192mg

## what makes it light
- uses low-fat milk instead of the traditional heavy cream
- uses reserved pasta water to develop creaminess instead of depending on cream, cheese, and more eggs

## Individual Chicken Potpies

Because the piecrust topping cooks on a baking sheet and is then placed over the filling, you don't need to use ovenproof bowls for the pies. Use a bowl or ramekin as a guide for cutting the dough. You can use 2 cups chopped leftover chicken in place of chicken breast tenders.

½ (14.1-ounce) package refrigerated pie dough (such as Pillsbury)
Cooking spray
⅛ teaspoon salt
2 tablespoons all-purpose flour
1 teaspoon dried rubbed sage
¼ teaspoon salt
¼ teaspoon black pepper
8 ounces chicken breast tenders, cut into bite-sized pieces
1¼ cups water
1½ cups frozen mixed vegetables
1 cup mushrooms, quartered
1 (10¾-ounce) can condensed reduced-fat, reduced-sodium cream of chicken soup

**1.** Preheat oven to 425°.

**2.** Cut 3 (4-inch) circles out of dough; discard remaining dough. Place dough circles on a baking sheet coated with cooking spray. Lightly coat dough with cooking spray; sprinkle evenly with ⅛ teaspoon salt. Pierce top of dough with a fork. Bake dough at 425° for 8 minutes or until golden.

**3.** Combine flour, sage, ¼ teaspoon salt, and pepper in a zip-top plastic bag; add chicken. Seal bag, and toss to coat. Heat a large non-stick skillet over medium-high heat. Coat pan with cooking spray. Add chicken mixture; cook 5 minutes, browning on all sides. Stir in water, scraping pan to loosen browned bits. Stir in vegetables, mushrooms, and soup; bring to a boil. Reduce heat, and cook 10 minutes. Spoon 1 cup chicken mixture into each of 3 (1-cup) ramekins or bowls; top each serving with 1 piecrust. **YIELD:** 3 servings (serving size: 1 pie).

CALORIES 452; FAT 18g (sat 7.6g, mono 7.5g, poly 2.2g); PROTEIN 24g; CARB 49g; FIBER 2.8g; CHOL 54mg; IRON 1.3mg; SODIUM 1,027mg; CALC 30mg

1

2

## Barbecued-Chicken Potpie

  1  teaspoon butter
Cooking spray
  2  cups chopped onion
  ½  cup chopped green bell pepper
  ⅓  cup diced seeded poblano chile or
     1 (4.5-ounce) can chopped green
     chiles, drained
  1  small garlic clove, minced
1½  teaspoons cumin seeds
  1  teaspoon ground coriander
  ¼  cup cider vinegar
  4  cups shredded cooked chicken breast
     (about 1½ pounds)
  2  tablespoons brown sugar
  1  ounce unsweetened chocolate, grated
  1  (12-ounce) bottle chili sauce
1½  cups lower-sodium chicken broth
     (such as Swanson Natural Goodness)
  1  (8-ounce) can refrigerated breadsticks
  ½  cup cornmeal

**1.** Preheat oven to 375°.

**2.** Melt butter in a large nonstick skillet coated with cooking spray over medium-high heat. Add onion, peppers, and garlic, and sauté 5 minutes. Stir in cumin and coriander, and cook 2 minutes. Stir in vinegar, scraping skillet to loosen browned bits. Add chicken and next 4 ingredients, and cook 15 minutes or until thick, stirring occasionally. Spoon chicken mixture into 11 x 7–inch baking dish coated with cooking spray.

**3.** Unroll breadstick dough, separating into strips; press cornmeal into strips. Place strips in a lattice fashion over chicken mixture. Bake at 375° for 25 minutes or until golden brown; let stand 15 minutes before serving. **YIELD:** 8 servings.

CALORIES 371; FAT 7.3g (sat 3.2g, mono 2.2g, poly 1.1g); PROTEIN 31.3g; CARB 44.3g; FIBER 2.2g; CHOL 74mg; IRON 3.1mg; SODIUM 862mg; CALC 37mg

3

## Biscuit-Topped Chicken Potpie

Serve a homemade potpie for dinner tonight. It tastes just like Mom's, but cooks in a fraction of the time.

- 1 tablespoon butter
- 2 cups chopped leek
- ¼ cup chopped shallot
- ¾ teaspoon chopped fresh or
  ¼ teaspoon dried thyme
- 1½ cups refrigerated diced potatoes with onions (such as Simply Potatoes)
- ⅓ cup dry white wine
- 1 teaspoon Dijon mustard
- 1 (14-ounce) can fat-free, lower-sodium chicken broth
- 2 cups chopped roasted chicken breast
- 1½ cups frozen mixed vegetables
- ¼ teaspoon salt
- ¼ teaspoon freshly ground black pepper
- 1½ tablespoons cornstarch
- 2 tablespoons water
- ⅔ cup half-and-half

Cooking spray

- 1¼ cups low-fat baking mix (such as Bisquick Heart Smart)
- ½ cup fat-free milk
- 1 large egg white, lightly beaten

**1.** Preheat oven to 425°.

**2.** Melt butter in a large nonstick skillet over medium-high heat. Add leek, shallot, and thyme; sauté 2 minutes. Add potatoes; sauté 2 minutes. Add wine; cook 1 minute or until liquid evaporates. Stir in mustard and broth; bring to a boil. Cook 4 minutes, stirring occasionally. Stir in chicken, mixed vegetables, salt, and pepper; cook 1 minute. Combine cornstarch and 2 tablespoons water in a small bowl, stirring with a whisk. Add cornstarch mixture and half-and-half to pan. Reduce heat, and simmer 2 minutes, stirring constantly. Spoon mixture into a 13 x 9–inch baking dish coated with cooking spray.

**3.** Lightly spoon baking mix into dry measuring cups; level with a knife. Combine baking mix, milk, and egg in a medium bowl, stirring with a whisk. Spoon batter over chicken mixture; spread evenly to cover. Bake at 425° for 20 minutes or until topping is golden and filling is bubbly. Let stand 10 minutes. **YIELD:** 6 servings (serving size: 1½ cups).

CALORIES 348; FAT 9.2g (sat 4.1g, mono 2.2g, poly 0.9g); PROTEIN 23.5g; CARB 43.3g; FIBER 4.4g; CHOL 55mg; IRON 3.1mg; SODIUM 634mg; CALC 131mg

## Speedy Chicken Potpie

Though you have to hustle, you really can get this chicken potpie on the table in 20 minutes. Start browning the chicken and bringing the broth to a boil right away, and get the pie dough in the oven as soon as it reaches 425°. Strips of pastry are a quick stand-in for the traditional crust on top.

Cooking spray
1 pound skinless, boneless chicken breast, cut into ½-inch pieces
¼ teaspoon salt
3 cups fat-free, lower-sodium chicken broth, divided
1 bay leaf
2 cups refrigerated diced potatoes with onion (such as Simply Potatoes)
⅔ cup frozen green peas and diced carrot blend
3 tablespoons all-purpose flour
½ teaspoon chopped fresh thyme
¼ teaspoon black pepper
¼ teaspoon dried rubbed sage
¼ (15-ounce) package refrigerated pie dough

**1.** Preheat oven to 425°.
**2.** Heat a large nonstick skillet over medium-high heat. Coat pan with cooking spray. Add chicken to pan; sprinkle with salt. Sauté 5 minutes or until browned and done.
**3.** While chicken cooks, bring 2¹/₂ cups broth and bay leaf to a boil in a large saucepan. Add potatoes; cover and cook over medium-high heat 8 minutes. Stir in peas and carrots; cover and cook 2 minutes. Stir in chicken. Combine remaining ¹/₂ cup broth and flour; stir into potato mixture. Reduce heat to medium; cook 2 minutes or until bubbly and thick. Remove bay leaf. Stir in thyme, pepper, and sage.
**4.** While potato mixture cooks, cut dough crosswise into 12 strips. Arrange on a parchment-lined baking sheet. Bake at 425° for 7 minutes or until browned and puffy. Top chicken mixture with dough strips. **YIELD**: 4 servings (serving size: 1¹/₄ cups chicken mixture and 3 piecrust strips).

CALORIES 341; FAT 8.5g (sat 2.9g, mono 2.5g, poly 0.7g); PROTEIN 30.4g; CARB 33.6g; FIBER 2.5g; CHOL 69mg; IRON 1.7mg; SODIUM 813mg; CALC 20mg

5

## Chicken Potpie

2 tablespoons butter
2 tablespoons olive oil
3 cups diced red potato (about 1 pound)
2 cups diced onion
2 cups sliced mushrooms (about 8 ounces)
1 cup diced celery
1 cup diced carrot
¼ cup chopped fresh parsley
2 teaspoons chopped fresh thyme
6½ tablespoons all-purpose flour
3 cups fat-free milk
½ cup fat-free, lower-sodium chicken broth
2 cups chopped cooked chicken breast (about 12 ounces)
1 cup frozen green peas
1 teaspoon salt
½ teaspoon freshly ground black pepper
6 (14 x 9–inch) sheets frozen phyllo dough, thawed
Cooking spray

**1.** Preheat oven to 375°.

**2.** Melt butter in a large Dutch oven over medium-high heat; add oil. Add potato and next 6 ingredients, and sauté 5 minutes. Reduce heat to medium-low; sprinkle flour over vegetables. Cook 5 minutes, stirring frequently. Stir in milk and broth. Increase heat to medium-high; bring to a boil. Reduce heat, and simmer 5 minutes or until thickened. Add chicken, peas, salt, and pepper.

**3.** Spoon mixture into a 3-quart baking dish. Place 1 phyllo sheet on a large cutting board or work surface (cover remaining dough to keep from drying); lightly spray with cooking spray. Repeat layers with cooking spray and remaining phyllo. Place phyllo layers loosely on top of mixture in dish. Place dish on a baking sheet. Bake at 375° for 30 minutes or until top is golden. **YIELD:** 6 servings.

CALORIES 354; FAT 11.2g (sat 3.8g, mono 5.3g, poly 1.2g); PROTEIN 24.2g; CARB 40g; FIBER 4.4g; CHOL 52mg; IRON 2.5mg; SODIUM 680mg; CALC 209mg

# Quick Chicken Noodle Soup

2 cups water
1 (32-ounce) carton fat-free, lower-sodium chicken broth
1 tablespoon olive oil
½ cup prechopped onion
½ cup prechopped celery
½ teaspoon salt

½ teaspoon freshly ground black pepper
1 medium carrot, chopped
6 ounces uncooked fusilli pasta
2½ cups shredded skinless, boneless rotisserie chicken breast
2 tablespoons chopped fresh flat-leaf parsley

**1.** Combine 2 cups water and chicken broth in a microwave-safe dish, and microwave at HIGH 5 minutes.

**2.** While broth mixture heats, heat a large saucepan over medium-high heat. Add oil to pan; swirl to coat. Add onion, celery, salt, pepper, and carrot; sauté 3 minutes or until almost tender, stirring frequently. Add hot broth mixture and pasta; bring to a boil. Cook 7 minutes or until pasta is almost al dente. Stir in chicken; cook 1 minute or until thoroughly heated. Stir in parsley.

**YIELD**: 6 servings (serving size: about 1 cup).

CALORIES 237; FAT 4.8g (sat 1g, mono 2.4g, poly 0.9g); PROTEIN 22.9g; CARB 23.9g; FIBER 1.7g; CHOL 50mg; IRON 1.8mg; SODIUM 589mg; CALC 28mg

**what makes it light**
uses skinless rotisserie chicken breast, which is low fat

> "This is great for wintertime when you want a nice easy meal that is filling and **makes you feel warm inside.** My husband didn't know it was light!
>
> from cookinglight.com

# Creamy Chicken-and-Rice Casserole

1 (6.9-ounce) package one-third-less-salt chicken-flavored rice-and-vermicelli mix with chicken broth and herbs (such as Rice-A-Roni)
1 tablespoon butter
2¼ cups hot water
Cooking spray
1½ pounds skinless, boneless chicken breast, cut into bite-sized pieces
1 cup presliced fresh mushrooms

½ teaspoon garlic powder
¾ cup fat-free sour cream
¼ teaspoon pepper
1 (10¾-ounce) can condensed reduced-fat, reduced-sodium cream of mushroom soup, undiluted
¼ cup crushed multigrain crackers (about 6 crackers)
1 tablespoon butter, melted
½ teaspoon poppy seeds

**1.** Preheat oven to 350°.
**2.** Cook rice mix in a large nonstick skillet according to package directions, using 1 tablespoon butter and $2^{1}/_{4}$ cups hot water. Remove mixture from pan; set aside. Wipe pan with a paper towel.
**3.** Heat skillet over high heat. Coat pan with cooking spray. Add chicken, mushrooms, and garlic powder; sauté 6 minutes or until chicken loses its pink color. Combine rice mixture, chicken mixture, sour cream, pepper, and soup in a bowl; stir well. Spoon mixture into a 2-quart casserole coated with cooking spray. Combine cracker crumbs, butter, and poppy seeds; stir well, and sprinkle over chicken mixture. Bake at 350° for 35 minutes or until thoroughly heated. **YIELD**: 6 servings (serving size: $1^{1}/_{3}$ cups).

CALORIES 373; FAT 9.1g (sat 3.5g, mono 2.9g, poly 2.3g); PROTEIN 32.1g; CARB 39.9g; FIBER 1.9g; CHOL 81mg; IRON 2mg; SODIUM 896mg; CALC 77mg

## what makes it light

- uses one-third-less-salt chicken-flavored rice-and-vermicelli mix
- uses less butter than traditional recipes
- uses fat-free sour cream
- uses reduced-fat, reduced-sodium condensed cream of mushroom soup
- uses multigrain crackers, which are healthier than traditional crackers (usually Ritz)

# recipe makeover
# cheesy chicken enchiladas

**The Reader:** Anna Marie "Rie" Lotti

**The Story:** "My son-in-law, Marc, is from a traditional Mexican family, and we're Italian. This is a dish we all love because it's cheesy and good," Rie says of this recipe that's been in her family for two decades. Rie notes their lifestyle has changed a lot since she started making the casserole: Both she and her husband, Tom, keep tabs on sodium, saturated fat, and calories since Tom was diagnosed with type 2 diabetes a few years ago. "I'm glad my daughter, Dawn, sent the recipe to *Cooking Light* for a makeover," she says.

**The Dilemma:** Plenty of cheese and sour cream, as well as canned cream of chicken soup, contributed to the hefty 773 calories per serving of this filling entrée. Plus, the soup and abundant 2 pounds of cheese added to the dish's sodium content.

**The Solution:** Using half the amount of cheese and opting for a reduced-fat Mexican blend in the filling cut 149 calories, 13.4 grams of fat (8.4 grams saturated), and 126 milligrams of sodium per serving. We topped the casserole with one-fourth the original amount of cheese and employed a sharp reduced-fat cheddar to trim 97 calories, 8.3 grams of fat (5.2 grams saturated), and 134 milligrams of sodium per serving.

In place of 2 cups of the full-fat sour cream, we used a combination of 1$\frac{2}{3}$ cups low-fat plain yogurt and $\frac{1}{3}$ cup butter to shave 29 calories and about 4 grams of fat (2.4 grams saturated) per serving. We substituted a reduced-fat, reduced-sodium version of canned cream of chicken soup for a savings of 1.5 grams of fat and 102 milligrams of sodium per serving. And, instead of frying the tortillas in oil, we brushed them with a prudent 1 tablespoon canola oil to keep fat and calories in check and pan-toasted them.

**The Feedback:** "The family thoroughly enjoyed the new version of the enchiladas," says Rie. **"The tortillas were tender, and the filling was flavorful and creamy with extra onion and garlic and the combined sour cream and butter."**

|  | BEFORE | AFTER |
|---|---|---|
| Calories per serving | 773 | 454 |
| Fat | 53.4g | 20.3g |
| Percent of total calories | 38% | 25% |

**Trade the traditional enchilada** sauce for a creamy, cheesy topping on this Mexican chicken recipe. Your family will never know they're enjoying a lightened meal. Serve with a salad of fresh mango, jícama, and shredded lettuce topped with a lime vinaigrette.

# Cheesy Chicken Enchiladas

2½ cups chopped cooked chicken breast
2 cups (8 ounces) preshredded reduced-fat 4-cheese Mexican blend cheese
1⅔ cups plain low-fat yogurt
⅓ cup butter, melted
¼ cup chopped onion
1 teaspoon minced garlic
¼ teaspoon freshly ground black pepper
1 (10¾-ounce) can condensed reduced-fat, reduced-sodium cream of chicken soup (such as Healthy Request), undiluted

1 (4.5-ounce) can chopped green chiles, drained
8 (8-inch) flour tortillas
1 tablespoon canola oil
Cooking spray
½ cup (2 ounces) finely shredded reduced-fat sharp cheddar cheese
¼ cup chopped green onions

**1.** Preheat oven to 350°.
**2.** Combine first 9 ingredients in a large bowl. Remove 1 cup chicken mixture; set mixture aside.
**3.** Heat a large skillet over medium-high heat. Working with 1 tortilla at a time, brush oil over both sides of tortilla. Add tortilla to pan; cook 5 seconds on each side or until toasted and soft. Remove from pan; arrange ½ cup chicken mixture down center of tortilla. Roll jelly-roll style; place filled tortilla, seam side down, in a 13 x 9–inch baking dish coated with cooking spray. Repeat procedure with remaining 7 tortillas, remaining oil, and remaining chicken mixture. Spread reserved 1 cup chicken mixture evenly over enchiladas. Cover and bake at 350° for 20 minutes. Uncover; sprinkle evenly with cheddar cheese and green onions; bake an additional 5 minutes or until cheese melts.

**YIELD:** 8 servings (serving size: 1 enchilada).

CALORIES 454; FAT 20.3g (sat 10.4g, mono 6.7g, poly 1.5g); PROTEIN 30.8g; CARB 36.6g; FIBER 2.2g; CHOL 73mg; IRON 2.3mg; SODIUM 757mg; CALC 347mg

**Serve a classic family-favorite** for an easy weeknight meal in minutes. Pair with a quick starch and a small green salad.

# Oven-Fried Chicken Parmesan

1.1 ounces all-purpose flour (about ¼ cup)
½ teaspoon dried oregano
¼ teaspoon salt
2 large egg whites, lightly beaten
¾ cup panko (Japanese breadcrumbs)
4 (6-ounce) skinless, boneless chicken breast halves

2 tablespoons olive oil, divided
Cooking spray
½ cup tomato-basil pasta sauce
½ cup (2 ounces) grated Parmigiano-Reggiano cheese
¾ cup (3 ounces) shredded part-skim mozzarella cheese

**1.** Preheat oven to 450°.

**2.** Combine first 3 ingredients in a shallow dish; place egg whites in a bowl. Place panko in a shallow dish. Dredge 1 breast half in flour mixture. Dip in egg whites; dredge in panko. Repeat procedure with remaining chicken, flour mixture, egg whites, and panko.

**3.** Heat 1 tablespoon oil in a large ovenproof skillet over medium-high heat. Add chicken to pan; cook 2 minutes. Add remaining 1 tablespoon oil. Turn chicken over; cook 2 minutes. Coat chicken with cooking spray; place pan in oven. Bake at 450° for 5 minutes. Turn chicken over; top each breast half with 2 tablespoons sauce, 2 tablespoons Parmigiano-Reggiano, and 3 tablespoons mozzarella. Bake 6 minutes or until chicken is done. **YIELD**: 4 servings (serving size: 1 breast half).

CALORIES 401; FAT 16.9g (sat 6.4g, mono 7.6g, poly 1.3g); PROTEIN 44.4g; CARB 15.9g; FIBER 0.6g; CHOL 95mg; IRON 1.8mg; SODIUM 719mg; CALC 352mg

## what makes it light

- uses less oil to brown the chicken before baking than traditional recipes
- uses less cheese on top than traditional recipes

# 5 ways with
# fried chicken

1

## Pan-Fried Chicken

The key to success with this recipe is even heat. If the oil gets too hot, the chicken may brown too quickly before fully cooking. If the oil is not hot enough, the chicken will absorb too much of it. You can lower the heat, or brown the chicken on the stovetop and then cook in a 350° oven until done.

    4.5  ounces all-purpose flour (about 1 cup)
    2.38 ounces whole-wheat flour (about
         ½ cup)
      1  teaspoon ground ginger
      ½  teaspoon hot paprika
      ½  teaspoon ground cinnamon
      ½  teaspoon freshly ground nutmeg
      ½  teaspoon fine sea salt
      2  bone-in chicken breast halves, skinned
      2  bone-in chicken thighs, skinned
      2  chicken drumsticks, skinned
      ¼  cup peanut oil

**1.** Sift together first 6 ingredients; place mixture in a large zip-top plastic bag. Sprinkle salt evenly over chicken. Add chicken, one piece at a time, to bag; seal. Shake bag to coat chicken. Remove chicken from bag, shaking off excess flour. Place chicken on a cooling rack; place rack in a jelly-roll pan. Reserve remaining flour mixture. Loosely cover chicken; chill $1^1/_2$ hours. Let chicken stand at room temperature 30 minutes. Return chicken, one piece at a time, to flour mixture, shaking bag to coat chicken. Discard excess flour mixture.

**2.** Heat peanut oil in a large skillet over medium-high heat. Add chicken to pan. Reduce heat to medium-low, and cook 25 minutes or until done, carefully turning every 5 minutes.

**3.** Line a clean cooling rack with brown paper bags; arrange chicken in a single layer on bags. Let stand 5 minutes. **YIELD:** 4 servings (serving size: 1 chicken breast half, or 1 thigh and 1 drumstick).

CALORIES 245; FAT 10.1g (sat 2g, mono 4.1g, poly 3g); PROTEIN 28.2g; CARB 9g; FIBER 0.8g; CHOL 87mg; IRON 1.8mg; SODIUM 240mg; CALC 17mg

# Lemon-Ginger Fried Chicken

1 teaspoon grated lemon rind
1 cup fresh lemon juice (about 4 lemons)
2 teaspoons minced peeled fresh ginger
1½ teaspoons minced garlic
2 bone-in chicken breast halves, skinned
2 bone-in chicken thighs, skinned
2 chicken drumsticks, skinned
4.5 ounces all-purpose flour (about 1 cup)
2 teaspoons ground ginger
1 teaspoon paprika
½ teaspoon ground red pepper
1 teaspoon kosher salt
½ teaspoon freshly ground black pepper
¼ cup peanut oil
¼ cup fat-free, lower-sodium chicken broth
2 tablespoons brown sugar
1 lemon, thinly sliced

**1.** Place rind, juice, and next 5 ingredients in a large zip-top plastic bag; seal and shake to coat. Marinate in refrigerator 1 hour, turning bag occasionally.

**2.** Sift together flour and next 3 ingredients. Place flour mixture in a large zip-top plastic bag. Remove chicken from marinade bag, reserving marinade. Sprinkle salt and black pepper evenly over chicken. Add chicken, one piece at a time, to flour mixture; seal bag and shake to coat chicken. Remove chicken from bag, shaking off excess flour mixture. Reserve remaining flour mixture. Place chicken on a wire rack; place rack in a jelly-roll pan. Cover and refrigerate 1½ hours. Let stand at room temperature 30 minutes.

**3.** Preheat oven to 350°.

**4.** Return chicken, one piece at a time, to flour mixture; seal bag and shake to coat chicken. Remove chicken from bag, shaking off excess flour mixture. Discard remaining flour mixture.

**5.** Heat oil in a large skillet over medium-high heat. Add chicken to pan; cook 3 minutes or until golden, turning once. Arrange chicken in a single layer in a shallow roasting pan. Combine broth and reserved marinade in a small bowl; carefully pour broth mixture into pan. Sprinkle chicken evenly with sugar, and top with lemon slices. Bake at 350° for 45 minutes or until golden and a thermometer registers 165°. **YIELD:** 4 servings (serving size: 1 breast half, or 1 thigh and 1 drumstick).

CALORIES 375; FAT 15.5g (sat 3.3g, mono 6.6g, poly 4.7g); PROTEIN 30.8g; CARB 30.5g; FIBER 2.4g; CHOL 85mg; IRON 2.6mg; SODIUM 578mg; CALC 48mg

2

## Oven-Fried Chicken ▾

- 1 cup low-fat buttermilk
- 2 large egg whites, beaten
- 4.5 ounces all-purpose flour (about 1 cup)
- ⅓ cup cornmeal
- 1 teaspoon salt, divided
- ¾ teaspoon freshly ground black pepper
- ¼ teaspoon ground red pepper
- 2 chicken breast halves, skinned (about 1 pound)
- 2 chicken thighs, skinned (about ½ pound)
- 2 chicken drumsticks, skinned (about ½ pound)
- 2 tablespoons canola oil
- Cooking spray

**1.** Preheat oven to 425°.
**2.** Cover a large baking sheet with parchment paper. Combine buttermilk and egg whites in a shallow dish; stir well with a whisk. Combine flour, cornmeal, ½ teaspoon salt, black pepper, and red pepper in a separate shallow dish; stir well. Sprinkle chicken evenly with remaining ½ teaspoon salt. Dip chicken in buttermilk mixture; dredge in flour mixture.
**3.** Heat oil in a large nonstick skillet over medium-high heat. Add chicken to pan; cook 4 minutes on each side or until lightly browned.

Place chicken on prepared baking sheet; lightly coat chicken with cooking spray. Bake at 425° for 30 minutes or until chicken is done. **YIELD:** 4 servings (serving size: 1 chicken breast half, or 1 drumstick and 1 thigh).

CALORIES 450; FAT 13.8g (sat 2.5g, mono 6.1g, poly 3.6g); PROTEIN 43.5g; CARB 35.3g; FIBER 1.7g; CHOL 109mg; IRON 3.2mg; SODIUM 803mg; CALC 88mg

## Buttermilk Oven-Fried Chicken with Coleslaw ▾

Coleslaw:
- 4 cups packaged coleslaw
- 3 tablespoons fat-free mayonnaise
- 1½ teaspoons sugar
- ½ teaspoon celery seeds
- 1½ teaspoons cider vinegar
- ⅛ teaspoon salt

Chicken:
- 1 cup low-fat buttermilk
- 4 (8-ounce) bone-in chicken breast halves, skinned
- 1.5 ounces all-purpose flour (about ⅓ cup)
- ⅓ cup cracker meal
- ½ teaspoon salt
- ½ teaspoon freshly ground black pepper
- 2 tablespoons butter

3

4

**1.** To prepare coleslaw, combine first 6 ingredients; toss to coat. Cover and chill.

**2.** Preheat oven to 425°.

**3.** To prepare chicken, combine buttermilk and chicken in a shallow dish, turning to coat.

**4.** Combine flour and cracker meal in a shallow dish. Transfer chicken from buttermilk to a work surface. Sprinkle chicken evenly with $^1/_2$ teaspoon salt and pepper. Working with one chicken breast half at a time, dredge chicken in flour mixture, shaking off excess; set aside. Repeat procedure with remaining chicken and flour mixture.

**5.** Melt butter in a large ovenproof nonstick skillet over medium-high heat. Add chicken to pan, meat side down; cook 4 minutes or until golden brown. Turn chicken over, and bake at 425° for 32 minutes or until a thermometer registers 165°. **YIELD:** 4 servings (serving size: 1 chicken breast half and $^3/_4$ cup slaw).

CALORIES 342; FAT 8.8g (sat 4.5g, mono 2.2g, poly 0.8g); PROTEIN 45.1g; CARB 18.5g; FIBER 2.6g; CHOL 123mg; IRON 2.3mg; SODIUM 672mg; CALC 95mg

## Oven-Fried Coconut Chicken ▶

The marinade infuses dark-meat chicken with a light coconut flavor; flaked coconut in the breading heightens the nutty taste. Find panko in your supermarket's ethnic food aisle.

1 tablespoon fresh lime juice
1 tablespoon hot pepper sauce
1 (13.5-ounce) can light coconut milk
4 (4-ounce) chicken thighs, skinned
4 (4-ounce) chicken drumsticks, skinned
¾ cup panko (Japanese breadcrumbs)
½ cup flaked sweetened coconut
½ teaspoon salt
¼ teaspoon freshly ground black pepper
Cooking spray

**1.** Combine first 3 ingredients in a large zip-top plastic bag. Add chicken to bag; seal. Marinate in refrigerator $1^1/_2$ hours, turning bag occasionally.

**2.** Preheat oven to 400°.

**3.** Combine panko, flaked coconut, salt, and black pepper in a shallow dish. Remove chicken from marinade; discard marinade. Dredge chicken, one piece at a time, in panko mixture. Place chicken on a baking sheet lined with parchment paper. Lightly coat chicken with cooking spray. Bake at 400° for 30 minutes or until golden brown. Carefully turn chicken over; bake an additional 30 minutes or until done. **YIELD:** 4 servings (serving size: 1 thigh and 1 drumstick).

CALORIES 256; FAT 8.6g (sat 4.4g, mono 1.6g, poly 1.2g); PROTEIN 27.7g; CARB 15.6g; FIBER 0.8g; CHOL 103mg; IRON 1.6mg; SODIUM 464mg; CALC 18mg

**This recipe first ran in the May 2005 issue of *Cooking Light* magazine** that profiled Chuck Williams, founder of Williams-Sonoma, and it's our hands-down best roast chicken.

# Roasted Chicken with Onions, Potatoes, and Gravy

1 (4-pound) roasting chicken
1¼ teaspoons salt, divided
¾ teaspoon freshly ground black pepper, divided
4 fresh oregano sprigs
1 lemon, quartered
1 celery stalk, cut into 2-inch pieces
Cooking spray
2 tablespoons butter, melted

2 pounds medium yellow onions, peeled and each cut into 8 wedges
2 pounds small red potatoes, cut into (1-inch) wedges
1.1 ounces all-purpose flour (about ¼ cup)
1 (14-ounce) can fat-free, lower-sodium chicken broth, divided
Lemon wedges (optional)
Oregano sprigs (optional)

**1.** Preheat oven to 425°.

**2.** Remove and discard giblets and neck from chicken. Trim excess fat. Starting at neck cavity, loosen skin from breast and drumsticks by inserting fingers, gently pushing between skin and meat. Combine $1/2$ teaspoon salt and $1/2$ teaspoon black pepper; rub under loosened skin and over breast and drumsticks. Place oregano sprigs, quartered lemon, and celery pieces into body cavity. Lift wing tips up and over back; tuck under chicken. Tie legs together with string. Place chicken, breast side up, on the rack of a broiler pan coated with cooking spray.

**3.** Combine $1/2$ teaspoon salt, remaining $1/4$ teaspoon pepper, melted butter, onions, and potatoes in a large bowl, and toss well to coat. Arrange onion mixture around chicken on rack. Place rack in pan. Bake at 425° for 20 minutes. Reduce oven temperature to 325° (do not remove pan from oven); bake an additional 1 hour and 10 minutes or until onions and potatoes are tender and a thermometer inserted into meaty part of chicken thigh registers 165°. Set chicken, onions, and potatoes aside; cover and keep warm.

**4.** Place a zip-top plastic bag inside a 2-cup glass measure. Pour pan drippings into bag; let stand 10 minutes (fat will rise to the top). Seal bag; carefully snip off 1 bottom corner of bag. Drain drippings into a small saucepan, stopping before fat layer reaches opening; discard fat. Combine remaining $1/4$ teaspoon salt, flour, and $1/2$ cup chicken broth in a small bowl, stirring with a whisk. Add flour mixture and remaining chicken broth to saucepan. Bring to a boil over medium-high heat. Reduce heat to medium; cook 5 minutes or until gravy thickens, stirring frequently with a whisk. Carve chicken; serve with gravy and onion mixture. Garnish with lemon wedges and oregano sprigs, if desired. **YIELD**: 6 servings (serving size: about 4 ounces chicken, $1^1/3$ cups onion mixture, and $1/3$ cup gravy).

CALORIES 430; FAT 11.6g (sat 4.5g, mono 3.8g, poly 2g); PROTEIN 36.9g; CARB 43.7g; FIBER 5.2g; CHOL 113mg; IRON 3.4mg; SODIUM 753mg; CALC 71mg

**? what makes it light**
- fat is removed from the broth before making the gravy
- portion size serves six instead of the usual four

"This dish was delicious! My family loved it—great comfort food that kept them coming back for seconds! It is also a great dish to prepare ahead of time when entertaining."

**from cookinglight.com**

# Turkey Tetrazzini

10 ounces uncooked vermicelli
2 teaspoons vegetable oil
1 pound turkey breast cutlets
¾ teaspoon onion powder, divided
½ teaspoon salt, divided
¼ teaspoon black pepper, divided
2 tablespoons dry sherry
2 (8-ounce) packages presliced mushrooms
¾ cup frozen green peas, thawed

¾ cup fat-free milk
⅔ cup fat-free sour cream
⅓ cup (about 1½ ounces) grated fresh Parmesan cheese
1 (10¾-ounce) can reduced-fat cream of chicken soup (such as Healthy Choice)
Cooking spray
⅓ cup dry breadcrumbs
2 tablespoons butter, melted

**1.** Preheat oven to 450°.
**2.** Cook pasta according to package directions, omitting salt and fat. Drain.
**3.** Heat oil in a large nonstick skillet over medium-high heat. Sprinkle turkey with $^1/_2$ teaspoon onion powder, $^1/_4$ teaspoon salt, and $^1/_8$ teaspoon pepper. Add turkey to pan; cook 2 minutes on each side or until done. Remove turkey from pan.
**4.** Add $^1/_4$ teaspoon onion powder, sherry, and mushrooms to pan. Cover and cook 4 minutes or until mushrooms are tender.
**5.** Combine peas, milk, sour cream, cheese, and soup in a large bowl. Chop turkey. Add $^1/_4$ teaspoon salt, $^1/_8$ teaspoon pepper, pasta, turkey, and mushroom mixture to soup mixture, tossing gently to combine. Spoon mixture into a 13 x 9–inch baking dish coated with cooking spray.
**6.** Combine breadcrumbs and butter, tossing to combine. Sprinkle over pasta mixture. Bake at 450° for 12 minutes or until bubbly. **YIELD:** 6 servings (serving size: about $1^2/_3$ cups).

CALORIES 459; FAT 14.8g (sat 5.9g, mono 4.4g, poly 2.8g); PROTEIN 30.5g; CARB 48.1g; FIBER 3.1g; CHOL 69mg; IRON 4mg; SODIUM 716mg; CALC 199mg

## what makes it light

- uses turkey breast, which is leaner than the traditional light-and-dark-meat mixed versions
- uses fat-free milk
- uses fat-free sour cream
- uses reduced-fat cream of chicken soup
- uses a minimal amount of butter

# sides & desserts

**Cook the fruit unpeeled to add flavor** and a pink hue. Then pass through a sieve to remove the peels. If you have a food mill, use it instead of a sieve. Or cool the fruit slightly, remove and discard the peels, and pulse in a food processor. Refrigerate for up to five days.

# Pear Applesauce

½ cup apple juice
2 pounds Fuji apples, cored and cut into wedges
2 pounds red Bartlett pears, cored and cut into wedges

2 (3-inch) cinnamon sticks
½ lemon, cut into 2 pieces
¼ cup packed brown sugar

**1.** Combine first 5 ingredients in a large saucepan; bring to a boil. Cover, reduce heat, and simmer 45 minutes or until fruit is tender. Discard cinnamon sticks and lemon. Press fruit mixture through a sieve over a bowl using the back of a spoon, and discard peels. Stir in brown sugar. Serve sauce at room temperature or chilled. **YIELD:** 16 servings (serving size: ¹/₄ cup).

CALORIES 80; FAT 0.4g (sat 0.1g, mono 0.1g, poly 0.1g); PROTEIN 0.3g; CARB 20.7g; FIBER 1.6g; CHOL 0mg; IRON 0.2mg; SODIUM 2.1mg; CALC 12mg

## what makes it light

• uses much less sugar than traditional recipes

"This slaw is a healthier version of an original family recipe. It is creamy and delicious, and **takes about five minutes to make.**"

from cookinglight.com

# New-Fashioned Apple and Raisin Slaw

½ cup light sour cream
3 tablespoons reduced-fat mayonnaise
1½ tablespoons white balsamic vinegar
1 teaspoon sugar
½ teaspoon black pepper
¼ teaspoon salt

2 cups unpeeled chopped Rome apple (about 1 medium)
1 cup golden raisins
1 (16-ounce) package cabbage-and-carrot coleslaw

**1.** Combine first 6 ingredients in a large bowl, stirring with a whisk. Add chopped apple, 1 cup raisins, and coleslaw; toss to combine. **YIELD:** 8 servings (serving size: 1 cup).

CALORIES 120; FAT 2.2g (sat 1.2g, mono 0.8, poly 0.2g); PROTEIN 2.3 g; CARB 25.3g; FIBER 3.3g; CHOL 0mg; IRON 0.8mg; SODIUM 162mg; CALC 31mg

## what makes it light

• uses light sour cream
• uses reduced-fat mayonnaise

30 minutes or less

**Check the beans 10 to 15 minutes ahead of time** to make sure they're not drying out.

# Bourbon Baked Beans

1 pound dried navy beans (about 2½ cups)
3 applewood-smoked bacon slices
1 cup finely chopped onion
5 cups water, divided
½ cup maple syrup, divided
¼ cup plus 2 tablespoons bourbon, divided

¼ cup Dijon mustard
1½ teaspoons Worcestershire sauce
¼ teaspoon freshly ground black pepper
1 tablespoon cider vinegar
1 teaspoon salt

**1.** Sort and wash beans; place in a large Dutch oven. Cover with water to 2 inches above beans; cover and let stand 8 hours or overnight. Drain beans. Wipe pan dry with a paper towel.

**2.** Preheat oven to 350°.

**3.** Heat pan over medium-high heat. Add bacon to pan, and cook 4 minutes or until crisp. Remove from pan, reserving $1^1/2$ tablespoons drippings in pan; crumble bacon. Add onion to drippings in pan; cook 5 minutes or until onion begins to brown, stirring frequently. Add beans, bacon, 4 cups water, $^1/4$ cup maple syrup, $^1/4$ cup bourbon, and next 3 ingredients to pan. Bring to a boil; cover and bake at 350° for 2 hours.

**4.** Stir in remaining 1 cup water, remaining $^1/4$ cup maple syrup, and remaining 2 tablespoons bourbon. Cover and bake 1 hour or until beans are tender and liquid is almost absorbed. Stir in vinegar and salt. **YIELD:** $6^1/2$ cups (serving size: $^1/2$ cup).

CALORIES 199; FAT 3.1g (sat 1.1g, mono 0.7g, poly 0.5g); PROTEIN 7.8g; CARB 31.8g; FIBER 5.6g; CHOL 4mg; IRON 2.1mg; SODIUM 307mg; CALC 66mg

## what makes it light

- uses much less sugar than traditional recipes
- uses less bacon than traditional recipes
- uses much less salt than traditional recipes

# broccoli casserole

**The Reader:** Trisha Prenger

**The Story:** Trisha has enjoyed this cheesy, simple casserole since childhood, when her mother prepared it for family meals. "My mother has had this recipe for at least 20 years. As children, my brother and I always liked the crunch of the water chestnuts in the casserole," she says. Since the recipe is easily assembled using ingredients found in most kitchens, Trisha says the casserole is now one of her family's favorites as a side dish for weeknight dinners. But as the mother of a two-year-old daughter, and with another baby on the way, she knows how important it is to make healthful food choices. "My husband, Eric, and I are trying to eat better overall and watch our fat intake," she notes. It's also important for her to cook dishes that are quick, easy, and tasty.

**The Dilemma:** "I knew my mom's version of the casserole was fattening because of the cream and mayonnaise," she says. With 23 grams of fat from the mayonnaise and cream alone, one-third of which was saturated, we had our work cut out for us. Furthermore, the original version contained about 20 percent of the American Heart Association's recommended daily dietary cholesterol intake (less than 300 milligrams) per serving.

**The Solution:** The mayonnaise, Miracle Whip, cream, and cheese added the bulk of the fat and calories to the original recipe. To match the sweet "tang" the Miracle Whip provided, we substituted fat-free mayonnaise, which also imparts a slightly sweet flavor, and shaved 118 calories and nearly 14 grams of fat per serving. Instead of using the cream, we cooked fat-free milk with flour and seasoned the mixture with a bit of salt and pepper to make a thick, rich-tasting sauce. A little fat-free cream cheese stirred into the milk sauce added more body and flavor. Swapping a homemade sauce for the cream cut another 11 grams of fat and 77 calories per portion. These changes also lowered the cholesterol to a manageable 15 milligrams per serving. Creative tweaking—like substituting flavorful sharp cheddar cheese for the original's milder Colby and adding a bit more chopped onion—allowed us to use several fat-free dairy products to cut calories, fat, and cholesterol without compromising taste. One final update: We used crispy panko (Japanese breadcrumbs) tossed with a little butter for a nice golden, crunchy topping.

**The Feedback:** Trisha prepared the heavy and light casseroles for a side-by-side family taste-testing. "My husband, mother, and I were very impressed and actually liked the lightened version better than the original recipe," Trisha says. They preferred the cheddar flavor of the lightened casserole over the "tangy-zesty" taste of the original. One other bonus, according to Trisha, was that there was more sauce in the lighter version, so the healthier version seemed creamier. This cheesier but lighter casserole, which is still quick to assemble, will remain a weeknight favorite for the Prenger family.

|  | BEFORE | AFTER |
|---|---|---|
| Calories per serving | 351 | 141 |
| Fat | 30.9g | 4.9g |
| Percent of total calories | 79% | 31% |

# Zesty Broccoli Casserole

3 (10-ounce) packages frozen broccoli
   florets, thawed
Cooking spray
1½ cups fat-free milk
2½ tablespoons all-purpose flour
  ½ teaspoon salt
  ¼ teaspoon freshly ground black pepper
  ¾ cup (3 ounces) shredded sharp
   cheddar cheese

½ cup (4 ounces) fat-free cream cheese,
  softened
1 cup fat-free mayonnaise
¾ cup chopped onion (about ½ medium)
1 (8-ounce) can sliced water chestnuts,
  rinsed and drained
¾ cup panko (Japanese breadcrumbs)
2 teaspoons butter, melted

**1.** Preheat oven to 375°.

**2.** Arrange broccoli in an even layer in an 11 x 7–inch baking dish coated with cooking spray;
set aside.

**3.** Combine milk, flour, salt, and pepper in a large saucepan over medium-high heat; bring to a
boil. Cook 1 minute or until thick, stirring constantly. Remove from heat. Add cheddar and
cream cheeses; stir until smooth. Stir in mayonnaise, onion, and water chestnuts. Spoon cheese
mixture evenly over broccoli.

**4.** Place panko in a small bowl. Drizzle with butter, and toss. Sprinkle breadcrumb mixture
evenly over cheese mixture. Lightly spray breadcrumb layer with cooking spray. Bake at 375°
for 25 minutes or until mixture begins to bubble and breadcrumbs brown. **YIELD:** 10 servings
(serving size: about ³/₄ cup).

CALORIES 141; FAT 4.9g (sat 2.6g, mono 1.3g, poly 0.7g); PROTEIN 8.6g; CARB 17.9g; FIBER 4.1g; CHOL 15mg; IRON 1mg;
SODIUM 484mg; CALC 173mg

"This is now 'my' coleslaw recipe! **Anyone who doesn't normally like coleslaw loves this!** Perfect combo of vinegar and mayo to satisfy the old debate of whether a vinegar- or mayo-based slaw is best. This is now my go-to recipe for company in the summer, and I always make this for the family at the beach. Doubles very easily for large groups, too."

**from cookinglight.com**

# Tangy Mustard Coleslaw

7 cups finely shredded green cabbage (about ½ head)
1 cup thinly vertically sliced red onion
1 cup grated carrot
¼ cup white wine vinegar
2 tablespoons sugar

2 tablespoons whole-grain mustard
2 tablespoons reduced-fat mayonnaise
⅛ teaspoon salt
⅛ teaspoon black pepper
⅛ teaspoon ground red pepper

**1.** Combine cabbage, onion, and 1 cup carrot in a large bowl. Combine white wine vinegar, sugar, mustard, mayonnaise, salt, black pepper, and red pepper in a small bowl; stir well with a whisk. Add mustard mixture to cabbage mixture, and toss well to coat. Cover and chill 20 minutes. Stir before serving. **YIELD:** 7 servings (serving size: about 1 cup).

CALORIES 58; FAT 0.8g (sat 0.1g, mono 0.1g, poly 0.3g); PROTEIN 1.5g; CARB 12.3g; FIBER 3g; CHOL 0mg; IRON 0.5mg; SODIUM 172mg; CALC 43mg

## what makes it light

- uses reduced-fat mayonnaise
- uses less salt than traditional recipes

30 minutes or less

"Yum! This is delicious. **It doesn't taste overly heavy, but it's not obviously light, either.** Was a hit at two dinners for my family and very easy. Nothing fancy—just good comfort food."

**from cookinglight.com**

# Corn Fritter Casserole

3 tablespoons butter, softened
3 large egg whites
1 (8-ounce) block fat-free cream
   cheese, softened
½ cup finely chopped onion
½ cup finely chopped red bell pepper
1 (15¼-ounce) can whole-kernel corn,
   drained

1 (14¾-ounce) can cream-style corn
1 (8½-ounce) package corn muffin mix
   (such as Jiffy)
¼ teaspoon black pepper
Cooking spray

**1.** Preheat oven to 375°.
**2.** Combine first 3 ingredients in a large bowl, stirring with a whisk until smooth. Stir in onion, bell pepper, whole-kernel corn, and cream-style corn; mix well. Add muffin mix and black pepper, stirring until well combined. Pour into an 11 x 7–inch baking dish coated with cooking spray. Bake at 375° for 50 minutes or until a wooden pick inserted in center comes out clean. **YIELD:** 9 servings (serving size: about ⅔ cup).

CALORIES 247; FAT 8.4g (sat 3.7g, mono 2.7g, poly 0.7g); PROTEIN 8.6g; CARB 36.7g; FIBER 1.9g; CHOL 31mg; IRON 1.3mg; SODIUM 629mg; CALC 72mg

## what makes it light
- uses egg whites
- uses fat-free cream cheese

"I give this recipe five stars because we can't live without it! I don't make conventional pickles like Mama used to do, but I have to have a jar of these in the refrigerator at all times during cuke season! **They are fantastic either with a sandwich or as a side-dish.** My husband, who refuses to touch a cucumber in any other form, wants them with just about every meal!"

from cookinglight.com

# Easy Refrigerator Pickles

6 cups thinly sliced pickling cucumbers (about 2 pounds)
2 cups thinly sliced onion
1½ cups white vinegar
¾ cup sugar
¾ teaspoon salt
½ teaspoon mustard seeds
½ teaspoon celery seeds
½ teaspoon ground turmeric
½ teaspoon crushed red pepper
¼ teaspoon freshly ground black pepper
4 garlic cloves, thinly sliced

**1.** Place 3 cups cucumber in a medium glass bowl; top with 1 cup onion. Repeat procedure with remaining 3 cups cucumber and remaining 1 cup onion.
**2.** Combine vinegar and remaining ingredients in a small saucepan; stir well. Bring to a boil; cook 1 minute. Pour over cucumber mixture; let cool. Cover and chill at least 4 days. **YIELD:** 7 cups (serving size: $^{1}/_{4}$ cup).

CALORIES 28; FAT 0.1g (sat 0g, mono 0g, poly 0.1g); PROTEIN 0.3g; CARB 7g; FIBER 0.3g; CHOL 0mg; IRON 0.1mg; SODIUM 64mg; CALC 7mg

## what makes it light
• uses a lot less sugar than traditional recipes
• naturally low fat

**Fried okra is a southern treat.** This version produces a crisp coating without frying.

# Oven-Fried Okra

1½ cups yellow cornmeal
¾ teaspoon kosher salt, divided
½ teaspoon freshly ground black pepper
Dash of ground red pepper
½ cup nonfat buttermilk

1 large egg, lightly beaten
1 pound fresh okra pods, trimmed and cut into ¾-inch slices (about 3 cups)
Cooking spray

**1.** Preheat oven to 450°.
**2.** Combine cornmeal, ¹/₂ teaspoon salt, black pepper, and red pepper in a shallow dish; set aside.
**3.** Combine buttermilk and egg in a large bowl, stirring with a whisk. Add okra; toss to coat. Let stand 3 minutes.
**4.** Dredge okra in cornmeal mixture. Place okra on a jelly-roll pan coated with cooking spray. Lightly coat okra with cooking spray. Bake at 450° for 35 to 40 minutes, stirring once. Sprinkle with remaining ¹/₄ teaspoon salt. **YIELD:** 8 servings (serving size: about ¹/₂ cup).

CALORIES 144; FAT 0.7g (sat 0.2g, mono 0.3g, poly 0.1g); PROTEIN 4.5g; CARB 29.3g; FIBER 2.6g; CHOL 27mg; IRON 1.3mg; SODIUM 204mg; CALC 68mg

## what makes it light

- uses kosher salt to keep sodium low
- uses nonfat buttermilk
- oven-fried, not deep-fried

By Patricia Miklik Doyle
has the USA's highest per-
oncentration of engin
ou've got this communit
art people, and ... they
lved," says Rick Davis, dire
Cummings Research Park.
m 1990 to 2009, metro
ville accounted for 24% of
a's population growth.
you come here, you see
of the place, and it's a
place to sell," says Da-
president of the
Alabama-Hunts-
NEW YORK

"This is exactly what you want potato salad to be. **The simple flavors all meld well together to create that taste we all expect and love.** Using low-fat mayo definitely did not compromise the flavor. Yet another great **Cooking Light** recipe where you don't even notice it's light."

**from cookinglight.com**

# Potato Salad 101

2 pounds small all-purpose white or red potatoes

3 tablespoons white vinegar

1 tablespoon canola oil

½ cup chopped celery

½ cup finely chopped red onion

2 tablespoons sweet pickle relish, drained

3 hard-cooked large eggs, chopped

¾ cup reduced-fat mayonnaise

2 tablespoons prepared mustard

½ teaspoon salt

¼ teaspoon freshly ground black pepper

**1.** Place potatoes in a saucepan, and cover with water. Bring to a boil. Reduce heat; simmer 10 minutes or until tender. Drain. Cool and peel. Cut potatoes into $1/2$-inch cubes. Place potatoes in a large bowl; sprinkle with vinegar and oil. Add celery, onion, pickle relish, and eggs; toss gently.
**2.** Combine mayonnaise, mustard, salt, and pepper. Spoon mayonnaise mixture over potato mixture; toss gently to coat. Cover and chill 1 to 24 hours. **YIELD:** 7 servings (serving size: 1 cup).

CALORIES 215; FAT 6.1g (sat 1.1g, mono 2.5g, poly 2g); PROTEIN 4.9g; CARB 35.9g; FIBER 1.9g; CHOL 91mg; IRON 0.9mg; SODIUM 536mg; CALC 26mg

## what makes it light

• uses reduced-fat mayonnaise
• uses canola oil, which is a healthy option

# 5 ways with
# mashed potatoes

## Buttermilk-Parmesan Mashed Potatoes

Be sure to purchase a crumbly wedge of Parmigiano-Reggiano for this superquick potato side dish.

- 2 pounds russet potatoes
- ⅔ cup fat-free milk
- 3 tablespoons butter
- ½ cup buttermilk
- ⅓ cup (1½ ounces) grated fresh Parmigiano-Reggiano cheese
- ½ teaspoon salt
- ¼ teaspoon freshly ground black pepper

**1.** Prick each potato several times with a fork. Place potatoes in microwave, and cook at HIGH 16 minutes or until tender, turning after 8 minutes. Let stand 2 minutes. Cut each potato in half lengthwise; scoop out flesh with a large spoon, and transfer to a bowl.

**2.** Combine milk and butter in a microwave-safe bowl, and microwave at HIGH 2 minutes or until butter melts. Add milk mixture to potatoes; mash with a potato masher to desired consistency. Stir in buttermilk and remaining ingredients. **YIELD:** 6 servings (serving size: $^3/_4$ cup).

CALORIES 240; FAT 7.9g (sat 4.9g, mono 1.9g, poly 0.3g); PROTEIN 7.5g; CARB 35.2g; FIBER 3.5g; CHOL 22mg; IRON 1.7mg; SODIUM 366mg; CALC 117mg

2

## Creamy Herbed Mashed Potatoes

Yukon golds make brilliant mashed potatoes, thanks to their balance of waxiness and starch. Because yellow potatoes are more flavorful than others, they don't need a lot of fat to taste rich. Mash them just until creamy—overworking the potatoes will make them gummy.

4 cups cubed peeled Yukon gold potato (about 2 pounds)
½ cup 2% reduced-fat milk
¼ cup low-fat sour cream
3 tablespoons butter
3 tablespoons chopped fresh chives
2 tablespoons chopped fresh parsley
½ teaspoon salt
¼ teaspoon freshly ground black pepper

**1.** Place potato in a saucepan; cover with water. Bring to a boil; cover, reduce heat, and simmer 10 minutes or until tender. Drain. Return potato to pan. Add milk and remaining ingredients; mash with a potato masher to desired consistency. **YIELD:** 6 servings (serving size: ³/4 cup).

CALORIES 215; FAT 7.1g (sat 4.5g, mono 1.8g, poly 0.3g); PROTEIN 4.5g; CARB 34.5g; FIBER 2.4g; CHOL 20mg; IRON 0.7mg; SODIUM 280mg; CALC 51mg

## Camembert Mashed Potatoes ▼

The buttery taste and creamy texture of Camembert cheese glorifies these potatoes. Camembert is similar in flavor and texture to Brie, which makes a fine substitute.

 1½ (8-ounce) rounds Camembert cheese
 11 cups cubed peeled Yukon gold potato
    (about 4½ pounds)
 ½ cup 1% low-fat milk
 ¾ teaspoon salt
 ¾ teaspoon freshly ground black pepper
 Chopped fresh chives (optional)
 Freshly ground black pepper (optional)

**1.** Cut cheese into 6 wedges. Carefully remove rind from cheese; discard rind. Chop cheese; let stand at room temperature while potato cooks.
**2.** Place potato in a large Dutch oven; cover with water. Bring to a boil. Reduce heat; simmer 12 minutes or until tender. Drain in a colander; return potato to pan. Add cheese, milk, salt, and $^3/_4$ teaspoon pepper; mash with a potato masher until smooth. Garnish with chives and additional pepper, if desired. **YIELD:** 12 servings (serving size: about $^2/_3$ cup).

CALORIES 198; FAT 4.4g (sat 2.8g, mono 1.3g, poly 0.1g); PROTEIN 7.9g; CARB 30.7g; FIBER 2g; CHOL 13mg; IRON 1.5mg; SODIUM 310mg; CALC 82mg

4

## Mashed Honey-Roasted Sweet Potatoes ▲

Prepare this dish up to a day ahead, and store, covered, in the refrigerator. To reheat, bake at 350°, covered, for 45 minutes.

 6 pounds sweet potatoes, peeled and
    cut into (1-inch) cubes
 Cooking spray
 5 tablespoons honey, divided
 4 tablespoons unsalted butter
 ¾ teaspoon salt

**1.** Preheat oven to 375°.
**2.** Place potato in a single layer on 2 large baking sheets coated with cooking spray. Lightly spray potato with cooking spray. Bake at 375° for 1 hour or until tender, stirring occasionally. Place potato, $^1/_4$ cup honey, butter, and salt in a large bowl, and beat with a mixer at medium speed until smooth. Drizzle with 1 tablespoon honey. **YIELD:** 12 servings (serving size: $^1/_2$ cup).

CALORIES 140; FAT 3.9g (sat 2.4g, mono 1.1g, poly 0.2g); PROTEIN 1.4g; CARB 26.2g; FIBER 2.4g; CHOL 10mg; IRON 0.4mg; SODIUM 154mg; CALC 24mg

3

# 5

## Mashed Yukon Gold Potatoes with Horseradish Butter

Horseradish is such a pungent ingredient that a little goes a long way. If you don't have a ricer or food mill, gently mash the potatoes with a potato masher. Just be sure not to overmash, or they will become rubbery.

Horseradish Butter:

    Cooking spray
  1 tablespoon minced shallots
  ¼ cup butter, softened
  1 tablespoon chopped fresh parsley
  2 teaspoons prepared horseradish

Potatoes:

  6½ cups cubed peeled Yukon gold potato (about 2½ pounds)
  1 bay leaf
  ¼ cup 1% low-fat milk
  ¼ cup fat-free, lower-sodium chicken broth
  ¼ cup reduced-fat sour cream
  1 teaspoon salt
  ¼ teaspoon freshly ground black pepper

**1.** To prepare horseradish butter, heat a small nonstick skillet over medium heat. Coat pan with cooking spray. Add shallots to pan; cook 1 minute. Remove from heat; cool.

**2.** Combine shallots, butter, parsley, and horseradish in a small bowl; blend well. Transfer butter mixture to a sheet of plastic wrap. Shape butter mixture into a 3-inch-long log, using plastic wrap to help mold. Wrap log tightly in plastic wrap, and refrigerate until firm.

**3.** To prepare potatoes, place potato and bay leaf in a large saucepan; cover with water. Bring to a boil. Cover, reduce heat, and simmer 20 minutes or until tender; drain. Discard bay leaf. Press potato through a ricer or food mill into a large bowl. Combine milk and broth in a microwave-safe dish. Microwave at HIGH 1 minute or until warm. Add milk mixture, sour cream, salt, and pepper to potato, stirring until well blended. Serve with horseradish butter.

**YIELD:** 8 servings (serving size: $^1/_2$ cup potatoes and $1^1/_2$ teaspoons horseradish butter).

CALORIES 182; FAT 6.7g (sat 4.2g, mono 1.8g, poly 0.3g); PROTEIN 4g; CARB 26.1g; FIBER 1.8g; CHOL 18mg; IRON 1.3mg; SODIUM 369mg; CALC 21mg

"This recipe was a great change from the usual potato au gratin! I was concerned that our kids would think it was 'icky' because of the strong flavor of the Gorgonzola, but they devoured it!

**from cookinglight.com**

# Potato-Gorgonzola Gratin

2 tablespoons butter
2½ tablespoons all-purpose flour
1 teaspoon chopped fresh thyme
2½ cups fat-free milk
¾ cup (3 ounces) crumbled Gorgonzola
   or other blue cheese
1½ teaspoons salt

¼ teaspoon freshly ground black pepper
3 pounds baking potatoes, peeled and
   cut into ⅛-inch-thick slices
Cooking spray
⅓ cup (1½ ounces) grated Parmigiano-
   Reggiano cheese

**1.** Preheat oven to 375°.

**2.** Melt butter in a small saucepan over medium-high heat. Add flour, and cook 2 minutes, stirring constantly with a whisk. Stir in thyme. Gradually add milk, stirring with a whisk; cook over medium heat until slightly thick (about 3 minutes), stirring constantly. Stir in Gorgonzola; cook 3 minutes or until cheese melts, stirring constantly. Stir in salt and pepper. Remove from heat.

**3.** Arrange one-fourth of potato in bottom of a 13 x 9–inch baking dish coated with cooking spray; spoon about $^3/_4$ cup sauce over potato. Repeat layers twice; arrange remaining potato over sauce. Sprinkle with Parmigiano-Reggiano. Cover and bake at 375° for 30 minutes. Uncover and bake an additional 40 minutes or until potatoes are tender. Remove from oven; let stand 10 minutes before serving. **YIELD:** 8 servings (serving size: about 1 cup).

CALORIES 254; FAT 7.9g (sat 5g, mono 2g, poly 0.2g); PROTEIN 10.6g; CARB 36.8g; FIBER 2.8g; CHOL 22mg; IRON 1.5mg; SODIUM 751mg; CALC 228mg

## what makes it light

- uses a minimal amount of butter
- uses fat-free milk
- uses two strong cheeses, which makes it possible to use less cheese to get great flavor

# 5 ways with

# fries

## Garlic Fries

These fries stand out. First, they're roasted at high heat until crisp and golden. Then they're tossed in melted butter, shredded Parmesan cheese, and chopped fresh parsley for a tasty finishing touch.

- 4 teaspoons canola oil
- ¾ teaspoon salt
- 3 pounds peeled baking potatoes, cut into ¼-inch-thick strips

Cooking spray
- 2 tablespoons butter
- 8 garlic cloves, minced (about 5 teaspoons)
- 2 tablespoons finely chopped fresh parsley
- 2 tablespoons freshly grated Parmesan cheese

**1.** Preheat oven to 400°.

**2.** Combine first 3 ingredients in a large zip-top plastic bag, tossing to coat. Arrange potato in a single layer on a baking sheet coated with cooking spray. Bake at 400° for 50 minutes or until potato is tender and golden brown, turning after 20 minutes.

**3.** Place butter and garlic in a large nonstick skillet, and cook over low heat 2 minutes, stirring constantly. Add potato, parsley, and Parmesan cheese to pan; toss to coat. Serve immediately. **YIELD:** 6 servings.

CALORIES 256; FAT 7.7g (sat 3.3g, mono 2g, poly 2g); PROTEIN 5.9g; CARB 42.3g; FIBER 3.5g; CHOL 12mg; IRON 1.9mg; SODIUM 386mg; CALC 55mg

1

## Oven Fries with Crisp Sage Leaves

As beautiful to look at as they are great to eat, these golden slices of potato are scented and subtly flavored with crisp cooked sage. They are an incredible snack or a perfect savory side to any meal, from chicken to filet mignon. You can double this recipe and use two baking sheets. For even browning, rotate the baking sheets halfway through the first 40 minutes of baking.

- 2 small baking potatoes (about 1 pound)
- 1 tablespoon extra-virgin olive oil
- ½ teaspoon kosher salt
- 12 fresh sage leaves

**1.** Preheat oven to 400°.

**2.** Cut each baking potato lengthwise into 6 equal slices. Place potato slices in a large bowl, and drizzle with olive oil. Sprinkle with salt; toss well to coat potato slices. Remove potato slices from bowl. Reserve remaining olive oil and salt in bowl; set aside. Arrange potato slices in a single layer on a baking sheet.

**3.** Bake at 400° for 40 minutes or until potato slices are golden brown on the bottom. Remove potato slices from oven (leave oven at 400°).

**4.** Add sage leaves to reserved olive oil and salt in bowl. Gently rub sage leaves along bottom of bowl, coating both sides with olive oil and salt. Working with one potato slice at a time, lift potato slice from baking sheet with a thin spatula. Lay 1 sage leaf on baking sheet, and cover with potato slice, browned side down. Repeat with remaining potato slices and sage leaves.

**5.** Bake at 400° for 10 minutes. Remove from heat. Using a thin spatula, carefully turn potato slices over with leaves on top. Bake at 400° for an additional 10 minutes or until bottoms begin to brown. Serve immediately.

**YIELD:** 3 servings (serving size: 4 potato slices).

CALORIES 205; FAT 4.7g (sat 0.7g, mono 3.3g, poly 0.4g); PROTEIN 3.5g; CARB 38.2g; FIBER 3.6g; CHOL 0mg; IRON 2.1mg; SODIUM 326mg; CALC 15mg

2

## Spicy Steak Fries ▼

Best served with burgers or steaks, these thick fries are a welcome change from deep-fried French fries.

- 1 tablespoon vegetable oil
- 2 large baking potatoes, each cut lengthwise into 12 wedges (about 1½ pounds)
- 2 teaspoons seasoning blend (such as Paul Prudhomme's Seafood Magic)
- ¼ teaspoon salt

**1.** Preheat oven to 400°.
**2.** Spread oil on a jelly-roll pan. Place potato wedges on pan. Sprinkle with seasoning; toss gently to coat. Bake at 400° for 40 minutes or until tender. Sprinkle with salt. **YIELD:** 4 servings (serving size: 6 wedges).

CALORIES 216; FAT 3.6g (sat 0.7g, mono 1g, poly 1.7g); PROTEIN 3.7g; CARB 42.9g; FIBER 3.1g; CHOL 0mg; IRON 2.3mg; SODIUM 275mg; CALC 17mg

## Herbed Sweet Potato Fries ▼

We guarantee you can't eat just one. And that's a good thing: Sweet potatoes are rich in beta carotene, vitamin C, and vitamin E.

- 2 cups frozen sweet potato fries (such as Alexia)
- Cooking spray
- 1 teaspoon chopped fresh thyme
- 1 teaspoon chopped fresh rosemary
- ¼ teaspoon salt
- ¼ teaspoon freshly ground black pepper

**1.** Preheat oven to 425°.
**2.** Arrange fries in a single layer on a baking sheet coated with cooking spray. Coat fries evenly with cooking spray; sprinkle remaining ingredients evenly over fries, tossing to coat.
**3.** Bake at 425° for 14 minutes or until golden. **YIELD:** 4 servings (serving size: $^1/_2$ cup).

CALORIES 86; FAT 3g (sat 0.3g, mono 0g, poly 0g); PROTEIN 1.2g; CARB 13.8g; FIBER 1.8g; CHOL 0mg; IRON 0.5mg; SODIUM 225mg; CALC 25mg

3  4

**5**

## Spicy Sweet Potato Fries

2½ cups frozen sweet potato fries
Butter-flavored cooking spray
¼ teaspoon kosher salt
⅛ teaspoon ground red pepper

**1.** Preheat oven to 425°.
**2.** Place potatoes in a single layer on a large baking sheet coated with cooking spray. Coat potatoes with cooking spray.
**3.** Bake at 425° for 16 minutes or until crisp and golden.
**4.** Combine salt and ground pepper in a small bowl. Remove fries from oven, and sprinkle with salt mixture. **YIELD:** 4 servings (serving size: ¹/₂ cup).

CALORIES 202; FAT 8.2g (sat 1.7g, mono 3.7g, poly 2.3g); PROTEIN 2.7g; CARB 32.1g; FIBER 4.1g; CHOL 0mg; IRON 1mg; SODIUM 304mg; CALC 54mg

"This dish was amazing! Took it to a dinner party, and everyone loved it! **This was my first time making a sweet potato casserole, and it was surprisingly simple.** Make sure to not skip the broiling part—it gives the crumble on top the perfect crunch! This is definitely a keeper! Thanks for another good recipe CL!"

**from cookinglight.com**

# Sweet Potato Casserole

Potatoes:

2 pounds sweet potatoes, peeled and chopped
¾ cup granulated sugar
¼ cup evaporated low-fat milk
3 tablespoons butter, melted
½ teaspoon salt
1 teaspoon vanilla extract
2 large eggs
Cooking spray

Topping:

1.5 ounces all-purpose flour (about ⅓ cup)
⅔ cup packed brown sugar
⅛ teaspoon salt
2 tablespoons melted butter
½ cup chopped pecans

**1.** Preheat oven to 350°.

**2.** To prepare potatoes, place potato in a Dutch oven; cover with water. Bring to a boil. Reduce heat, and simmer 20 minutes or until tender; drain. Cool 5 minutes.

**3.** Place potato in a large bowl; add granulated sugar, evaporated milk, 3 tablespoons melted butter, $^{1}/_{2}$ teaspoon salt, and vanilla. Beat with a mixer at medium speed until smooth. Add eggs; beat well. Pour potato mixture into a 13 x 9–inch baking pan coated with cooking spray.

**4.** To prepare topping, weigh or lightly spoon flour into a dry measuring cup; level with a knife. Combine flour, brown sugar, and $^{1}/_{8}$ teaspoon salt; stir with a whisk. Stir in 2 tablespoons melted butter. Sprinkle flour mixture evenly over potato mixture; arrange pecans evenly over top. Bake at 350° for 25 minutes or just until golden. Remove casserole from oven.

**5.** Preheat broiler.

**6.** Broil casserole 45 seconds or until topping is bubbly. Let stand 10 minutes before serving.

**YIELD:** 12 servings (serving size: about $^{2}/_{3}$ cup).

CALORIES 258; FAT 9.2g (sat 3.6g, mono 3.6g, poly 1.5g); PROTEIN 3.3g; CARB 42g; FIBER 2.5g; CHOL 43mg; IRON 1.2mg; SODIUM 199mg; CALC 54mg

## what makes it light

- uses less sugar than traditional recipes
- uses evaporated low-fat milk
- uses a minimal amount of butter

**Easy to prepare and rich in flavor,** the casserole pairs fabulously with roasted chicken, ham, or pork chops. This simple dish has become a staff favorite, and we believe it will be in your home, too.

# Squash-Rice Casserole

8 cups sliced zucchini (about
   2½ pounds)
1 cup chopped onion
½ cup fat-free, lower-sodium chicken
   broth
2 cups cooked rice
1 cup (4 ounces) shredded reduced-fat
   sharp cheddar cheese

1 cup fat-free sour cream
¼ cup (1 ounce) grated fresh Parmesan
   cheese, divided
¼ cup Italian-seasoned breadcrumbs
1 teaspoon salt
¼ teaspoon black pepper
2 large eggs, lightly beaten
Cooking spray

**1.** Preheat oven to 350°.
**2.** Combine first 3 ingredients in a Dutch oven; bring to a boil. Cover, reduce heat, and simmer 20 minutes or until tender. Drain; partially mash with a potato masher.
**3.** Combine zucchini mixture, rice, cheddar cheese, sour cream, 2 tablespoons Parmesan cheese, breadcrumbs, salt, pepper, and eggs in a bowl; stir gently. Spoon mixture into a 13 x 9–inch baking dish coated with cooking spray; sprinkle with remaining 2 tablespoons Parmesan cheese. Bake at 350° for 30 minutes or until bubbly. Remove casserole from oven.
**4.** Preheat broiler. Broil 1 minute or until lightly browned. **YIELD:** 8 servings (serving size: 1 cup).

CALORIES 197; FAT 5.5g (sat 2.7g, mono 1.5g, poly 0.4g); PROTEIN 12.7g; CARB 24g; FIBER 1.4g; CHOL 65mg; IRON 1.5mg; SODIUM 623mg; CALC 209mg

## what makes it light

- uses fat-free, lower-sodium chicken broth
- uses reduced-fat sharp cheddar cheese
- uses fat-free sour cream

**Here's our lightened rendition of a traditional yellow squash casserole;** it's just as delicious, just minus the guilt. Meat-and-three casseroles are usually laden with mayo, cream, butter, cheese, or any combination of the four.

# Yellow Squash Casserole

8 cups sliced yellow squash (about 2 pounds)
1 tablespoon water
6 ounces hot turkey Italian sausage (about 2 links)
½ cup chopped onion
2 garlic cloves, minced
2 (1-ounce) slices day-old white bread
½ cup fat-free sour cream
⅓ cup (1½ ounces) diced provolone cheese
¼ teaspoon salt
¼ teaspoon black pepper
1 (10¾-ounce) can condensed reduced-fat, reduced-sodium cream of mushroom soup, undiluted
Cooking spray

**1.** Preheat oven to 350°.
**2.** Combine squash and water in a large microwave-safe bowl. Cover with plastic wrap; vent. Microwave at HIGH 6 to 10 minutes or until tender. Drain well.
**3.** Remove casing from sausage. Cook sausage, onion, and garlic in a large nonstick skillet over medium-high heat until browned, stirring to crumble. Drain.
**4.** Place bread in a food processor, and pulse 10 times or until coarse crumbs form to measure 1 cup. Combine squash, sausage mixture, $^1/_2$ cup breadcrumbs, sour cream, cheese, salt, pepper, and soup. Spoon squash mixture into a 2-quart casserole coated with cooking spray.
**5.** Top with remaining $^1/_2$ cup breadcrumbs. Spray breadcrumbs with cooking spray. Bake at 350° for 30 minutes. **YIELD:** 12 servings (serving size: $^2/_3$ cup).

CALORIES 85; FAT 2.9g (sat 1.2g, mono 0.5g, poly 0.6g); PROTEIN 4.8g; CARB 10.3g; FIBER 1.8g; CHOL 12mg; IRON 0.7mg; SODIUM 279mg; CALC 91mg

**?** **what makes it light**
- uses turkey Italian sausage
- uses fat-free sour cream
- uses reduced-fat, reduced-sodium cream of mushroom soup

# 5 ways with

# cookies

## Snickerdoodles

Extremely easy to make, these cookies are just as good for a special occasion as they are an everyday snack.

- 7.9 ounces all-purpose flour (about 1¾ cups)
- ½ teaspoon baking soda
- ½ teaspoon cream of tartar
- 1 cup sugar
- ¼ cup butter, softened
- 1 tablespoon corn syrup
- 1 teaspoon vanilla
- 1 large egg
- 3 tablespoons sugar
- 2 teaspoons ground cinnamon
- Cooking spray

**1.** Preheat oven to 375°.

**2.** Weigh or lightly spoon flour into dry measuring cups; level with a knife. Combine flour, baking soda, and cream of tartar, stirring with a whisk.

**3.** Combine 1 cup sugar and butter in a large bowl, and beat with a mixer at medium speed until well blended. Add corn syrup, vanilla, and egg; beat well. Gradually add flour mixture to sugar mixture, beating just until combined. Cover and chill 10 minutes.

**4.** Combine 3 tablespoons sugar and cinnamon, stirring with a whisk.

**5.** With moist hands, shape dough into 42 (1-inch) balls. Roll balls in sugar mixture. Place balls 2 inches apart onto baking sheets coated with cooking spray. Flatten balls with bottom of a glass. Bake at 375° for 5 minutes (cookies will be slightly soft). Cool on baking sheets 2 minutes. Remove cookies from pans; cool completely on wire racks. **YIELD:** 42 cookies (serving size: 1 cookie).

CALORIES 54; FAT 1.3g (sat 0.7g, mono 0.1g, poly 0.4g); PROTEIN 0.7g; CARB 10.1g; FIBER 0.2g; CHOL 8mg; IRON 0.3mg; SODIUM 28mg; CALC 3mg

1

## 2

## Lemon-Honey Drop Cookies

One cookinglight.com reader describes these cookies as "little lemony morsels of loveliness." We think you'll wholeheartedly agree.

- ½ cup granulated sugar
- 7 tablespoons butter, softened
- 2 teaspoons grated lemon rind
- ⅓ cup honey
- ½ teaspoon lemon extract
- 1 large egg
- 7.9 ounces all-purpose flour (about 1¾ cups)
- 1 teaspoon baking powder
- ½ teaspoon salt
- ¼ cup plain fat-free yogurt
- Cooking spray
- 1 cup powdered sugar
- 2 tablespoons fresh lemon juice
- 2 teaspoons grated lemon rind

**1.** Preheat oven to 350°.

**2.** Beat first 3 ingredients with a mixer at medium speed until light and fluffy. Add honey, extract, and egg; beat until well blended. Weigh or lightly spoon flour into dry measuring cups; level with a knife. Combine flour, baking powder, and salt, stirring well with a whisk. Add flour mixture to sugar mixture alternately with yogurt, beginning and ending with flour mixture. Drop by level tablespoons 2 inches apart onto baking sheets coated with cooking spray. Bake at 350° for 12 minutes or until lightly browned.

**3.** Combine powdered sugar and juice in a small bowl; stir with a whisk. Brush powdered sugar mixture evenly over hot cookies. Sprinkle evenly with 2 teaspoons rind. Remove cookies from pan; cool on wire racks. **YIELD:** 32 cookies (serving size: 1 cookie).

CALORIES 89; FAT 2.8g (sat 1.6g, mono 0.8g, poly 0.2g); PROTEIN 1.1g; CARB 15.3g; FIBER 0.2g; CHOL 14mg; IRON 0.4mg; SODIUM 81mg; CALC 15mg

## Chocolate Chip Cookies ▼

Store up to one week in an airtight container—if they last that long. We suggest keeping a dozen in the freezer for emergencies.

- 10 ounces all-purpose flour (about 2¼ cups)
- 1 teaspoon baking soda
- ¼ teaspoon salt
- 1 cup packed brown sugar
- ¾ cup granulated sugar
- ½ cup butter, softened
- 1 teaspoon vanilla extract
- 2 large egg whites
- ¾ cup semisweet chocolate chips
- Cooking spray

**1.** Preheat oven to 350°.
**2.** Weigh or lightly spoon flour into dry measuring cups; level with a knife. Combine flour, baking soda, and salt, stirring with a whisk.
**3.** Combine sugars and butter in a large bowl; beat with a mixer at medium speed until well blended. Add vanilla and egg whites; beat 1 minute. Add flour mixture and chips; beat until blended.

**4.** Drop dough by level tablespoons 2 inches apart onto baking sheets coated with cooking spray. Bake at 350° for 10 minutes or until lightly browned. Cool on pans 2 minutes. Remove from pans; cool completely on wire racks. **YIELD:** 4 dozen (serving size: 1 cookie).

CALORIES 88; FAT 3g (sat 1.8g, mono 0.5g, poly 0.1g); PROTEIN 1g; CARB 14.6g; FIBER 0.2g; CHOL 5mg; IRON 0.4mg; SODIUM 56mg; CALC 5mg

## Peanut Butter Icebox Cookies ▼

For a chocolate-peanut butter variation add one ounce of grated semisweet chocolate to the flour mixture.

- 4.5 ounces all-purpose flour (about 1 cup)
- ¼ teaspoon baking soda
- ⅛ teaspoon salt
- 3 tablespoons butter, softened
- 2 tablespoons chunky peanut butter
- ½ cup packed brown sugar
- ¼ cup granulated sugar
- 1 teaspoon vanilla extract
- 1 large egg white
- Cooking spray

3

4

**1.** Weigh or lightly spoon flour into a dry measuring cup; level with a knife. Combine flour, baking soda, and salt; set aside. Beat butter and peanut butter at medium speed of a mixer until light and fluffy. Gradually add sugars, beating at medium speed until well blended. Add vanilla and egg white, and beat well. Add flour mixture; stir well. Turn dough out onto wax paper; shape into a 6-inch log. Wrap log in wax paper; freeze 3 hours.

**2.** Preheat oven to 350°.

**3.** Cut log into 24 ($^{1}/_{4}$-inch) slices, and place slices 1 inch apart on a baking sheet coated with cooking spray. Bake at 350° for 8 to 10 minutes. Remove from pan, and cool on wire racks. **YIELD:** 2 dozen (serving size: 1 cookie).

CALORIES 69; FAT 2.4g (sat 0.4g, mono 0.7g, poly 0.5g); PROTEIN 1.2g; CARB 10.8g; FIBER 0.2g; CHOL 9mg; IRON 0.4mg; SODIUM 53mg; CALC 7mg

## Oatmeal-Raisin Cookies ▶

Fast, simple, and satisfying, oatmeal-raisin cookies are a sure-to-please staple in the American home. They're easy to prepare because they're made with ingredients you probably have on hand.

> ½ cup granulated sugar
> ½ cup packed brown sugar
> ⅓ cup butter, softened
> 1 teaspoon vanilla extract
> ⅛ teaspoon salt
> 1 large egg
> 4.5 ounces all-purpose flour (about 1 cup)
> 1 cup regular oats
> ½ cup raisins
> Cooking spray

**1.** Preheat oven to 350°.

**2.** Beat first 6 ingredients at medium speed of a mixer until light and fluffy. Weigh or lightly spoon flour into a dry measuring cup, and level with a knife. Add flour and oats to egg mixture; beat until blended. Stir in raisins. Drop by level tablespoons 2 inches apart onto baking sheets coated with cooking spray. Bake at 350° for 15 minutes or until golden brown. Cool on pan 3 minutes. Remove cookies from pan; cool on wire racks. **YIELD:** 2 dozen (serving size: 1 cookie).

CALORIES 101; FAT 3.1g (sat 1.7g, mono 0.9g, poly 0.2g); PROTEIN 1.5g; CARB 17.3g; FIBER 0.6g; CHOL 16mg; IRON 0.6mg; SODIUM 43mg; CALC 10mg

"These are perfect!!! They remind me of my childhood and those muggy southern summer afternoons spent by my neighbor's pool. They are smooth and sweet and tangy, finishing with an unexpected crunch. **The combination of textures is addictive if the flavor isn't already enough to hook you.** I finished them with a light dusting of powdered sugar. Next time I will use a doily as a stencil before I powder them up for added elegance."

**from cookinglight.com**

# Easy Lemon Squares

Crust:
- ¼ cup granulated sugar
- 3 tablespoons butter, softened
- 4.5 ounces all-purpose flour (about 1 cup)

Topping:
- 3 large eggs
- ¾ cup granulated sugar
- 2 teaspoons grated lemon rind
- ⅓ cup fresh lemon juice
- 3 tablespoons all-purpose flour
- ½ teaspoon baking powder
- ⅛ teaspoon salt
- 2 teaspoons powdered sugar

**1.** Preheat oven to 350°.

**2.** To prepare crust, beat ¼ cup granulated sugar and butter at medium speed of a mixer until creamy. Weigh or lightly spoon 4.5 ounces flour into a dry measuring cup; level with a knife. Gradually add flour to sugar mixture, beating at low speed until mixture resembles fine crumbs. Gently press mixture into bottom of an 8-inch square baking pan. Bake at 350° for 15 minutes; cool on a wire rack.

**3.** To prepare topping, beat eggs at medium speed until foamy. Add ¾ cup granulated sugar and next 5 ingredients, and beat until well blended. Pour mixture over partially baked crust. Bake at 350° for 20 to 25 minutes or until set. Cool on wire rack. Sift powdered sugar evenly over top.

**YIELD:** 16 servings (serving size: 1 square).

CALORIES 118; FAT 3.2g (sat 1.7g, mono 1g, poly 0.3g); PROTEIN 2.2g; CARB 20.5g; FIBER 0.3g; CHOL 47mg; IRON 0.6mg; SODIUM 68mg; CALC 16mg

## what makes it light

- uses less butter than traditional recipes
- uses fewer eggs than traditional recipes

# recipe makeover
# butterscotch bars

**The Reader:** Carol Bischoff

**The Story:** Carol has always had a sweet tooth. She says these rich butterscotch bars, with a buttery crust and gooey-nutty center, are irresistible. But she and her husband now have goals to stay fit and eat more healthfully, so she sent the recipe to *Cooking Light* for a makeover.

**The Dilemma:** Plenty of butter, butterscotch chips, sweetened condensed milk, and walnuts contributed to the hefty 223 calories per serving. One bar had 5 grams of saturated fat per serving, about one-third the daily allotment per American Heart Association diet recommendations.

**The Solution:** We started with the middle layer. First, we swapped fat-free sweetened condensed milk for the regular version to maintain sweetness and richness with fewer calories. Then we reduced the amount of butterscotch chips by a third and omitted 2 tablespoons butter in this part of the recipe without compromising flavor or texture. These three changes trimmed 42 calories

and 2½ grams of fat (nearly 2 grams saturated) per serving. We also slightly tweaked the base layer, which serves double-duty as the crumb topping. Eliminating 3 tablespoons of butter and ½ cup brown sugar shaved 20 calories and 1 gram of fat per bar. Lastly, to keep calories in check, we used fewer walnuts and finely chopped and toasted them to extend their flavor and crunch. This cut another 10 calories and about 1 gram of fat.

**The Feedback:** Carol and her husband liked the lighter bars. Her husband thought the oatmeal was more prominent, which added a pleasingly hearty texture to the dessert. "There were many excellent changes, and I like this healthier version of my longtime dessert favorite," Carol says.

| | BEFORE | AFTER |
|---|---|---|
| Calories per serving | 223 | 148 |
| Fat | 9.8g | 5.1g |
| Percent of total calories | 5.4% | 2.7% |

**A small square of these rich bars is enough to satisfy a dessert craving.** The flour and oats mixture is somewhat dry after combining, but it serves as both a solid base for the soft butterscotch chip layer and a crumbly, streusel-like topping.

# Butterscotch Bars

1 cup packed brown sugar
5 tablespoons butter, melted
1 teaspoon vanilla extract
1 large egg, lightly beaten
9 ounces all-purpose flour (about 2 cups)
2½ cups quick-cooking oats
½ teaspoon salt

½ teaspoon baking soda
Cooking spray
¾ cup fat-free sweetened condensed milk
1¼ cups butterscotch morsels (about 8 ounces)
⅛ teaspoon salt
½ cup finely chopped walnuts, toasted

**1.** Preheat oven to 350°.

**2.** Combine sugar and butter in a large bowl. Stir in vanilla and egg. Weigh or lightly spoon flour into dry measuring cups; level with a knife. Combine flour, oats, $1/2$ teaspoon salt, and baking soda in a bowl. Add oat mixture to sugar mixture; stir with a fork until combined (mixture will be crumbly). Place 3 cups oat mixture into the bottom of a 13 x 9–inch baking pan coated with cooking spray; press into bottom of pan. Set aside.

**3.** Place sweetened condensed milk, butterscotch morsels, and $1/8$ teaspoon salt in a microwave-safe bowl; microwave at HIGH 1 minute or until butterscotch morsels melt, stirring every 20 seconds. Stir in walnuts. Scrape mixture into prepared pan, spreading evenly over crust. Sprinkle evenly with remaining oat mixture, gently pressing into butterscotch mixture. Bake at 350° for 30 minutes or until topping is golden brown. Place pan on a wire rack; run a knife around outside edge. Cool completely. **YIELD:** 36 servings (serving size: 1 bar).

CALORIES 148; FAT 5.1g (sat 2.7g, mono 0.9g, poly 1.1g); PROTEIN 2.6g; CARB 23.4g; FIBER 0.8g; CHOL 11mg; IRON 0.8mg; SODIUM 87mg; CALC 31mg

"The hard thing to remember is this: just because they're lower in fat, doesn't mean you can eat half the pan. Hahaha! **These are very tasty brownies, and have been a big hit every time I've made them.**"

**from cookinglight.com**

# Ooey-Gooey Peanut Butter-Chocolate Brownies

¾ cup fat-free sweetened condensed milk, divided
¼ cup butter, melted and cooled
¼ cup fat-free milk
1 (18.25-ounce) package devil's food cake mix

1 large egg white, lightly beaten
Cooking spray
1 (7-ounce) jar marshmallow creme (about 1¾ cups)
½ cup peanut butter morsels

**1.** Preheat oven to 350°.

**2.** Combine ¼ cup condensed milk, butter, and next 3 ingredients in a bowl (batter will be very stiff). Coat bottom of a 13 x 9–inch baking pan with cooking spray. Press two-thirds of batter into prepared pan using floured hands; pat evenly (layer will be thin).

**3.** Bake at 350° for 10 minutes. Combine ½ cup condensed milk and marshmallow creme in a bowl; stir in morsels. Spread marshmallow mixture evenly over brownie layer. Carefully drop remaining batter by spoonfuls over marshmallow mixture. Bake at 350° for 27 to 30 minutes. Cool completely in pan on a wire rack. **YIELD:** 2 dozen (serving size: 1 brownie).

CALORIES 176; FAT 5g (sat 2.1g, mono 1.6g, poly 1.1g); PROTEIN 2.6g; CARB 29.9g; FIBER 0.8g; CHOL 6mg; IRON 0.8mg; SODIUM 212mg; CALC 30mg

## what makes it light

- uses fat-free sweetened condensed milk
- uses a minimal amount of butter
- uses fat-free milk
- uses an egg white instead of a whole egg

"Having been raised on 'the real thing,' with gobs of eggs and full-fat cream cheese, I was skeptical—but this was fabulous! **The texture was right on, and the taste was wonderful.** For cheese-cake I'll use this recipe exclusively from now on. If you make this for guests they probably will never know it's low fat unless you tell them!"

from cookinglight.com

# New York Cheesecake

Crust:

3 ounces all-purpose flour (about ⅔ cup)

3 tablespoons sugar

2 tablespoons chilled butter, cut into small pieces

1 tablespoon ice water

Cooking spray

Filling:

4 cups fat-free cottage cheese

2 cups sugar

2 (8-ounce) blocks ⅓-less-fat cream cheese, softened

1.1 ounces all-purpose flour (about ¼ cup)

½ cup fat-free sour cream

1 tablespoon grated lemon rind

1 tablespoon vanilla extract

¼ teaspoon salt

5 large eggs

**1.** Preheat oven to 400°.

**2.** To prepare crust, weigh or lightly spoon 3 ounces flour into a dry measuring cup; level with a knife. Place flour and 3 tablespoons sugar in a food processor; pulse 2 times or until combined. Add butter; pulse 6 times or until mixture resembles coarse meal. With processor on, slowly pour ice water through food chute, processing just until blended (do not allow dough to form a ball).

**3.** Firmly press mixture into bottom of a 9-inch springform pan coated with cooking spray. Bake at 400° for 10 minutes or until lightly browned; cool on a wire rack.

**4.** Reduce oven temperature to 325°.

**5.** To prepare filling, strain cottage cheese through a cheesecloth-lined sieve for 10 minutes; discard liquid. Place cottage cheese in food processor; process until smooth.

**6.** Place 2 cups sugar and cream cheese in a large bowl; beat with a mixer at medium speed until smooth. Weigh or lightly spoon 1.1 ounces flour into a dry measuring cup; level with a knife. Add flour, sour cream, and remaining ingredients to cream cheese mixture; beat well. Add cottage cheese, stirring until well blended. Pour mixture into prepared crust.

**7.** Bake at 325° for 1 hour and 30 minutes or until almost set. Turn oven off. Cool cheesecake in closed oven 1 hour. Remove cheesecake from oven; run a knife around outside edge. Cool to room temperature. Cover and chill at least 8 hours. **YIELD:** 16 servings (serving size: 1 wedge).

**Note:** You can also make the cheesecake in a 10 x 2½–inch springform pan. Bake at 300° for 1 hour and 30 minutes or until almost set. Turn oven off. Cool cheesecake in closed oven 30 minutes.

CALORIES 291; FAT 9.8g (sat 5.7g, mono 3g, poly 0.5g); PROTEIN 12.9g; CARB 37.7g; FIBER 0.2g; CHOL 98mg; IRON 0.7mg; SODIUM 410mg; CALC 93mg

# recipe makeover
## sour cream pound cake

**The Reader:** Don Milburn

**The Story:** Don loves to cook and has always enjoyed the recipe for this cake, given to him by his mother. But he came to us for help because "all the old-time recipes never considered calories or fat content."

**The Dilemma:** This cake was indeed heavy, weighed down by 2½ sticks of butter and a cup of sour cream.

**The Solution:** We didn't want to lose any lushness in the cake, so we only slightly decreased the amount of butter from 1 cup to ¾ cup—cutting about 30 calories and 3 grams of fat from each slice. Switching to fat-free sour cream removed another 3 grams of fat from each serving. Using only 1½ tablespoons of butter instead of 4 tablespoons for the glaze shaved almost 2 grams of fat per serving. To replace flavor lost in the glaze, we switched from granulated sugar to brown sugar, which has a rich, full caramel-like flavor.

**The Feedback:** Don enjoyed our version so much that he made it for a family celebration. He didn't tell anyone in the family that it was a light adaptation, and "no one knew there was a difference."

|  | BEFORE | AFTER |
|---|---|---|
| Calories per serving | 427 | 325 |
| Fat | 19.4g | 11g |
| Percent of total calories | 41% | 30% |

# Sour Cream Pound Cake with Rum Glaze

Cake:

Cooking spray
- 3 tablespoons dry breadcrumbs
- 12 ounces cake flour (about 3 cups)
- 1 teaspoon baking powder
- ¼ teaspoon baking soda
- ¼ teaspoon salt
- ¾ cup butter, softened
- 2 cups granulated sugar
- 3 large eggs

- ¼ cup fat-free milk
- 1 tablespoon dark rum
- 2 teaspoons vanilla extract
- 1 cup fat-free sour cream

Glaze:
- ½ cup packed brown sugar
- 2 tablespoons dark rum
- 2 tablespoons water
- 1½ tablespoons butter

**1.** Preheat oven to 350°.

**2.** To prepare cake, coat a 10-inch tube pan with cooking spray; dust with breadcrumbs. Set aside.

**3.** Weigh or lightly spoon flour into dry measuring cups; level with a knife. Combine flour, baking powder, baking soda, and salt, stirring well with a whisk. Place butter and granulated sugar in a large bowl; beat with a mixer at medium speed until light and fluffy. Add eggs, 1 at a time, beating well after each addition. Add milk, 1 tablespoon rum, and vanilla; beat until combined. Beating at low speed, add flour mixture and sour cream alternately to sugar mixture, beginning and ending with flour mixture; beat until just combined.

**4.** Spoon batter into prepared pan. Bake at 350° for 1 hour or until a wooden pick inserted in center comes out clean. Cool in pan 10 minutes. Loosen cake from sides of pan using a narrow metal spatula. Place a plate upside down on top of cake; invert onto plate. Invert cake again. Pierce cake liberally with a wooden pick.

**5.** While cake bakes, prepare glaze. Combine brown sugar, 2 tablespoons rum, and water in a small saucepan; bring to a boil, stirring until sugar dissolves. Add $1^1/_2$ tablespoons butter, stirring until butter melts. Drizzle half of warm glaze evenly over warm cake; allow mixture to absorb into cake. Drizzle remaining glaze over cake. Cool cake completely. **YIELD:** 16 servings (serving size: 1 slice).

CALORIES 325; FAT 11g (sat 6.3g, mono 3.2g, poly 0.5g); PROTEIN 3.6g; FIBER 0.6g; CHOL 68mg; IRON 1.5mg; SODIUM 232mg; CALC 58mg

# 5 ways with

# cakes

## Texas Sheet Cake

Rich in chocolate, this easy charmer boasts a sweet, fudgy icing that would melt in your mouth if not for the pecans.

        Cooking spray
    2  teaspoons all-purpose flour
    9  ounces all-purpose flour (about 2 cups)
    2  cups granulated sugar
    1  teaspoon baking soda
    1  teaspoon ground cinnamon
    ¼  teaspoon salt
    ¾  cup water
    ½  cup butter
    ½  cup unsweetened cocoa, divided
    ½  cup low-fat buttermilk
    1  tablespoon vanilla extract, divided
    2  large eggs
    6  tablespoons butter
    ⅓  cup fat-free milk
    3  cups powdered sugar
    ¼  cup chopped pecans, toasted

**1.** Preheat oven to 375°.
**2.** Coat a 13 x 9–inch pan with cooking spray, and dust with 2 teaspoons flour. Set aside.
**3.** Weigh or lightly spoon 9 ounces flour into dry measuring cups; level with a knife. Combine flour and next 4 ingredients in a large bowl, stirring well with a whisk. Combine $^{3}/_{4}$ cup water, $^{1}/_{2}$ cup butter, and $^{1}/_{4}$ cup cocoa in a small saucepan; bring to a boil, stirring frequently. Add to flour mixture. Beat at medium speed with an electric mixer until well blended. Add buttermilk, 1 teaspoon vanilla, and eggs; beat well. Pour batter into prepared pan. Bake at 375° for 22 minutes or until a wooden pick inserted in center comes out clean. Place on a wire rack.
**4.** Combine 6 tablespoons butter, fat-free milk, and remaining $^{1}/_{4}$ cup cocoa in a saucepan; bring to a boil, stirring constantly. Remove from heat. Gradually stir in powdered sugar and remaining 2 teaspoons vanilla. Spread over hot cake. Sprinkle cake with pecans. Cool completely on wire rack. **YIELD:** 20 servings (serving size: 1 piece).

CALORIES 298; FAT 10g (sat 5.5g, mono 3.2g, poly 0.7g); PROTEIN 3.1g; CARB 49.8g; FIBER 0.5g; CHOL 44mg; IRON 1.1mg; SODIUM 188mg; CALC 25mg

1

# Cranberry Upside-Down Coffee Cake

Serve this buttery cake for a make-ahead brunch dish or at the end of a casual meal.

**Cake:**
- Cooking spray
- 1 tablespoon all-purpose flour
- 1 cup fresh cranberries
- ½ cup coarsely chopped pitted dates
- 2 tablespoons chopped walnuts
- 1 teaspoon grated orange rind
- ½ cup butter, softened and divided
- ½ cup packed dark brown sugar
- 2 tablespoons fresh orange juice
- ¼ teaspoon ground cinnamon
- 6.75 ounces all-purpose flour (about 1½ cups)
- 1 teaspoon baking powder
- ½ teaspoon salt
- 1 cup granulated sugar
- 1 teaspoon vanilla
- 1 large egg
- ½ cup nonfat buttermilk

**Glaze:**
- 1 cup powdered sugar
- 1 teaspoon butter, melted
- 2 tablespoons fresh orange juice

**1.** Preheat oven to 350°.

**2.** To prepare cake, coat a 9-inch square baking pan with cooking spray; dust with 1 tablespoon flour. Combine cranberries, dates, walnuts, and rind in a bowl. Melt 2 tablespoons butter in a small saucepan over medium heat. Stir in brown sugar, 2 tablespoons juice, and cinnamon; cook 3 minutes, stirring constantly. Pour brown sugar mixture into prepared pan. Sprinkle cranberry mixture evenly over brown sugar mixture.

**3.** Weigh or lightly spoon 6.75 ounces flour into dry measuring cups; level with a knife. Combine flour, baking powder, and salt in a bowl, stirring well with a whisk. Place granulated sugar and remaining 6 tablespoons butter in a large bowl; beat with a mixer at medium speed until well blended. Add vanilla and egg; beat well. Add flour mixture and buttermilk alternately to granulated sugar mixture, beginning and ending with flour mixture. Spoon batter over cranberry mixture.

**4.** Bake at 350° for 40 minutes or until a wooden pick inserted in center comes out clean. Cool in pan 5 minutes on a wire rack; run a knife around outside edges. Invert cake onto a plate; cool.

**5.** To prepare glaze, combine powdered sugar and remaining ingredients in a small bowl, stirring until smooth. Drizzle over cake. Cut cake into squares. **YIELD:** 12 servings (serving size: 1 square).

CALORIES 312; FAT 9.1g (sat 5.1g, mono 1g, poly 2.3g); PROTEIN 3g; CARB 55.7g; FIBER 1.4g; CHOL 39mg; IRON 1.2mg; SODIUM 236mg; CALC 32mg

# 3

## Carrot Cake with Toasted Coconut Cream Cheese Frosting

This cake keeps for up to three days in the refrigerator and also freezes well.

Cake:

- 3.4 ounces all-purpose flour (about ¾ cup)
- ¼ cup quick-cooking oats
- 1½ teaspoons ground cinnamon
- 1 teaspoon baking powder
- ½ teaspoon baking soda
- ¼ teaspoon salt
- 1 cup granulated sugar
- ¼ cup canola oil
- 1 (2½-ounce) jar carrot baby food
- 2 large eggs, lightly beaten
- 1¼ cups finely grated carrot (about 4 ounces)
- ½ cup golden raisins
- Cooking spray

Frosting:

- ⅓ cup (3 ounces) ⅓-less-fat cream cheese, softened
- 1 tablespoon butter, softened
- 1¼ cups powdered sugar, sifted
- ½ teaspoon vanilla extract
- ¼ cup flaked sweetened coconut, toasted

**1.** Preheat oven to 325°.
**2.** To prepare cake, weigh or lightly spoon flour into a dry measuring cup; level with a knife. Place flour and next 5 ingredients in a food processor; pulse 6 times or until well blended. Place flour mixture in a large bowl. Combine granulated sugar, canola oil, baby food, and eggs; stir with a whisk. Add to flour mixture; stir just until moist. Stir in grated carrot and raisins. Spoon batter into an 8-inch square baking pan coated with cooking spray.
**3.** Bake at 325° for 40 minutes or until a wooden pick inserted in center comes out clean. Cool in pan on a wire rack.
**4.** To prepare frosting, combine cream cheese and butter in a large bowl. Beat with a mixer at high speed until creamy. Gradually add powdered sugar and vanilla, beating at low speed until smooth (do not overbeat). Spread over cake; sprinkle with coconut. Cover and chill. **YIELD:** 12 servings (serving size: 1 piece).

CALORIES 262; FAT 8.8g (sat 2.7g, mono 3.6g, poly 1.6g); PROTEIN 3.2g; CARB 44.1g; FIBER 1.2g; CHOL 44mg; IRON 0.9mg; SODIUM 201mg; CALC 47mg

## Old-Fashioned Caramel Layer Cake

Hands down, this is one of the best-tasting cake recipes we have ever created. The caramel frosting is sweet perfection.

Cake:

- Cooking spray
- 1 tablespoon all-purpose flour
- 1½ cups granulated sugar
- ½ cup butter, softened
- 2 large eggs
- 1 large egg white
- 10.1 ounces all-purpose flour (about 2¼ cups)
- 2½ teaspoons baking powder
- ½ teaspoon salt
- 1¼ cups fat-free milk
- 2 teaspoons vanilla extract

Frosting:

- 1 cup packed dark brown sugar
- ½ cup evaporated fat-free milk
- 2½ tablespoons butter
- 2 teaspoons light-colored corn syrup
- Dash of salt
- 2 cups powdered sugar
- 2½ teaspoons vanilla extract

**1.** Preheat oven to 350°.

**2.** To prepare cake, coat 2 (9-inch) round cake pans with cooking spray; line bottoms with wax paper. Coat wax paper with cooking spray; dust with 1 tablespoon flour.

**3.** Beat granulated sugar and $^1/_2$ cup butter at medium speed of a mixer until well blended (about 5 minutes). Add eggs and egg white, 1 at a time, beating well after each addition. Weigh or lightly spoon 10.1 ounces flour into dry measuring cups; level with a knife. Combine flour, baking powder, and salt; stir well with a whisk. Add flour mixture to sugar mixture alternately with $1^1/_4$ cups milk, beginning and ending with flour mixture. Stir in 2 teaspoons vanilla.

**4.** Pour batter into prepared pans, and sharply tap pans once on counter to remove air bubbles. Bake at 350° for 30 minutes or until a wooden pick inserted in center comes out clean. Cool in pans 10 minutes on a wire rack; remove from pans. Carefully peel off wax paper; cool completely on wire rack.

**5.** To prepare frosting, combine brown sugar and next 4 ingredients in a medium saucepan, and bring to a boil over medium-high heat, stirring constantly. Reduce heat, and simmer until thick (about 5 minutes), stirring occasionally. Remove from heat. Add powdered sugar and $2^1/_2$ teaspoons vanilla; beat at medium speed of a mixer until smooth and slightly warm. Cool 2 to 3 minutes (frosting will be thin but thickens as it cools).

**6.** Place 1 cake layer on a plate; spoon $^1/_2$ cup frosting on to cake layer spreading to cover. Top with remaining cake layer. Frost top and sides of cake. Store cake loosely covered in refrigerator. **YIELD:** 18 servings (serving size: 1 slice).

CALORIES 307; FAT 7.5g (sat 4.4g, mono 2.2g, poly 0.4g); PROTEIN 3.8g; CARB 56.7g; FIBER 0.4g; CHOL 43mg; IRON 1.2mg; SODIUM 251mg; CALC 97mg

4

## Red Velvet Cupcakes

Throw out that old recipe that calls for shortening. This version is healthier—and even more delicious. As one cookinglight.com reader says, "The icing is to die for."

Cupcakes:

    Cooking spray
    10  ounces cake flour (about 2½ cups)
    3  tablespoons unsweetened cocoa
    1  teaspoon baking soda
    1  teaspoon baking powder
    1  teaspoon kosher salt
    1½  cups granulated sugar
    6  tablespoons unsalted butter, softened
    2  large eggs
    1¼  cups nonfat buttermilk
    1½  teaspoons white vinegar
    1½  teaspoons vanilla extract
    2  tablespoons red food coloring (about 1 ounce)

Frosting:

    5  tablespoons butter, softened
    4  teaspoons nonfat buttermilk
    1  (8-ounce) block cream cheese, softened
    3½  cups powdered sugar (about 1 pound)
    1¼  teaspoons vanilla extract

**1.** Preheat oven to 350°.
**2.** To prepare cupcakes, place 30 paper muffin cup liners in muffin cups; coat with cooking spray.
**3.** Weigh or lightly spoon cake flour into dry measuring cups; level with a knife. Combine cake flour, unsweetened cocoa, baking soda, baking powder, and salt in a medium bowl; stir with a whisk. Place granulated sugar and unsalted butter in a large bowl; beat with a mixer at medium speed until well blended (about 3 minutes). Add eggs, 1 at a time, beating well after each addition. Add flour mixture and $1^1/_4$ cups nonfat buttermilk alternately to sugar mixture, beginning and ending with flour mixture. Add white vinegar, $1^1/_2$ teaspoons vanilla, and food coloring; beat well.

**4.** Spoon batter into prepared muffin cups. Bake at 350° for 20 minutes or until a wooden pick inserted in center comes out clean. Cool in pan 10 minutes on a wire rack; remove from pan. Cool completely on wire racks.
**5.** To prepare frosting, beat 5 tablespoons butter, 4 teaspoons nonfat buttermilk, and cream cheese with a mixer at high speed until fluffy. Gradually add powdered sugar; beat until smooth. Add $1^1/_4$ teaspoons vanilla; beat well. Spread frosting evenly over cupcakes.
**YIELD:** 30 cupcakes (serving size: 1 cupcake).

CALORIES 205; FAT 7.3g (sat 4.5g, mono 2g, poly 0.3g); PROTEIN 2.3g; CARB 33.5g; FIBER 0.3g; CHOL 34mg; IRON 0.9mg; SODIUM 168mg; CALC 35mg

5

# Maple-Walnut Apple Crisp

1.5 ounces all-purpose flour (about ⅓ cup)

½ cup packed light brown sugar

⅓ cup regular oats

¼ teaspoon ground cinnamon

¼ cup chilled butter, cut into small pieces

3 tablespoons chopped walnuts

7 cups sliced peeled Rome apple (about 3 pounds)

¼ cup maple syrup

½ teaspoon ground cinnamon

**1.** Preheat oven to 375°.

**2.** Weigh or lightly spoon flour into a dry measuring cup; level with a knife. Combine flour, sugar, oats, and ¼ teaspoon cinnamon in a medium bowl; cut in butter with a pastry blender or 2 knives until mixture is crumbly. Stir in walnuts.

**3.** Combine apple and remaining ingredients in a large bowl; toss well. Spoon apple mixture into an 8-inch square baking dish or 1½-quart casserole. Sprinkle with crumb mixture. Bake at 375° for 45 minutes or until golden brown. Serve warm. **YIELD:** 9 servings.

CALORIES 208; FAT 7.1g (sat 3.4g, mono 1.9g, poly 1.3g); PROTEIN 1.8g; CARB 36.5g; FIBER 2.3g; CHOL 14mg; IRON 0.9mg; SODIUM 58mg; CALC 27mg

# Old-Fashioned Strawberry Shortcakes

3½ cups halved strawberries, divided
⅓ cup sugar
⅓ cup orange juice
2 teaspoons vanilla extract
1 teaspoon lemon juice
5.6 ounces all-purpose flour (about 1¼ cups)
3 tablespoons sugar
1 teaspoon baking powder

¼ teaspoon baking soda
⅛ teaspoon salt
3 tablespoons chilled butter, cut into small pieces
½ cup low-fat buttermilk
Cooking spray
6 tablespoons frozen reduced-calorie whipped topping, thawed
Whole strawberries (optional)

**1.** Combine 1 cup strawberry halves, $^1/_3$ cup sugar, orange juice, vanilla, and lemon juice in a bowl, and mash with a potato masher. Stir in $2^1/_2$ cups strawberry halves. Cover and chill.

**2.** Preheat oven to 425°.

**3.** Weigh or lightly spoon flour into dry measuring cups; level with a knife. Combine flour, 3 tablespoons sugar, baking powder, baking soda, and salt in a bowl; cut in butter with a pastry blender or 2 knives until mixture resembles coarse meal. Add buttermilk, stirring just until moist (dough will be sticky).

**4.** Turn dough out onto a lightly floured surface, and knead lightly 4 times with floured hands. Pat dough into a 6 x 4-inch rectangle. Cut dough into 6 squares. Place 1 inch apart on a baking sheet coated with cooking spray. Bake at 425° for 12 minutes. Cool on a wire rack.

**5.** Split shortcakes in half horizontally using a serrated knife; place each bottom half on a dessert plate. Spoon $^1/_4$ cup strawberry mixture over each bottom half. Top with shortcake tops; spoon $^1/_4$ cup strawberry mixture over each top. Top each serving with 1 tablespoon whipped topping; garnish with whole strawberries, if desired. **YIELD:** 6 servings.

CALORIES 270; FAT 7.2g (sat 1.9g, mono 2.7g, poly 2.1g); PROTEIN 4.3g; CARB 47.3g; FIBER 3g; CHOL 0mg; IRON 1.7mg; SODIUM 183mg; CALC 93mg

**what makes it light**

- uses less sugar than traditional recipes
- uses low-fat buttermilk
- uses reduced-calorie whipped topping

**For extra-delicious decadence** add a scoop of vanilla low-fat ice cream to your warm serving of cobbler.

# Lattice-Topped Blackberry Cobbler

1 cup granulated sugar, divided
6 tablespoons butter, softened
1 large egg yolk
½ teaspoon vanilla extract
¾ cup whole almonds, toasted
6 ounces all-purpose flour (about 1⅓ cups)
¼ teaspoon baking powder

¼ teaspoon salt
3 tablespoons ice water
10 cups fresh blackberries
3 tablespoons cornstarch
1 tablespoon fresh lemon juice
Cooking spray
2 tablespoons turbinado sugar

**1.** Place ⅓ cup granulated sugar and butter in a large bowl; beat with a mixer until combined (about 1 minute). Add egg yolk, beating well. Stir in vanilla.
**2.** Place almonds in a food processor; pulse 10 times or until finely ground. Weigh or lightly spoon flour into dry measuring cups; level with a knife. Combine nuts, flour, baking powder, and salt, stirring well with a whisk. Gradually add nut mixture to butter mixture, beating at low speed just until a soft dough forms, adding 3 tablespoons ice water, as necessary. Turn dough out onto a lightly floured surface; knead lightly 6 times or until smooth. Divide dough into 2 equal portions; wrap each portion in plastic wrap. Chill 1 hour or until firm.
**3.** Preheat oven to 375°.
**4.** Combine remaining ⅔ cup granulated sugar, blackberries, cornstarch, and lemon juice; toss gently. Arrange berry mixture in a 13 x 9–inch glass or ceramic baking dish coated with cooking spray.
**5.** Unwrap dough. Roll each dough portion into a 13 x 9–inch rectangle on a lightly floured surface. Cut one rectangle, crosswise, into (1-inch-wide) strips. Cut remaining rectangle, lengthwise, into (1-inch-wide) strips. Arrange strips in a lattice pattern over fruit mixture; sprinkle dough with turbinado sugar. Bake at 375° for 50 minutes or until golden. Let stand 10 minutes.
**YIELD:** 12 servings (serving size: about ⅔ cup).

CALORIES 301; FAT 11.5g (sat 4.1g, mono 4.6g, poly 1.8g); PROTEIN 5.7g; CARB 47g; FIBER 8.6g; CHOL 32mg; IRON 2mg; SODIUM 103mg; CALC 75mg

## what makes it light
• uses a lot less sugar for the amount of blackberries than traditional recipes

**Simply good. Nothing says summer like fresh, juicy peaches,**
and here's a fantastic application that pairs down-home flavor with a
healthy twist.

# Peach Cobbler

9 ounces all-purpose flour (about
  2 cups)
1 tablespoon granulated sugar
¼ teaspoon salt
6 tablespoons chilled butter, cut into
  6 pieces
6 tablespoons ice water
Cooking spray
6 cups sliced peeled peaches (about
  3¾ pounds)

¾ cup packed brown sugar, divided
2½ tablespoons all-purpose flour
1 tablespoon vanilla extract
1 teaspoon ground cinnamon
¼ cup slivered almonds
1 large egg
1 teaspoon water
1 tablespoon granulated sugar

**1.** Preheat oven to 375°.
**2.** Weigh or lightly spoon 9 ounces flour into dry measuring cups; level with a knife. Place flour, sugar, and salt in a food processor; pulse 2 to 3 times. Add butter pieces; pulse 10 times or until mixture resembles coarse meal. With processor on, slowly add ice water through food chute, processing just until combined (do not form a ball).
**3.** Gently press dough into a 4-inch circle. Slightly overlap 2 lengths of plastic wrap on a slightly damp surface. Place dough on plastic wrap; cover with 2 additional lengths of overlapping plastic wrap. Roll dough, still covered, into a 15 x 13–inch rectangle. Place in freezer 5 minutes or until plastic wrap can be easily removed; remove top sheets. Fit dough, uncovered side down, into a rectangular 2-quart baking dish coated with cooking spray, allowing dough to extend over edges; remove remaining plastic wrap.
**4.** Combine peaches, $^{1}/_{2}$ cup brown sugar, $2^{1}/_{2}$ tablespoons flour, vanilla, and cinnamon in a large bowl; toss gently. Spoon into prepared dish; fold edges of dough over peach mixture. Sprinkle $^{1}/_{4}$ cup brown sugar over mixture; sprinkle with almonds.
**5.** Combine egg and water in a small bowl. Brush egg mixture over dough; sprinkle with granulated sugar. Bake at 375° for 45 minutes or until filling is bubbly and crust is lightly browned. Let stand 30 minutes before serving. **YIELD:** 10 servings.

CALORIES 302; FAT 9.2g (sat 1.6g, mono 4.3g, poly 2.7g); PROTEIN 4.5g; CARB 51.5g; FIBER 2.8g; CHOL 11mg; IRON 1.9mg; SODIUM 149mg; CALC 39mg

## what makes it light
• uses much less sugar than traditional recipes
• uses less fat to make the crust than traditional recipes

"This pie is absolutely amazing! I was a little unsure whether it would taste good with all the fat-free and low-cal ingredients. It turned out so good, and everyone I served it to raved about it! In fact, the lighter ingredients made the pie so much better, and I think this type of pie could be too sweet if full-fat ingredients were used. The chocolate shavings were the perfect touch! I have made it a bunch of times and plan on doing so again this weekend!

**from cookinglight.com**

# Frozen Peanut Butter Pie

1⅔ cups chocolate graham cracker crumbs (about 8½ cookie sheets)

7 tablespoons sugar, divided

2 large egg whites, lightly beaten

Cooking spray

1¼ cups fat-free milk

⅔ cup reduced-fat crunchy peanut butter

½ teaspoon vanilla

½ cup (4 ounces) fat-free cream cheese, softened

1 (8-ounce) container frozen fat-free whipped topping, thawed

3 tablespoons finely chopped salted, dry-roasted peanuts

¼ cup shaved milk chocolate (about 1 ounce)

**1.** Preheat oven to 350°.

**2.** Combine crumbs, 3 tablespoons sugar, and egg whites; toss with a fork until moist. Press into bottom and up sides of a 9-inch deep-dish pie plate coated with cooking spray. Prick crust with a fork before baking. Bake at 350° for 10 minutes. Remove from oven; cool on a wire rack.

**3.** Combine milk and remaining ¼ cup sugar in a heavy saucepan over medium-low heat. Cook 2 minutes or until sugar dissolves, stirring constantly; transfer mixture to a bowl. Add peanut butter and vanilla, stirring with a whisk until combined. Cover and chill 30 minutes.

**4.** Place cream cheese in a large bowl, and beat with a mixer at medium speed until light and fluffy. Add milk mixture, beating on low speed until combined. Fold in whipped topping; pour mixture into prepared piecrust. Freeze, uncovered, 8 hours or overnight or until hard. Sprinkle with peanuts and shaved chocolate. Transfer pie to refrigerator 30 minutes before slicing. **YIELD:** 10 servings (serving size: 1 wedge).

CALORIES 259; FAT 8.7g (sat 1.9g, mono 3.8g, poly 2g); PROTEIN 9.4g; CARB 35.5g; FIBER 1.6g; CHOL m2g; IRON 0.6mg; SODIUM 249mg; CALC 136mg

# 5 ways with

# pies

## Apple Pie

This traditional pie calls for Cortland apples, but we found that Pacific Rose apples also work well.

|       |                                                        |
| ----- | ------------------------------------------------------ |
| 11.25 | ounces all-purpose flour (about 2½ cups)               |
| ¾     | teaspoon salt                                          |
| 6     | tablespoons chilled butter, cut into small pieces      |
| 2     | tablespoons vegetable shortening, cut into small pieces |
| 1     | tablespoon fresh lemon juice                           |
| ¾     | cup ice water                                          |
| 2½    | cups thinly sliced peeled Braeburn apple (about 1 pound) |
| 2½    | cups thinly sliced peeled Cortland apple (about 1 pound) |
| 1     | cup sugar                                              |
| 1.1   | ounces all-purpose flour (about ¼ cup)                 |
| ¼     | teaspoon ground cinnamon                               |
| ⅛ to ¼ | teaspoon ground allspice                              |
|       | Cooking spray                                          |
| 1     | tablespoon chilled butter, cut into small pieces       |
| ½     | teaspoon vanilla extract                               |
| 1     | tablespoon whole milk                                  |

**1.** Weigh or lightly spoon 11.25 ounces flour into dry measuring cups; level with a knife. Combine flour and salt in a large bowl; cut in 6 tablespoons butter and vegetable shortening with a pastry blender or 2 knives until mixture resembles coarse meal. Add lemon juice. Sprinkle surface with ice water, 1 tablespoon at a time, and toss with a fork until moist and crumbly. Shape dough into a ball, and wrap in plastic wrap. Chill 1 hour.

**2.** Divide dough into 2 equal portions. Gently press each portion into a 1-inch-thick circle on heavy-duty plastic wrap; cover and freeze 10 minutes.

**3.** Preheat oven to 350°.

**4.** Place apples in a large bowl. Combine sugar, 1.1 ounces flour, cinnamon, and allspice in a small bowl. Sprinkle sugar mixture over apples; toss well to coat.

**5.** Working with 1 dough portion at a time, roll dough into a 12-inch circle on a lightly floured surface. Fit dough circle into a 9-inch pie plate coated with cooking spray, allowing dough to extend over the edge. Roll remaining dough portion into a 10-inch circle on a lightly floured surface. Spoon apple mixture into prepared pie plate, and dot with 1 tablespoon butter. Drizzle

1

apple mixture with ¹/₂ teaspoon vanilla. Top with 10-inch dough circle. Press edges of dough together. Fold edges under, and flute. Brush surface of dough with milk. Cut 3 (1-inch) slits in the top of dough to allow steam to escape. Bake at 350° for 1 hour or until apples are tender. **YIELD:** 10 servings (serving size: 1 wedge).

CALORIES 326; FAT 10.8g (sat 6g, mono 2.8g, poly 1.2g); PROTEIN 3.8g; CARB 54.1g; FIBER 2.3g; CHOL 21mg; IRON 1.7mg; SODIUM 233mg; CALC 14mg

## Coconut Cream Pie ▶

This pie takes a brief turn under the broiler to brown the peaks of the Italian meringue.

Crust:
  ½ (15-ounce) package refrigerated pie dough (such as Pillsbury)

Filling:
  1.1 ounces all-purpose flour (about ¼ cup)
  ½ cup sugar
  ⅛ teaspoon salt
  2 large eggs
  ¾ cup 2% reduced-fat milk
  ¾ cup light coconut milk
  ¼ teaspoon coconut extract
  ¼ teaspoon vanilla extract

Meringue:
  3 large egg whites
  ⅔ cup sugar
  ¼ cup water
  1 tablespoon flaked sweetened coconut, toasted

**1.** Prepare and bake piecrust in a 10-inch deep-dish pie plate. Cool completely on a wire rack.

**2.** To prepare filling, weigh or lightly spoon flour into a dry measuring cup; level with a knife. Combine flour, ¹/₂ cup sugar, salt, and eggs in a large bowl; stir well with a whisk.

**3.** Heat milk and coconut milk over medium-high heat in a small, heavy saucepan to 180° or until tiny bubbles form around edge (do not boil). Gradually add hot milk mixture to sugar mixture, stirring constantly with a whisk.

Place mixture in pan; cook over medium heat until thick and bubbly (about 10 minutes), stirring constantly.

**4.** Remove from heat. Spoon custard into a bowl; place bowl in a large ice-filled bowl 10 minutes or until custard comes to room temperature, stirring occasionally. Remove bowl from ice. Stir in extracts; spoon mixture into prepared crust. Cover and chill 8 hours or until firm.

**5.** Preheat broiler with rack in middle of oven.

**6.** To prepare meringue, place egg whites in a large bowl; beat with a mixer at high speed until soft peaks form. Combine ²/₃ cup sugar and water in a saucepan; bring to a boil. Cook, without stirring, until candy thermometer registers 238°. Pour hot sugar syrup in a thin stream over egg whites, beating at high speed until stiff peaks form.

**7.** Spread meringue over chilled pie, and sprinkle with coconut. Broil 1 minute or until meringue is lightly browned; cool 5 minutes on a wire rack. Serve immediately. **YIELD:** 10 servings (serving size: 1 wedge).

CALORIES 281; FAT 9.3g (sat 5.6g, mono 2.6g, poly 0.4g); PROTEIN 5.3g; CARB 45.6g; FIBER 0.6g; CHOL 63mg; IRON 1.4mg; SODIUM 208mg; CALC 28mg

## Key Lime Pie ▼

Key lime pie is traditionally made with egg yolks, sweetened condensed milk, and lime juice from yellowish green Key limes. We guarantee that this lightened version will be a family favorite.

- 2 large eggs
- 2 large egg whites
- ½ cup Key lime juice (such as Nellie and Joe's Famous Key West Lime Juice)
- 1 teaspoon grated lime rind
- 1 (14-ounce) can fat-free sweetened condensed milk
- 1 (6-ounce) reduced-fat graham cracker crust
- 1½ cups frozen reduced-calorie whipped topping, thawed
- Grated lime rind (optional)

**1.** Preheat oven to 350°.
**2.** Beat eggs and egg whites at medium speed of a mixer until well blended. Gradually add juice, rind, and milk to egg mixture, beating until well blended. Spoon mixture into crust, and bake at 350° for 20 minutes or until almost set (the center will not be firm but will set up as it chills). Cool pie on a wire rack. Cover loosely, and chill 4 hours. Spread whipped topping evenly over filling. Garnish with grated lime rind, if desired. **YIELD:** 8 servings (serving size: 1 wedge).

CALORIES 288; FAT 5.9g (sat 3g, mono 1.5g, poly 1.1g); PROTEIN 7.6g; CARB 49.2g; FIBER 0.8g; CHOL 56mg; IRON 0.6mg; SODIUM 198mg; CALC 141mg

4

## Lemon Meringue Pie ▲

Crust:
- 1¼ cups graham cracker crumbs (about 8 cookie sheets)
- 2 tablespoons sugar
- 1 tablespoon butter, melted
- 1 large egg white, lightly beaten
- Cooking spray

Filling:
- 2 teaspoons grated lemon rind
- ½ cup fresh lemon juice (about 3 lemons)
- 1 (14-ounce) can fat-free sweetened condensed milk
- 1 (6-ounce) carton lemon fat-free yogurt (such as Yoplait)
- 1½ teaspoons unflavored gelatin
- 3 tablespoons water

Meringue:
- ⅔ cup sugar
- ¼ cup water
- 3 large egg whites
- ¼ teaspoon cream of tartar

**1.** Preheat oven to 325°.
**2.** To prepare crust, combine first 4 ingredients in a bowl; toss with a fork until moist. Press into a 9-inch pie plate coated with cooking spray. Bake at 325° for 15 minutes or until lightly browned; cool on a wire rack.

3

**3.** To prepare filling, combine lemon rind and next 3 ingredients in a medium bowl, and set aside. Sprinkle gelatin over 3 tablespoons water in a small microwave-safe bowl; let stand 1 minute. Microwave at HIGH 15 seconds, stirring until gelatin dissolves. Stir gelatin mixture thoroughly into yogurt mixture. Spoon filling into prepared crust. Press plastic wrap onto surface of filling; chill 1 hour or until almost firm.

**4.** To prepare meringue, combine $^2/_3$ cup sugar and $^1/_4$ cup water in a small saucepan; bring to a boil. Cook, without stirring, until candy thermometer registers 240°. Beat egg whites and cream of tartar at high speed of a mixer until foamy. Pour hot sugar syrup in a thin stream over egg white mixture, beating at high speed until stiff peaks form. Remove plastic wrap from filling. Spread meringue evenly over filling, sealing to edge of crust.

**5.** Preheat broiler with rack in middle of oven.

**6.** Broil 1 minute or until meringue is lightly browned, and cool pie on wire rack. Chill until set. **YIELD:** 9 servings (serving size: 1 wedge).

CALORIES 293; FAT 2.9g (sat 1.1g, mono 0.9g, poly 0.6g); PROTEIN 6.8g; CARB 59.9g; FIBER 0.1g; CHOL 9mg; IRON 0.6mg; SODIUM 178mg; CALC 141mg

**1.** To prepare crust, weigh or lightly spoon flour into a dry measuring cup; level with a knife. Combine flour, granulated sugar, baking powder, and $^1/_4$ teaspoon salt in a bowl. Add milk and butter; toss with a fork until moist.

**2.** Press mixture gently into a 4-inch circle on heavy-duty plastic wrap; cover with additional plastic wrap. Roll dough, still covered, to an 11-inch circle. Freeze 10 minutes or until plastic wrap can be easily removed.

**3.** Remove 1 sheet of plastic wrap; fit dough into a 9-inch pie plate coated with cooking spray. Remove top sheet of plastic wrap. Fold edges under; flute.

**4.** Preheat oven to 350°.

**5.** To prepare filling, beat egg and next 4 ingredients at medium speed of a mixer until well blended. Stir in pecan halves and vanilla extract. Pour mixture into prepared crust. Bake at 350° for 20 minutes, then cover with foil. Bake an additional 20 minutes or until a knife inserted 1 inch from the edge comes out clean. Do not overbake. Cool pie on a wire rack. **YIELD:** 10 servings (serving size: 1 wedge).

CALORIES 288; FAT 9.2g (sat 1.5g, mono 5.1g, poly 2g); PROTEIN 4.3g; CARB 48.1g; FIBER 1g; CHOL 25mg; IRON 1.1mg; SODIUM 253mg; CALC 52mg

## Classic Pecan Pie ▶

Crust:

- 4.5 ounces all-purpose flour (about 1 cup)
- 2 tablespoons granulated sugar
- ½ teaspoon baking powder
- ¼ teaspoon salt
- ¼ cup fat-free milk
- 1 tablespoon butter, melted
- Cooking spray

Filling:

- 1 large egg
- 4 large egg whites
- 1 cup light or dark-colored corn syrup
- ⅔ cup packed dark brown sugar
- ¼ teaspoon salt
- 1 cup pecan halves
- 1 teaspoon vanilla extract

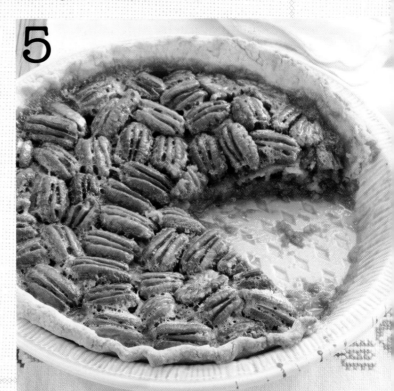

5

"Awesome! I have had some delicious banana puddings in my day, and this recipe ranks right up there. It's great out of the oven or out of the fridge. You have to try this recipe!"

from cookinglight.com

# Banana Pudding

1.5 ounces all-purpose flour (about ⅓ cup)

Dash of salt

2½ cups 1% low-fat milk

1 (14-ounce) can fat-free sweetened condensed milk

2 large egg yolks

2 teaspoons vanilla extract

3 cups sliced ripe banana, divided

45 reduced-fat vanilla wafers, divided

4 large egg whites (at room temperature)

¼ cup sugar

**1.** Preheat oven to 325°.

**2.** Combine flour and salt in a medium saucepan. Gradually add milks and yolks; stir well. Cook over medium heat 8 minutes or until thick, stirring constantly. Remove from heat; stir in vanilla.

**3.** Arrange 1 cup banana slices in bottom of a 2-quart baking dish. Spoon one-third of pudding mixture over banana. Arrange 15 wafers on top of pudding. Repeat layers twice, arranging last 15 wafers around edge of dish. Push cookies into pudding.

**4.** Beat egg whites at high speed of a mixer until foamy. Gradually add sugar, 1 tablespoon at a time, beating until stiff peaks form. Spread meringue evenly over pudding, sealing to edge of dish. Bake at 325° for 25 minutes or until golden. **YIELD:** 10 servings (serving size: $^3/_4$ cup).

CALORIES 255; FAT 2.9g (sat 1g, mono 0.9g, poly 0.2g); PROTEIN 7.9g; CARB 49.5g; FIBER 0.1g; CHOL 51mg; IRON 0.4mg; SODIUM 155mg; CALC 161mg

## what makes it light

• uses low-fat milk
• uses fat-free sweetened condensed milk
• uses reduced-fat vanilla wafers

**Adding cornstarch to this homey pudding lessens the possibility of its curdling.** To prevent the custard from tipping and taking on ice water, make sure the bowl you use for the ice bath is only slightly larger than the custard bowl.

# Bittersweet Chocolate Pudding

½ cup granulated sugar
⅓ cup unsweetened cocoa
3 tablespoons cornstarch
3 tablespoons dark brown sugar
⅛ teaspoon salt

4 cups 2% reduced-fat milk
3 large egg yolks, lightly beaten
2 ounces bittersweet chocolate, chopped
1 teaspoon vanilla extract

**1.** Combine first 5 ingredients in a large saucepan. Gradually add milk, stirring with a whisk. Bring to a boil over medium heat, stirring constantly. Cook 1 minute, stirring constantly.
**2.** Place egg yolks in a bowl. Gradually add hot milk mixture to egg yolks, stirring constantly. Return milk mixture to pan. Cook over medium heat 5 minutes or until mixture is thick, stirring constantly. Remove mixture from heat, and add chopped chocolate and vanilla extract, stirring until chocolate melts. Spoon pudding into a small bowl. Place bowl in a large ice-filled bowl 15 minutes or until pudding is cool, stirring occasionally. Remove bowl from ice; cover and chill. **YIELD:** 6 servings (serving size: $^3/_4$ cup).

CALORIES 282; FAT 9.5g (sat 5.1g, mono 2.4g, poly 0.5g); PROTEIN 8.4g; CARB 43g; FIBER 2.4g; CHOL 119mg; IRON 1.2mg; SODIUM 138mg; CALC 222mg

### what makes it light
- uses reduced-fat milk
- uses less sugar than traditional recipes
- doesn't use butter, which some puddings do

**Raisin-studded bread pudding and buttery,** bourbon-spiked sauce combine in this time-honored dessert.

# New Orleans Bread Pudding with Bourbon Sauce

Pudding:
- ¼ cup raisins
- 2 tablespoons bourbon
- 1¼ cups 2% reduced-fat milk
- ½ cup sugar
- 1 tablespoon vanilla extract
- ½ teaspoon ground cinnamon
- ¼ teaspoon ground nutmeg
- Dash of salt

- 3 large eggs, lightly beaten
- 4½ cups (½-inch) cubed French bread (about 8 ounces)
- Cooking spray

Sauce:
- ½ cup sugar
- ¼ cup light-colored corn syrup
- ¼ cup butter
- ¼ cup bourbon

**1.** To prepare pudding, combine raisins and 2 tablespoons bourbon in a bowl. Let stand 30 minutes. Drain mixture in a sieve over a bowl, reserving liquid.

**2.** Combine reserved liquid, milk, and next 6 ingredients in a large bowl, stirring well with a whisk. Add bread, tossing gently to coat. Spoon mixture into an 8-inch square baking dish coated with cooking spray. Sprinkle evenly with raisins, pressing gently into bread mixture. Cover with foil; chill 30 minutes or up to 4 hours.

**3.** Preheat oven to 350°.

**4.** Place dish in a 13 x 9–inch baking pan; add hot water to pan to a depth of 1 inch. Bake, covered, at 350° for 20 minutes. Uncover and bake an additional 10 minutes or until a knife inserted in center comes out clean.

**5.** To prepare sauce, combine $^1/_2$ cup sugar, corn syrup, and butter in a small saucepan over medium heat. Bring to a simmer; cook 1 minute, stirring constantly. Remove from heat; stir in $^1/_4$ cup bourbon. Serve each bread pudding piece warm with about 1 tablespoon sauce. **YIELD:** 9 servings.

CALORIES 309; FAT 8.2g (sat 4.3g, mono 2.7g, poly 0.6g); PROTEIN 5.6g; CARB 47.6g; FIBER 1g; CHOL 87mg; IRON 1.1mg; SODIUM 272mg; CALC 74mg

## ? what makes it light
- uses reduced-fat milk
- uses fewer eggs than traditional recipes
- uses less butter than traditional recipes
- uses less sugar than traditional recipes

**Nutty caramel coats delicate baked custard in this rich dessert, also referred to as "flan."** Although we specify cooking the caramel until golden, you can cook it longer for a deep amber color; the bitter notes of the darker caramel add a nice contrast to the sweet custard.

# Classic Crème Caramel

4 cups 2% reduced-fat milk
1 vanilla bean, split lengthwise
Cooking spray
1²/₃ cups sugar, divided

¼ cup water
¼ teaspoon kosher salt
6 large eggs
3 tablespoons heavy whipping cream

**1.** Preheat oven to 225°.

**2.** Heat milk and vanilla bean over medium-high heat in a medium, heavy saucepan to 180° or until tiny bubbles form around edge (do not boil); remove pan from heat. Cover and set aside.

**3.** Coat 10 (6-ounce) custard cups with cooking spray; arrange cups on a jelly-roll pan.

**4.** Combine 1 cup sugar and $^1/_4$ cup water in a small, heavy saucepan; cook over medium-high heat until sugar dissolves, stirring frequently. Continue cooking 7 minutes or until golden (do not stir). Immediately pour into prepared custard cups, tipping quickly until caramelized sugar coats bottom of cups.

**5.** Combine remaining $^2/_3$ cup sugar, salt, and eggs in a large bowl, stirring with a whisk. Remove vanilla bean from milk mixture; reserve bean for another use. Gradually pour warm milk mixture into egg mixture, stirring constantly with a whisk; stir in cream. Strain egg mixture through a sieve into a large bowl; pour about $^1/_2$ cup egg mixture over caramelized sugar in each custard cup. Bake at 225° for 2 hours or until custards are just set. Remove from oven; cool to room temperature. Place plastic wrap on surface of custards; chill overnight.

**6.** Loosen edges of custards with a knife or rubber spatula. Place a dessert plate, upside down, on top of each cup; invert onto plate. Drizzle any remaining caramelized syrup over custards. **YIELD:** 10 servings (serving size: 1 custard).

CALORIES 236; FAT 6.5g (sat 3.1g, mono 2.2g, poly 0.5g); PROTEIN 7.1g; CARB 38.4g; FIBER 0g; CHOL 140mg; IRON 0.6mg; SODIUM 139mg; CALC 138mg

## what makes it light

- uses reduced-fat milk
- uses less heavy cream than traditional recipes

"This recipe is fantastic, very easy, and full of peach flavor. **It's simple but not too sweet** like commercial ice cream. Would recommend this to anyone who loves a taste of summer."

**from cookinglight.com**

# Peach Ice Cream

3 cups sliced peeled peaches (about
   1½ pounds)
1 cup half-and-half

½ cup sugar
½ cup whole milk
1 teaspoon vanilla extract

**1.** Place peaches in a blender or food processor; process until finely chopped. Combine peaches and remaining ingredients in a large bowl. Pour peach mixture into freezer can of an ice-cream freezer; freeze according to manufacturer's instructions. Spoon ice cream into a freezer-safe container; cover and freeze 2 hours or until firm. **YIELD:** 8 servings (serving size: $^{1}/_{2}$ cup).

CALORIES 125; FAT 4g (sat 2.5g, mono 1.2g, poly 0.2g); PROTEIN 1.8g; CARB 21.3g; FIBER 1.2g; CHOL 13mg; IRON 0.1mg; SODIUM 20mg; CALC 53mg

## what makes it light

- uses less sugar than traditional recipes
- uses less cream than traditional recipes by substituting a mix of milk and half-and-half

# Nutritional Analysis

## How to Use It and Why

Glance at the end of any *Cooking Light* recipe, and you'll see how committed we are to helping you make the best of today's light cooking. With chefs, registered dietitians, home economists, and a computer system that analyzes every ingredient we use, *Cooking Light* gives you authoritative dietary detail like no other magazine. We go to such lengths so you can see how our recipes fit into your healthful eating plan. If you're trying to lose weight, the calorie and fat figures will probably help most. But if you're keeping a close eye on the sodium, cholesterol, and saturated fat in your diet, we provide those numbers, too. And because many women don't get enough iron or calcium, we can also help there, as well. Finally, there's a fiber analysis for those of us who don't get enough roughage.

Here's a helpful guide to put our nutritional analysis numbers into perspective. Remember, one size doesn't fit all, so take your lifestyle, age, and circumstances into consideration when determining your nutrition needs. For example, pregnant or breast-feeding women need more protein, calories, and calcium. And women older than 50 need 1,200mg of calcium daily, 200mg more than the amount recommended for younger women and men.

## We Use These Abbreviations in Our Nutritional Analysis

| | | | |
|---|---|---|---|
| sat | saturated fat | CHOL | cholesterol |
| mono | monounsaturated fat | CALC | calcium |
| poly | polyunsaturated fat | g | gram |
| CARB | carbohydrates | mg | milligram |

### Daily Nutrition Guide

| | Women Ages 25 to 50 | Women over 50 | Men over 24 |
|---|---|---|---|
| **Calories** | 2,000 | 2,000 or less | 2,700 |
| **Protein** | 50g | 50g or less | 63g |
| **Fat** | 65g or less | 65g or less | 88g or less |
| **Saturated Fat** | 20g or less | 20g or less | 27g or less |
| **Carbohydrates** | 304g | 304g | 410g |
| **Fiber** | 25g to 35g | 25g to 35g | 25g to 35g |
| **Cholesterol** | 300mg or less | 300mg or less | 300mg or less |
| **Iron** | 18mg | 8mg | 8mg |
| **Sodium** | 2,300mg or less | 1,500mg or less | 2,300mg or less |
| **Calcium** | 1,000mg | 1,200mg | 1,000mg |

The nutritional values used in our calculations either come from The Food Processor, Version 8.9 (ESHA Research), or are provided by food manufacturers.

# Metric Equivalents

The information in the following charts is provided to help cooks outside the United States successfully use the recipes in this book. All equivalents are approximate.

## Cooking/Oven Temperatures

|  | Fahrenheit | Celsius | Gas Mark |
|---|---|---|---|
| **Freeze Water** | 32° F | 0° C | |
| **Room Temp.** | 68° F | 20° C | |
| **Boil Water** | 212° F | 100° C | |
| **Bake** | 325° F | 160° C | 3 |
|  | 350° F | 180° C | 4 |
|  | 375° F | 190° C | 5 |
|  | 400° F | 200° C | 6 |
|  | 425° F | 220° C | 7 |
|  | 450° F | 230° C | 8 |
| **Broil** |  |  | Grill |

## Liquid Ingredients by Volume

| ¼ tsp | = | 1 ml | | | | |
|---|---|---|---|---|---|---|
| ½ tsp | = | 2 ml | | | | |
| 1 tsp | = | 5 ml | | | | |
| 3 tsp | = | 1 tbl | = | ½ fl oz | = | 15 ml |
| 2 tbls | = | ⅛ cup | = | 1 fl oz | = | 30 ml |
| 4 tbls | = | ¼ cup | = | 2 fl oz | = | 60 ml |
| 5⅓ tbls | = | ⅓ cup | = | 3 fl oz | = | 80 ml |
| 8 tbls | = | ½ cup | = | 4 fl oz | = | 120 ml |
| 10⅔ tbls | = | ⅔ cup | = | 5 fl oz | = | 160 ml |
| 12 tbls | = | ¾ cup | = | 6 fl oz | = | 180 ml |
| 16 tbls | = | 1 cup | = | 8 fl oz | = | 240 ml |
| 1 pt | = | 2 cups | = | 16 fl oz | = | 480 ml |
| 1 qt | = | 4 cups | = | 32 fl oz | = | 960 ml |
| | | | | 33 fl oz | = | 1000 ml = 1l |

## Dry Ingredients by Weight

(To convert ounces to grams, multiply the number of ounces by 30.)

| 1 oz | = | ¹⁄₁₆ lb | = | 30 g |
|---|---|---|---|---|
| 4 oz | = | ¼ lb | = | 120 g |
| 8 oz | = | ½ lb | = | 240 g |
| 12 oz | = | ¾ lb | = | 360 g |
| 16 oz | = | 1 lb | = | 480 g |

## Length

(To convert inches to centimeters, multiply the number of inches by 2.5.)

| 1 in | = | | | 2.5 cm | |
|---|---|---|---|---|---|
| 6 in | = | ½ ft | = | 15 cm | |
| 12 in | = | 1 ft | = | 30 cm | |
| 36 in | = | 3 ft | = 1 yd = | 90 cm | |
| 40 in | = | | | 100 cm | = 1m |

## Equivalents for Different Types of Ingredients

| Standard Cup | Fine Powder (ex. flour) | Grain (ex. rice) | Granular (ex. sugar) | Liquid Solids (ex. butter) | Liquid (ex. milk) |
|---|---|---|---|---|---|
| 1 | 140 g | 150 g | 190 g | 200 g | 240 ml |
| ¾ | 105 g | 113 g | 143 g | 150 g | 180 ml |
| ⅔ | 93 g | 100 g | 125 g | 133 g | 160 ml |
| ½ | 70 g | 75 g | 95 g | 100 g | 120 ml |
| ⅓ | 47 g | 50 g | 63 g | 67 g | 80 ml |
| ¼ | 35 g | 38 g | 48 g | 50 g | 60 ml |
| ⅛ | 18 g | 19 g | 24 g | 25 g | 30 ml |

# index